Social Cognitive Theory

Social Cognitive Theory

An Agentic Perspective on Human Nature

Albert Bandura[†]

Edited by Daniel Cervone

Published by John Wiley & Sons, Inc., Hoboken, New Jersey.
Published simultaneously in Canada.

For general information on our other products and services or for technical support, please contact our Customer Care Department within the United States at (800) 762-2974, outside the United States at (317) 572-3993 or fax (317) 572-4002.

Wiley also publishes its books in a variety of electronic formats. Some content that appears in print may not be available in electronic formats. For more information about Wiley products, visit our web site at www.wiley.com.

Library of Congress Cataloging-in-Publication Data

Name: Bandura, Albert, 1925-2021, author.
Title: Social cognitive theory : an agentic perspective on human nature /
   Albert Bandura.
Description: Hoboken, NJ : John Wiley & Sons, Inc., [2023] | Includes
   bibliographical references and index.
Identifiers: LCCN 2022050634 (print) | LCCN 2022050635 (ebook) | ISBN
   9781394161454 (paperback) | ISBN 9781394161478 (adobe pdf) | ISBN
   9781394161461 (epub)
Subjects: LCSH: Social perception. | Self-efficacy.
Classification: LCC BF323.S63 B36 2023 (print) | LCC BF323.S63 (ebook) |
   DDC 302/.12—dc23/eng/20221212
LC record available at https://lccn.loc.gov/2022050634
LC ebook record available at https://lccn.loc.gov/2022050635

Cover Design: Wiley

Set in 9.5/12.5pt STIXTwoText by Straive, Chennai, India

Contents

Author Biography

Professor Albert Bandura (December 4, 1925–July 26, 2021) was the David Starr Jordan Professor of Social Science in Psychology at Stanford University. Born and raised in the Canadian village of Mundare, in Alberta, he earned his Bachelor's degree at the University of British Columbia in 1949, after which he entered the graduate program in Psychology at the University of Iowa, receiving his PhD in 1952. He subsequently completed a postdoctoral internship at the Wichita Guidance Center and then joined the Stanford University faculty in 1953, remaining there for his entire professional career.

As a result of his considerable contributions, Professor Bandura was renowned as one the of the most influential psychologists of modern times. He was the originator of Social Cognitive Theory, a comprehensive, multifaceted conception of human nature in which personal agency plays a central role.

Professor Bandura's early work included the seminal Bobo Doll experiments, conducted from 1961 to 1963, which demonstrated how aggressive behaviors can be acquired and elicited in children through observation, modeling, and imitation of an adult's behavior. This research spawned in-depth study of social learning and behavior change processes, culminating in his influential book *Principles of Behavior Modification* in 1969. Emphasizing the interplay of cognitive, behavioral, and environmental influences, this work catalyzed the transition from prevailing behaviorist and psychoanalytic conceptions to a more complex, interactional theory of personality and psychological change. The book served as a springboard for the development of powerful cognitive-behavioral treatments that have advanced to dominate the clinical landscape.

Subsequently, Professor Bandura expanded Social Cognitive Theory by analyzing self-regulatory and motivational processes. He emphasized how self-efficacy beliefs shape human behavior and underlie the exercise of personal agency. In doing so, he enriched our understanding of the important role played by beliefs about our abilities in guiding our choice of goals and our efforts to attain them. The concept of personal agency was central to his own life path, in which he charted unknown intellectual territory and maintained a remarkable focus on developing his ideas.

Professor Bandura incorporated moral decision making into Social Cognitive Theory to further enlarge its scope. In his book, *Moral Disengagement: How People Do Harm and Live With Themselves,* he identified a set of eight mechanisms that individuals and social systems might enlist to absolve themselves from feelings of guilt or remorse and to evade responsibility for their actions. He identified how these mechanisms are related to many of the pressing social and corporate problems of our time.

During the course of his long career, Professor Bandura was the recipient of many honorary degrees and awards, including the Award for Outstanding Lifetime Contribution to Psychology from the American Psychological Association in 2004; the Grawemeyer Award for Psychology in 2008; the Lifetime Career Award from the International Union of Psychological Science in 2012; the Order of Canada, one of the country's highest civilian honors, in 2015; and the National Medal of Science, bestowed upon him by President Barack Obama in 2016.

Toward the end of his career, he focused on harnessing the power of social learning, modeling, and self-efficacy to address such exigent global concerns as climate change, social injustice towards girls and women, family planning, and public health crises. He collaborated with the Population Media Center to develop mass media serial dramas that were broadcast in targeted areas of the world as a means of modeling practical strategies to achieve positive social change. Throughout his life and career, his guiding motivation had been to foster practices to promote human betterment and to ensure environmental sustainability.

Dr. Bandura by his childhood home in Mundare, Alberta, 2010. Source: Photo courtesy of Dr. Mary Bandura.

Foreword

In October of 2021, I received in the mail a box full of papers. It contained the most poignant of notes to self:

> *I was often reminded that it is not the miles traveled, but the tread left that is important. When I checked I still had enough remaining tread to complete this farewell novel.*
> *I did not have enough tread to complete my farewell novel.*

Professor Albert Bandura, the most impactful psychologist of his historical era, recognized that he could not bring his final book to fruition. The papers were those that had been on his desk at the time of his passing in July of that year.

I have no way of knowing the following, but Professor Bandura might also have recognized something else: that he had advanced so far on his project that anybody with an understanding of Social Cognitive Theory *could* bring the work to fruition. He had outlined the volume as a whole; had completed a substantial amount of the writing; and had left notes indicating the book's precise purpose and intended audience. I thank Dr. Mary Bandura, representative of the Albert Bandura Trust, for granting me the extraordinary honor of serving as editor.

Bandura's Goal for the Work

Professor Bandura's aim for *Social Cognitive Theory: An Agentic Perspective on Human Nature* was straightforward. He wanted to present, concisely, the multiple interrelated aspects of his Social Cognitive Theory. This aim is significant for reasons that go beyond the sheer importance of his scientific contributions. It had been decades since Professor Bandura had written a similarly comprehensive theoretical volume: his magnum opus, *Social Foundations of Thought and Action*, published in 1986. There had been significant theoretical and empirical advances since that time. Furthermore, after the many years, the 1986 volume is no longer easily available. The present work thus stands as the definitive, accessible presentation of Professor Bandura's major intellectual gift to psychology: Social Cognitive Theory.

The book also is significant because, despite his fame, many may not properly understand that Social Cognitive Theory is, in fact, his major intellectual gift. In academia, scholars commonly are exposed to one part of Professor Bandura's work without necessarily seeing the whole. As he himself notes in Chapter 3 of this volume, one of his contributions, self-efficacy theory, "has received such attention that writers have sometimes appeared to conflate [it] with the entire social cognitive framework. This is a mistake." Something similar happens outside of academia. Professor Bandura's name is associated commonly with one or another isolated idea or experiment—self-efficacy theory; moral disengagement; the Bobo Doll study—rather than with his overarching theoretical framework. Consider how the *New York Times* (29 July 2021) identified the creator of Social Cognitive Theory in their headline announcing his passing: "Leading psychologist of aggression." That is not wrong, but one hardly could call it comprehensively "right." *The Times* did explain to readers that the "single principle undergirding his work . . . was the idea of personal agency"—but only because, in the very last interview conducted for the piece, I interrupted *The Times* writer to say something like "no, no, for heaven's sakes, the single principle undergirding his work is the idea of personal agency." Professor Bandura furnished so many trees that observers sometimes missed the forest.

The present volume clarifies for today's reader, and for posterity, that the many parts of Albert Bandura's theoretical and empirical work were parts of a whole. The whole is Social Cognitive Theory: a comprehensive framework for understanding persons and their capacity for agency.

Agency

In *Social Cognitive Theory*, Bandura balances two central ideas: *determinants* (a term that appears repeatedly throughout this volume) and *agency* (the book's overarching theme). It is not an easy balancing act. The philosopher McCann (1998) stated the core concern: whether an explanation of agency "can be made commensurate with our notions of an orderly universe" (p. 170). "Agency" implies freedom of choice; "determinants" imply its absence. Is there a "compatibilist" (McKenna & Coates, 2021) position that might reconcile the two?

Scholars have been asking this question since the days of the Stoics—in fact, apparently since a particular Stoic, Chrysippus. His writings primarily are lost. But sources from his time (third century BCE) report that his compatibalism was an original effort to reconcile the existence of causes with the recognition that people are agents who contribute to their own actions and thus bear responsibility for them (White, 1985, p. 98). Similar compatibilist efforts recur in subsequent eras. For example, as Professor Bandura notes in Chapter 1, medieval Scholastics needed to reconcile belief in the causal power of a divine Creator with observations of evil in the created world. They did so by concluding that God had endowed people with the power of free choice, thus enabling them to choose evil or to prove their moral worth.

Moving to the modern era, one of scientific psychology's most famous intellectual positions addressed compatibilism—and argued against it. In his operant behaviorism, B. F. Skinner did not balance environmental determinism and personal agency; he instead tipped the balance entirely to determinism. Note that, for there to be personal agency, persons must possess psychological attributes with causal force—"personal powers," as Harré (1998, p. 15) called them. Skinner's psychology jettisoned such powers: "We do not need to try to discover what personalities, states of mind, feelings, traits of character, plans, purposes, intentions . . . really are in order to get on with a scientific analysis of behavior" (Skinner, 1971, p. 20). "A scientific analysis shifts both the responsibility [for individual action] and the achievement [that a person might realize] to the environment" (Skinner, 1971, p. 30). In the present text, Professor Bandura addresses the limitations of the Behaviorist position directly in some passages, whereas in others its anti-agency argument seems to "lurk in the background." His Presidential Address to the *American Psychological Association* confronted the behaviorist conception head on (Bandura, 1974).

Although many late-20th century psychologists remained enamored with Behaviorism's anti-agency position, contemporaneous scholars in other fields acknowledged human agency and analyzed its key features. Contributions from philosophy are particularly constructive. Hacker (1996), drawing on the work of Wittgenstein (1953), explained that "what is distinctive of human agency is . . . the capacity to reflect on the possible reasons for acting and to deliberate about alternative courses of action in the light of the reasons one has" (p. 192). Taylor (1985) presented—as an essentially consensual position—the idea that "a person is a being who has a sense of self, has a notion of the future and the past, can hold values, make choices; in short, can adopt life-plans" (p. 97). Frankfurt precisely identified an agentic capacity unique to humans: "It seems to be peculiarly characteristic of humans . . . that they are able to form . . . 'second-order desires'" (Frankfurt, 1971, p. 6). All animals have desires, but humans "may also want to have (or not to have) certain desires and motives. They are capable of wanting to be different, in their preferences and purposes, from what they are" (Frankfurt, 1971, p. 7). This second-order capability, Frankfurt (1971) explained, arises from human's "capacity for reflective self-evaluation" (p. 7). (Professor Bandura advances a highly similar argument in Chapter 4 of this text: "The metacognitive capability to reflect on oneself and on the adequacy of one's capabilities, thoughts, and actions is the most distinctly human core property of agency.")

Scholarship on agency of course was not confined to discourse in academic philosophy. King (2009) explains that in the sociological analyses known as critical social theory, society consists not only of institutional structures but also of "individuals, whose agency and consciousness must be recognized" (p. 263).

This brief review of scholarly conceptions of agency raises three questions, two of which will be addressed immediately. First, if scholars outside of psychology have so thoroughly recognized human's agentic capacities, why did Bandura feel a need to sound the theme here? The answer plainly lies in scholarship *inside* of psychology. To a curious degree, the field's major paradigms historically have downplayed agentic capabilities. Consider the paradigms Bandura critiques at the start of his 1986 text. In psychodynamic theory, "an unconscious mental life . . . orchestrates behavior" (p. 5). In trait theory, in at least some prominent accounts, "human actions are governed by traits" (Bandura, 1986, p. 5). Since neither one's unconscious processes nor one's trait levels are thought to be agentically controllable, these perspectives provided little insight into the psychology of personal agency. And Behaviorism, of course, was no help. What about the discipline's dominant late-20th century paradigm, cognitive science? As Bruner summarized in 1990, "cognitive science . . . despite all its hospitality toward goal-directed behavior, is still chary of a concept of agency" (p. 9). Hence the need for a comprehensive agentic perspective on human nature.

The second question is this: What does Social Cognitive Theory add to scholarship on agency, above and beyond contributions in other fields? This answer, too, is plain. Bandura offers more than merely an agentic "perspective." He also provides a careful delineation of psychological processes that underpin agentic capabilities; measures for assessing these agentic processes; research paradigms capable of revealing how the psychological processes function in interaction with social environments; and applications of this basic theory and research that prove to dramatically improve the well-being of individuals and societies (see especially Chapter 6 of this text). These unique contributions are what made Professor Bandura the most highly cited figure in psychology and the social sciences.

The third of the questions can be introduced with an anecdote.

A Theory of . . .

Colleagues in Brazil recently asked me to record opening remarks for a conference of theirs on Social Cognitive Theory. In my video, I posed this question to the conference attendees: What is Social Cognitive Theory a theory *of*?

At other conferences, this question would be odd. Attendees would answer in a common voice and wonder why the question had been asked. "Hey, you attendees at a conference on Darwin's theory of natural selection, what's it a theory of?" Everyone says "the evolution of species." "Greetings, conference on Newtonian mechanics . . . " Everyone says "the motion of objects." But attendees at the Social Cognitive Theory conference provided answers that were diverse, as I saw for myself when organizers analyzed responses and sent me a word cloud. If my online Portuguese-to-English translation device is working, the most common responses were that Social Cognitive Theory is a theory of "human behavior," of "learning," and of "psychological functioning." These answers, like *The Times* headline, are not wrong but hardly are comprehensively right.

What would be comprehensively right? The writers quoted above suggest something. They were interested in agency, but as part of a larger project. More broadly, they were interested in *persons*. Hacker (2013, p. 1) explains that "we have projects and interests, we make choices and decisions, act voluntarily and intentionally, and are responsible for what we do. So we are persons." Frankfurt (1971) placed his analysis of second-order desires into an essay titled "Freedom of the Will and the Concept of a Person" (1971). And Charles Taylor, as quoted above, explained that the beings with a sense of self, a concept of future and past, values, and plans, are persons. (Philosophers sometimes remind us that if beings from another planet swoop in, extend their greetings, declare their intentions, and ask to call home, we do not see them as humans but do treat them as persons.)

This, finally, answers our "theory of?" question. Social Cognitive Theory can best be understood as a theoretical framework for understanding *persons*. In the standard nomenclature of psychology's subdisciplines, it is a theory of personality:

> Social cognitive theory provides an integrated theory of personality that addresses the complexity of human self-development, adaption, and change from an agentic perspective (Bandura, 1999b). Walter Mischel, who valiantly fought the trait war for decades, also provides a theory of personality that integrates intrapersonal determinants with conditionally manifested dispositions (Mischel & Shoda, 1999).
>
> (Bandura, 2015, p. 1041)

And this brings the scope of Bandura's achievement into view. In this book, he provides the intellectual world with a remarkably comprehensive, eminently practical, thoroughly data-based, integrated account of the development and psychological capacities of persons. It stands out from other personality theories that have dotted psychology's landscape not only in its rigor and scope, but in its multifaceted exploration of personal agency.

Persons

Despite our having reached this conclusion, there is one more thing to say. In his writing cited above, Charles Taylor did not present "a conception" of persons; he presented two of them. Their difference highlights a psychological process that is critical to Social Cognitive Theory, that figures prominently in this volume (see especially Chapters 4 and 5), yet that is sometimes overlooked in reviews of Bandura's work.

Taylor (1985) was addressing this question: "What is special about agents who are also persons?" (p. 97). In one conception of persons, what separates us from our animal friends (who do things purposefully and thus are agents) is computational power. People have greater agency than animals because of "their ability to envisage a longer time scale, to understand more complex cause-effect relationships, and thus engage in calculations" (Taylor, 1985, pp. 101–102). In this first conception of persons, you could put persons and non-human animals in the same situation and the people would (at least in some cases) outshine the animals by virtue of their greater ability to mentally represent environmental conditions, to predict short- and long-term contingencies in the environment, and to reflect consciously on their options for coping with prospective external events. If faced with a prototype survival dilemma—"can I get this piece of food without that predator in the distance seeing me?"—animals might assess the respective locations of the food and the predator, and their current state of hunger. People might do the same, but while envisioning a more complex range of strategies ("I'll come back later when the predator is napping"; "I'll get my friend to climb a nearby tree and make noise to distract the predator and will get the food then."). In this conception, persons and animals could be said to be at different locations on a common dimension: "This conception sees the superiority of man over animal as lying in greater strategic capacity" (Taylor, 1985, p. 112).

The greater-capacity conception of persons is entirely sensible. With all due respect to the other species, we do have greater cognitive capacities. This first conception of persons is central to Social Cognitive Theory, which analyzes a range of human cognitive capabilities involving forethought and strategic planning.

In the second conception of persons, however, one recognizes that in some cases you could *not* put people and non-human animals in "the same situation." People experience the following situations: embarrassing situations; humiliating situations; situations that enlarge their conception of self; situations that fill them with pride or shame. Animals do not experience these. The human experiences arise because people respond to *the personal significance of* situations and "there are matters of significance for human beings which are particularly human, and have no analogue with animals" (Taylor, 1985, p. 102). Our hypothetical human forager may well make food and predator calculations. But the situation's personal significance may be shaped be something else entirely—not by predictions about the objective external world ("predator at 200 yards cannot hear my rustling in the trees") but instead by an "internal world" of personal beliefs and conceptions of self-worth ("It will be really humiliating if I return to the village empty-handed, especially since I forgot to share food with my neighbors the last time I went out foraging").

Taylor notes that these matters of personal significance often include moral and ethical considerations. The great developmental psychologist Jerome Kagan recognized this, too: "One of the unique qualities of *Homo sapiens* is the continual disposition to apply a symbolic good–bad evaluation to most events (Bandura, 1996; Osgood, Suci, & Tannenbaum 1957). Humans are the only species that evaluate symbolically their acts, ideas, and feelings with a moral gloss and are motivated to regard themselves as good" (Kagan, 1996, p. 905). In short, in this second conception of persons, people are not just animals who execute more elaborate calculations than the other animals. "Humans are really different" (Shweder, 1999).

As you surely noticed, Kagan recognized something else, too: that this process of subjective evaluation—of good–bad "gloss"—is central to Bandura's Social Cognitive Theory. In Social Cognitive Theory, people are not merely animals with more computational ability than pigeons and rats. Sure, they are that. But they are more than that. People are self-evaluating agents. They evaluate their own actions in relation to socially acquired standards and react affectively to action—standard discrepancies. Furthermore, in a feature distinctive to the social cognitive approach, these affective self-evaluations contribute directly to future action. In Chapter 4, Bandura explicates the role of self-evaluative reactions in goal-directed motivation. In Chapter 5, he explains their role in moral agency. People commonly adhere to moral rules even if no one would notice a violation because *someone* would notice: they themselves: "People behave prosocially because they anticipate that acting well will bring self-satisfaction and self-respect, they refrain from transgressing norms because they know that antisocial conduct—even if it is not detected by external social systems—will give rise to self-reproof" (Chapter 5). The significance of these morally-charged circumstances cannot be explained solely in terms of external environmental features and calculations about those features—the explanation that follows from Taylor's person conception #1. Instead, in these cases that Bandura analyzes, "significance . . . is such that we cannot explain it without taking into account that it is significant for us" (Taylor, 1985, p. 111). A simple indication of the breadth of the social cognitive framework is that—in theory and in empirical methods—it encompasses *both* of the conceptions of persons identified by Taylor.

We earlier noted observers' tendency to conflate a single concept or research program of Professor Bandura's with Social Cognitive Theory as a whole. You now can see why Professor Bandura called out this mistake—and authored this book.

On the Completion of *Social Cognitive Theory*

As noted at the outset, Professor Bandura was not able himself to bring his final book to completion. Especially in light of his historical stature in the field, I would like to clarify precisely how this volume was completed.

My editing drew on three sets of materials: writing that Professor Bandura prepared for this volume; prior theoretical publications (listed below) by Professor Bandura that addressed the topics covered in the book's chapters; and material in the Stanford University archives, which contains personal papers including highly detailed lecture notes that Professor Bandura had prepared over the years. The first two sets of materials overlap; Professor Bandura had been incorporating into his book sections of material from his prior papers. His writing process fit the book's purpose; as noted, he was aiming to bring the various established parts of Social Cognitive Theory together in one monograph-length presentation, and thus was combining new writing with ideas expressed in prior material. My own editing simply brought this process to completion.

Regarding the text's word-by-word style, editing did include a large number of small stylistic changes to Professor Bandura's original text. He wanted this book's content to be accessible to both professionals and students, but sadly did not live to complete final editing toward this goal. With the encouragement of the Albert Bandura Trust, I edited text to enhance its accessibility to student readers at the graduate and advanced-undergraduate levels. This process included the addition of a small amount of original text designed merely to enhance the chapter-to-chapter flow of material.

Finally, the text also contains a small amount of original substantive material added by myself. In all cases, these additions are demarcated. Brief additions, including added references, appear in the main text in brackets. Longer passages that extend or update points raised in the main text appear in footnotes.

Albert Bandura

This volume is concerned with Social Cognitive Theory, not its creator. Yet, I would be remiss if I did not comment on the Author in closing.

I will focus on a simple question: How did Al Bandura accomplish all this? How did he generate such a wide array of compelling research results, formulate a theory of such exceptional breadth, and thus impact the field to such an extraordinary degree? Superficially, his professional activities—teaching courses; conducting research with students and colleagues; writing empirical and theoretical papers—resembled those of thousands of other university-based psychologists. He did not run a large center or institute. He did not found a professional association or scientific journal to promote his work. Yet, he was the most eminent psychologist of his era (Haggbloom et al., 2002) and the most highly cited living author not merely in psychology, but in the overall social sciences or humanities (http://www.timeshighereducation.co.uk/405956.article). What personal qualities fueled these achievements?

As I contemplate this question, two ideas come to mind. A thought experiment can introduce the first. Imagine you have run a study that identifies a mediator of some established effect; that is, people know that independent variable X affects outcome Y, and you find that mediator M—a person-based process—substantially accounts for the X → Y influence. If you are like most people, you would report your results in a paper titled something like "M mediates the effects of X on Y," and move on. However, if you had the analytical skills one associates with an exceptional natural scientist or engineer, you might do something more. You might delineate classes of factors that affect X and organize them into a taxonomy, identify classes of processes that are affected *by* X and account for its influence on Y, and combine these into a systematic, comprehensive theoretical model. Alternatively, suppose you had a different set of conceptual skills, namely, those creative, imaginative abilities one associates with "visionaries." In this case, you might have the insight that your X is not just "a statistical mediator" but, instead, is a distinctive and pervasive class of human thought. Furthermore, you might recognize that your study's implications extend far beyond your original outcome Y to an indefinitely wide range of outcomes that are crucial to human welfare.

Or there is a third alternative: You are Albert Bandura. In this case, you possess exceptional levels of *both types* of intellectual skills, the analytical and the visionary. You rapidly transform your "mediator study" into a scientifically systematic and intellectually far-reaching enterprise.

As readers may recognize, I have outlined—abstractly—the history of self-efficacy theory. Its impact has been vast; enter *self-efficacy* into a Google Scholar search, and you get a "results" number so large that you think it's a typographical error. Yet, the enterprise began with a simple mediator study: "Cognitive Processes Mediating Behavioral Change" (Bandura, Adams, & Beyer, 1977). In someone else's hands, the reported research result might have been an isolated contribution to a narrow domain of study. In Professor Bandura's, it became one of the highest-impact conceptions in psychology's history.

The second idea can be introduced with a joke: Someone is wandering the streets of Manhattan, looking for America's best music school. He asks, "How do you get to Juilliard." The answer: "Practice."

How do you become Al Bandura? I was never there to see the following, but my understanding when in graduate school was that Al entered his at-home study in the morning right after breakfast and read-and-wrote continuously until lunch. Every day. The Bandura family has since confirmed this and added that, on most days, he returned to his study from 8 p.m. until midnight. The probability of hearing Professor Bandura say "I was distracted today; couldn't find time for writing" was zero. This extraordinarily consistent, disciplined schedule surely was key to his developing a theoretical framework of unrivaled comprehensiveness. It should come as no surprise that, when interviewed for the eventual obituary that appeared in the *New York Times*, Professor Bandura commented on the enduring value of self-regulatory skills.

Soon after Professor Bandura's passing, a colleague who was at Stanford in the 1980s commented to me that "Al compartmentalized." Yes, he had diverse interests. He found time for gardening and for opera. He dispensed tips on picnic spots in Napa Valley and hiking trails in the High Sierra. He once spontaneously delivered to me an extraordinarily detailed and well-structured lecture on the elaborate classification system used to categorize German wines. (I cannot recall why he delivered this lecture—but I still recall the classifications.) Yet he compartmentalized. He was always able to focus on work. In the Department, Al Bandura was never "having a bad day." One can speculate that there must have been some outside-of-work bad days here or there—but one only can speculate. Professor Bandura was remarkably able to put aside personal concerns to focus on scientific advance.

========

In any field of scholarship, the contributions of the most famous figures are likely to be underestimated. Great scholars invent intellectual tools that others use without thinking about the inventor. We plot points in x—y coordinate systems without considering Descartes. We run computer programs without contemplating Von Neumann and others who devised a computer architecture with stored programs. Such is the case with Al Bandura.

When Professor Bandura began his career, psychologists looking for a comprehensive framework for understanding persons had three primary options: psychodynamic theory, trait theory, and radical behaviorism. As he recognized more clearly than perhaps anyone else, all three shared two curious qualities, the second of which followed from the first. All three incorporated one-way determinism; personal qualities were said to be caused by indelible early-life experiences, inherited dispositions, or external reinforcers. As a result of the one-way causal models, all three obscured from view the agentic capabilities that are the focus of this book; the mid-20th century theories left little room for reciprocal person-based causality.

And what intellectual tools are available to psychological scientists who start their careers today? There's barely a psychoanalyst or radical behaviorist in sight, and anyone who thinks that people inherit five universal personality traits that determine their life course is embarrassingly ill-informed. Instead, today's "default conception" of persons is a systems view in which not only psychological structures but also biological ones develop in interaction with the social world, and interact with one another reciprocally. A second feature of today's default conception of humans is that people influence their life course through agentic processes; publications on goals, self-concept, self-control strategies, and self-efficacy beliefs appear at the rate of literally thousands of papers a year. An agentic social-cognitive framework is the new "default" conceptual system for innumerable investigators—many of whom do not even contemplate its origins.

Was Al Bandura individually responsible for this sea change in psychological science? Of course not. His own Social Cognitive Theory would tell us that the foundation of his beliefs was a social-scientific world that provided critical seeds for his theory's growth. But no other individual is more responsible for this profound change in psychology's conception of human nature than Albert Bandura. Professor Bandura was the world's most highly cited psychologist. But perhaps the greatest indication of his impact is that so many people are social cognitive theorists without even knowing it.

Acknowledgments

I thank Professor Bandura's longtime Executive Assistant, Ms. Karen Saltzman, for making available to me electronic versions of Professor Bandura's publications— and for sending me a box of papers. I also thank the Stanford University archives for access to material in the Bandura Archives.

I am grateful to Professor Roberta Azzi for emailing incisive questions about Social Cognitive Theory that indirectly contributed to the development of some material in the text—and for sending a word cloud.

Gratitude also is expressed to Professor Tracy L. Caldwell for a highly valuable administrative suggestion that facilitated the book's preparation.

Thank you to Darren Lalonde and the entire team at John Wiley and Sons for their support throughout the process.

Finally, thanks are extended again to Mary Bandura for the great honor of bringing her Father's project to a close.

Daniel Cervone
University of Illinois Chicago

Source Publications

The chapters in this book include revised material from the following publications by Professor Bandura:

Bandura, A. (1971). Analysis of modeling processes. In A. Bandura (Ed.), *Psychological modeling: Conflicting theories*. Routledge

Bandura, A. (1978). Social learning theory of aggression. *Journal of Communication, 28*, 12–29.

Bandura, A. (1989). Human agency in social cognitive theory. *American Psychologist, 44*(9), 1175–1184.

Bandura, A. (1989). Social cognitive theory. In R. Vasta (Ed.), *Annals of child development. Vol. 6. Six theories of child development* (pp. 1–60) JAI Press.

Bandura, A. (1991). Social cognitive theory of moral thought and action. In W. M. Kurtines & J. L. Gewirtz (Eds.), *Handbook of moral behavior and development* (Vol. 1, pp. 45–103). Erlbaum.

Bandura, A. (1991). Self-regulation of motivation through anticipatory and self-reactive mechanisms. In R. A. Dienstbier (Ed.), *Perspectives on motivation: Nebraska symposium on motivation* (Vol. 38, pp. 69–164). University of Nebraska Press.

Bandura, A. (2000). Cultivate self-efficacy for personal and organizational effectiveness. In E. A. Locke (Ed.), *Handbook of principles of organizational behavior* (pp. 120–136). Blackwell Publishing.

Bandura, A. (2008). Toward an agentic theory of the self. In H. W. Marsh, R. G. Craven, & D. M. McInerey (Eds.), *Self-processes, learning, and enabling human potential* (pp. 15–49). Information Age.

Bandura, A. (2011) Social and policy impact of social cognitive theory. In M. M. Mark, S.I. Donaldson & B. Campbell (Eds.), *Social psychology and evaluation* (pp. 33–70). Guilford.

Bandura, A. (2018). Toward a psychology of human agency: Pathways and reflections. *Perspectives on Psychological Science, 13*(2), 130–136.

Bandura, A., Barbaranelli, C., Caprara, G. V., & Pastorelli, C. (2001). Self-efficacy beliefs as shapers of children's aspirations and career trajectories. *Child Development, 72*, 187–206.

Bandura, A., & Locke, E. (2003). Negative self-efficacy and goal effects revisited. *Journal of Applied Psychology, 88,* 87–99.

Preface

As my father's ideas progressed and the Star Wars films became wildly popular, he coined the phrase "May the Efficacy Force be with you." He used it as his signature phrase when signing books and wanted it inscribed on his headstone, which it is. Self-efficacy is central among the psychological constructs he posited as influencing behavior, and reflects beliefs in one's ability to master particular challenges. To wish someone the "Efficacy Force" is to hope that they are inspired to develop confidence in their ability to succeed at their life pursuits, thereby establishing a sense of control over their life course. It is a wish that they create visions of what they want to accomplish, figure out how to pursue them, and get back in the saddle when they run into trouble during their efforts. It is a wish that they take the reins of life and steer their own course.

My father certainly felt the "Efficacy Force" as he tirelessly developed a psychological theory of personality that put the capacity for human agency front and center. This framework emphasizes how people actively mediate their experiences through their intentions, reflections, and judgments, which are situated in historical, interpersonal, and cultural contexts. The complex interplay of these factors generates how we navigate our world, how we create our realities, and how we transform ourselves. Social Cognitive Theory (SCT) treats people as the authors of their experience by assigning conscious, intentional thought a primary role in psychological functioning. People are not simply buffeted about by environmental contingencies or unconscious processes, as was emphasized by behavioral and psychoanalytic models, or by static personality traits. We play a far more active and deliberate role in shaping and controlling our destinies. Moral decision making features centrally; SCT describes the ways individuals and social systems either maintain or renounce responsibility for their conduct, and how this governs both humane and inhumane conduct. This approach to human nature, while complex, is intuitively sensible. People relate to a theory that emphasizes their lived experience, personal responsibility, and ways to exercise control. It fosters optimism and empowerment.

In keeping with his theory, my father practiced what he preached in many areas of life. He and my mother Virginia, transplants from the Canadian and American midwestern plains, cultivated a life in California nourished by their culinary, artistic, musical, and political interests. They were locavores. They loved fresh, simple, flavorful foods, inspired by childhood memories of farm fresh corn, berries and cream, homemade pickles, plum pierogi; the list goes on. They created a bountiful garden offering up an ever-expanding array of fruits and vegetables. My mother honed her cooking skills and they sought out wonderful restaurants all over the Bay Area. The "Efficacy Force" empowered this adventure, leading to a rich food and wine culture in our home that brought great pleasure to friends and family.

Perhaps the strongest spark fueling my father's efficacious pursuit of SCT was his desire to see it put to social good. He often said that the value of a psychological theory is reflected by how useful it is in promoting individual and social change. As SCT became established it was applied to diverse clinical and social issues, proving to be a powerful tool for change. Modeling, guided mastery experiences, and self-management training helped people develop skills, cope with fears, and build resilience. They do so by enhancing self-efficacy, thereby providing a sense of control that often translates into a more general sense of personal agency. People become active agents of their own development; if you can succeed in one area, why not in others? These principles formed the basis of highly effective programs designed to treat clinical problems and promote health, education, athletic achievement, business management, and effective parenting practices. They can be creatively applied to most social domains to impart skill and enhance performance.

The extension of SCT to global issues of family planning, population growth, and environmental sustainability was the ultimate application of these principles, leading to my father's collaboration with organizations, such as the Population Media Center, that use various media to tackle social problems in different countries. Serial dramas employing popular stars were developed to portray social dilemmas and solutions that engage viewers in a voyage of discovery that enables change in their own lives. Transformative stories depicted how girls and women could overcome obstacles to gaining an education, utilizing family planning, and accessing contraception. Families and young men were depicted grappling with cultural practices that damage girls and restrict their opportunities, such as genital mutilation and forced early marriage. Cultural stereotypes that contribute to unwanted pregnancies, such as the attribution of masculinity to those having many children, were challenged. These dramas carefully scripted models in traditional roles, positive alternative roles, and those struggling with the transformation from one to the other, showing a path to life changes. They have proven remarkably effective in increasing gender equity, girls' educational attainment, use of family planning, as well as influencing other practices that are environmentally destructive and limit opportunity. Nowhere is the arc of my father's career more clearly evidenced than in the journey from his early modeling studies, in which children learned to imitate aggressive models, to the application of these findings via powerful media applications promoting social change. He was thrilled by these developments and their implications for creating a more just, sustainable world.

In his early nineties, my father embarked on writing yet another book. He wanted to present a succinct, accessible description of SCT and its applications. As he was unable to finish it before his death, I invited one of his former students, Dr. Daniel Cervone, to complete the work. There is perhaps no one better qualified to take on this project; Dan has contributed to the theoretical structure of SCT through his research and his writings, and has a deep understanding of the framework. He writes with clarity and humor, and proposed a strategy that preserved our father's voice while seamlessly knitting together the core features of the theory. He knew my father well and they had a strong personal relationship. I am grateful for his enthusiasm and tireless efforts to bring this to completion. I felt the winds of the "Efficacy Force" behind him!

I also want to thank the team at Wiley & Sons for their support and patience as we all navigated how to use previously published material to bring this to fruition. They embraced the project and were positive and responsive throughout the process.

David Maxfield provided both financial and moral support for this project. He and his wife Kathy were very caring and had a warm friendship with my father. Their visits brightened his days.

Finally, I am indebted to Karen Salzman, my father's Executive Assistant, for organizing and helping manage these writings, which was no easy task. She provided the supportive bedrock and friendship that enabled him to continue writing and communicating with his professional world.

I hope this updated, concise presentation of Social Cognitive Theory inspires continuing growth in new ideas and applications to make this world a better place, as my father hoped it would.

Mary Bandura

Dr. Bandura in his garden at his home in Stanford, CA, 2009. Source: Photo courtesy of Dr. Mary Bandura.

1

A Psychology of Human Agency

Across historical eras, conceptions of human nature have changed markedly. Theological conceptions predominated in earlier times. Human nature was viewed as preordained by divine design. In the late 19th century, Darwinian principles began to supplant religious doctrines. Human nature was said to result from environmental pressures acting on random gene mutations and reproductive recombinations.

Different as they may be, the theological and the Darwinian frameworks have something in common: They leave little room for human agency. The nature of humans reflects either the purposes of the Divine or the purposeless algorithm that is natural selection.

That purposeless algorithm, however, gave rise to a purposeful species. The abilities to communicate using symbols, to deliberate upon the physical and social worlds, and to plan and intentionally alter the environment in preparation for future events conferred considerable functional advantages. These cognitive capabilities thus became the hallmark of humans.

These human cognitive capabilities are recognized widely. Yet, their implications for understanding causal processes contributing to human nature are often underappreciated. The emergence of language and forethought converted our species into agents: beings who could transcend the dictates of their immediate environment, select and shape the external circumstances they encounter, and thereby guide the course of individual and societal development. Planful cognitive agency augmented aimless environmental selection. Contemporary technological advances have greatly expanded the power of human agency in these coevolutionary processes.

Through cognitive self-regulation, humans can envision the future and act on it in the present. They can evaluate and modify ongoing current behaviors to best serve not only present needs, but also long-term aims. These self-referent cognitive abilities are central to Social Cognitive Theory's agentic perspective on human nature.

On Agency and "Free Will"

Scholarly debates over human agency have a long history. Medieval theologians recognized the dissonance of two ideas: 1) the Creator is omniscient and benevolent, yet 2) created a world that contains evil, including moral evils perpetrated by people who were made in the Creator's image. The doctrine of "free will" provided a way out of this conceptual conundrum. By granting the power of free choice, the Creator enabled people to prove their moral worth in a world of temptations and evils.

The free will position, whose proponents granted humans the power of free choice in the likeness of absolute agency, was debated by philosophers for centuries. A recurrent limitation of these debates is that free will was enigmatic: an autonomous causative force whose origins, exact nature, and independent functioning in the midst of environmental pressures were shrouded in ambiguity. Preoccupation with the metaphysical incompatibility of free will and determinism diverted attention from more fruitful analysis of the capacity of humans to bring their personal influence to bear on events (Nahmias, 2002).

Progress can be made by reframing the issue of free will in terms of the exercise of agency. Agency describes broad capability; to be an "agent" is to be able to influence intentionally one's functioning and life circumstances. This agentic framing invites specification of the psychological mechanisms and causal structures that enable persons to act as agents.

Human agency operates principally through cognitive and other self-regulatory processes. Their analysis provides insights into the constructive and proactive role that cognition plays in human action, while advancing the understanding of human capabilities beyond earlier debates about an amorphous "free will."

Nonagentic Approaches in Contemporary Psychology

Psychology has undergone wrenching paradigm shifts during its relatively brief history. Yet, what is surprising is that competing paradigms each have questioned the human capacity for agency. The substantial influence of these paradigms underscores the significance of the agentic perspective on human nature advanced in this volume.

In much of the 20th century, experimental psychology's guiding paradigm was behaviorism. Behaviorists proposed an input-output model. Stimuli and responses were linked by an intervening but noncausal black box. Investigators harbored the belief that stimuli—in particular, those stimuli that function as response consequences—alter behavior in an automatic, unconscious manner. Skinner's (1971) contention that "a person does not act upon the world, the world acts upon him" (p. 211) epitomized the behavioristic denial of human agency.

This line of theorizing was eventually put out of vogue by psychological models inspired by a new technology: computers. Creative theorists filled the behavioristic black box with symbolic representations, rules, and computational operations. The mind as a symbol manipulator, in the likeness of a linear computer, became the conceptual model for the times.

Cognitive processing theories modeled on serial computer architectures were, in turn, superseded by connectionist models which recognized that mental events occur in parallel. In parallel processing models, interconnected, multilayered, neuronal-like subsystems work simultaneously. Sensory organs deliver up information to a multitude of sub-systems acting as the mental machinery that processes the inputs and, through some intermediate integrating system, generates a coherent output automatically and nonconsciously.

These alternative theories differ in what they place in the mediating system. Radical behaviorism posits a noncausal connector; computerized cognitivism posits a linear central processor; and parallel distributed connectionism posits interconnected, neuronal-like subunits. But the theories share the same bottom-up causation: input → throughput → output. In each model, environments act on biological machinery that generates outputs automatically and nonconsciously.

These nonagentic conceptions strip humans of a functional consciousness, a self-identity, and thus an agentic capability. As Harré (1983) emphasized, such conceptions of human nature attribute personal actions to subpersonal parts. In actuality, however, it is conscious, intentional *people*—not subpersonal parts of people—who plan actions and act on the environment. People create, preserve, transform, and even destroy environments, rather than merely reacting to them as given "inputs." Nonagentic conceptions overlook the socially embedded interplay between the exercise of personal agency and the nature of the environments that individuals experience. In so doing, they provide a truncated image of human nature.

Agency, Consciousness, and the Brain

Consciousness is the very substance of mental life. Conscious experience makes life not only manageable, but meaningful; a conscious life is a life worth living.

Without the capacity for deliberative and reflective conscious activity, humans would be mindless automatons. With it, they are mindful agents.

Consciousness encompasses multiple functions. For example, the function of consciously experiencing an event that is happening *to* oneself differs from the function of interacting purposefully in an ongoing activity as a planful agent (Korsgaard, 1989a and 1989b). In addition to these nonreflective and reflectively self-aware components, consciousness also serves a conceptual function; people can consciously deliberate on ideas and experiences, which they do mainly through the medium of language. In this conceptual function, people purposefully access and deliberatively process information in order to construct, select, and ultimately evaluate and regulate courses of action. The human mind is generative, creative, proactive, and reflective, not just reactive.

One must distinguish the psychological functions of conscious thought from the physiological functions that enable people to think consciously. With this distinction in hand, one encounters a formidable explanatory challenge: bridging the gap between a physicalistic account for brain functions and a (nondualistic) cognitivism. How do people activate brain processes to realize given intentions and purposes?

Consciousness is an emergent brain activity with higher-level control functions, rather than simply an epiphenomenal byproduct of lower-level processes. Indeed, if the neuronal processes of common activities were automatically reflected in consciousness, conscious experience would be hopelessly cluttered; a mind numbing array of contents would foreclose any functionality of conscious reflection. When one is driving a car, for example, one's consciousness is filled with thoughts of other matters rather than with the ongoing neuronal or biomechanical aspects of driving.

Emergent properties differ in kind from their lower-level bases. For example, the fluidity and viscosity of water are emergent properties, not simply the combined properties of the individual hydrogen and oxygen components (Bunge, 1977). Through their interactive effects, components are transformed into new phenomena. Van Gulick (2001) made the important distinction between emergent properties and emergent causal powers over events at the lower level.

In the metatheory enunciated by Sperry (1991, 1993; also see Eccles, 1974), cognitive agents regulate their actions by cognitive downward causation and also undergo upward activation by sensory stimulation. The patterns of neural activities characterizing interpretive and deliberative thought processes have a downward regulatory function over lower-level neural events that lead to action in this conception of cognitive functionalism (Sperry, 1993). These regulatory functions are central to the exercise of human agency. In the case of humans, most of this interpretative thought operates through language, drawing on a vast knowledge base. The core agentic capabilities of intentionality, forethought, self-reaction, and self-reflection operate as hierarchically organized determinants.

In acting as agents, individuals obviously lack awareness of, and direct control over, neuronal processes and structures. Yet, they exercise second-order control over these processes. They do so by intentionally engaging in activities known to be functionally related to given outcomes. The intentional pursuit of these activities, in turn, activates and modifies subpersonal neuronal events. An illustrative analogy is that, in driving, drivers intentionally engage in deliberate acts that are under their control (e.g., steering, braking, stepping on the gas pedal, turning on the car's air conditioner). These acts *indirectly* control mechanical, chemical, and electrical processes (hydraulic mechanisms, microcombustion, electrochemical processes) of which the driver is unaware. The deliberate planning of a trip indirectly puts the underlying processes to work.

Consider also dual-level control in skill acquisition. Baseball pitchers practice to throw the ball in precise locations that are designed to discombobulate batters. As pitchers exert direct control over this practicing, they enlist and thus exert indirect control over neurophysiological machinery that is active when they pitch. Enactments of controllable activities at the macro, behavioral level trigger subserving events at the more micro, neural level.

The fact that individuals have no awareness of their brain processes does not mean that they are just quiescent hosts of automata that dictate their behavior. Neural systems are biological tools that people use to pursue goals and accomplish tasks that give meaning, direction, and satisfaction to life (Bandura 1997; Harré & Gillet, 1994). Neuroimaging can shed light on how agentic causal beliefs and activities develop functional neuronal structures and orchestrate neurodynamics.[1]

This analysis of agency, consciousness, and the brain highlights the paramount role of intentional action in personal development—where "development" includes growth in knowledge, skills, behavioral capacities, and also the neural structures which support them. Because intentional action is such a driver of development, a scientific analysis of human agency requires, first and foremost, explication of the *psychological* capacities that enable persons to act as agents. These capacities are the central focus of Social Cognitive Theory.

---

1 Bandura's point about how social activities develop neural structures aligns with additional developments in cognitive science and neuroscience. Consider Cecilia Heyes's (2018, 2021) research and theory on "cognitive gadgets." As she explains, it is through sociocultural experience that people acquire mental tools ("gadgets") with neural underpinnings. These neurally-grounded tools are not genetically prespecified; they are acquired experientially. A classic case is the gadget you are using now, for reading. The human brain did not "evolve for reading," which is a relatively recent cultural invention. But when people go to the effort of learning how to read, they unknowingly (unless they have watched a lot of neuroscience videos) create interconnections among previously independent brain regions that detect shapes, encode sounds, and encode meaning (DeHaene, 2009). The activity of learning how to read thus creates a new, functionally coherent neural system, exactly as Bandura's writing suggests.

Core Properties of Human Agency

Social Cognitive Theory adopts an agentic perspective on human development, adaptation, and change (Bandura, 1986, 2001a). In this view, personal qualities are not merely a static result of environmental and biological determinants. They also are part of the causal structure. People are not mere passive observers of their behavior and development. They are self-organizing, proactive, self-reflecting, and self-regulating agents who contribute causally to their life circumstances and personal growth.

In Social Cognitive Theory, the agentic aspects of psychosocial functioning are manifested though three core psychological properties: forethought, self-reactiveness, and self-reflection. These agentic properties are introduced here, and are examined in greater detail in subsequent chapters of this text.

Forethought

Future states of affairs have no present material existence, so cannot be a cause of current behavior. But through cognitive representations, visualized futures can be brought into the present and can serve as guides and motivators of current behavior. In forethought, the first of the three core agentic properties, people form intentions that include action plans and strategies; set goals for personal achievement; and visualize the likely outcomes of their goal-directed actions. In this form of anticipatory self-guidance, behavior is governed by visualized goals and anticipated outcomes rather than being pulled by an unrealized future state.

Forethought contributes directly to human agency. It enables people to transcend the dictates of their immediate environment and to shape and regulate the present to realize desired futures. When projected over the long-term on matters of value, a forethoughtful perspective provides direction, coherence, and meaning to one's life.

Self-Reactiveness

The second agentic property is self-reactiveness.[2] Agents are not only planners and forethinkers. They are also self-regulators. Individuals manage their behavior

---

2 The term "self-reactiveness" in Bandura's writing here corresponds to the class of psychological phenomena also referred to as "self-evaluative reactions" in earlier writing in Social Cognitive Theory (e.g., Bandura & Cervone, 1983, 1986; Bussey & Bandura, 1992; Cervone, Jiwani, & Wood, 1991; Simon, 1979b; and see Chapter 4). Although less concise, the term "self-evaluative reactions" explicitly references the dynamic psychological process through which people appraise and then respond to the acceptability, adequacy, and excellence of their actions in relation to personal standards of performance. This class of psychological phenomena is pervasive, yet it is not easy to name; Kagan (1998, p. 151) notes that "curiously, no word in English names . . . with precision" the momentary pleasant feeling that results when behavior meets a valued personal standard of performance.

by self-sanctions within a self-governing system. They do so by adopting behavioral standards against which they evaluate their performances. They respond with positive or negative evaluative self-reactions depending on how well their behavior measures up to their adopted standards (Bandura, 1991a).

Self-reactiveness is central to goal-based motivation. Goals, in and of themselves, may fail to spur people to action. Goals acquire motivational force when they activate self-reactive influences that, in turn, govern motivation and action. Particular characteristics of goals—especially their specificity, challenge level, and temporal proximity—are key to the activation of evaluative self-reactions and other aspects of self-referent thinking. Chapter 4 of this book is devoted to the self-regulatory mechanisms through which people can shape their future.

Personal standards and evaluative self-reactions are particularly central in the moral domain. Social Cognitive Theory moves beyond analyses of moral reasoning by addressing the explanatory gap between moral thought and moral conduct. Moral reasoning is linked to moral conduct through self-regulatory mechanisms rooted in moral standards that are coupled with contingent self-sanctions (Bandura, 1991b, 2016). Self-regard and self-contempt are roused by actions that, respectively, adhere to or violate moral standards. Chapter 5 of this text is devoted to moral standards and the psychological mechanisms through which people sometimes disengage them.

Self-Reflection

The third agentic property is self-reflection. People do not only react evaluatively to their current actions. They also contemplate past and future activities. They reflect on their efficacy for action, on the soundness of their thoughts, on the rightness of their values, and on the meaning and morality of their pursuits. It is at this higher level of self-reflectiveness that individuals address conflicts between alternative courses of action and competing values, and favor one course over another. The metacognitive capability to reflect on oneself and on the adequacy of one's capabilities, thoughts, and actions is the most distinctly human core property of agency.

In Social Cognitive Theory, people's capacity to act as intentional agents stems from multifacted psychological mechanisms that work in concert. Yet, among these mechanisms of agency, one is particularly central: Self-efficacy beliefs, that is, people's beliefs about their capabilities to exert control over the diverse challenges of their lives. Self-efficacy beliefs are of paramount importance for three reasons. One is that they directly influence thoughts, actions, and emotions as people engage in activities. Second, reflections on self-efficacy influence *other* self-regulatory processes that, in turn, affect self-regulated behavior; these include determinants such as goals and aspirations, outcome expectations, affective proclivities, and perceptions of impediments and opportunities in the social environment. Thirdly, self-efficacy beliefs partly determine whether people even *undertake* a given challenging activity. Individuals often can select the environments they experience. Self-reflections on efficacy guide the selections. People tend to avoid challenges and contexts in which they doubt their efficacy for adequate performance. Chapter 3 of this volume analyzes perceived self-efficacy as a foundation of agency.

Three Modes of Human Agency

Theorizing and research on human agency have centered primarily on agency exercised individually. However, this is not the only way in which people affect how they live their lives. Social Cognitive Theory identifies three different modes of human agency: individual, proxy, and collective.

The individual form of agency is causally influential in activity domains whose outcomes are, at least in principle, controllable personally. However, in many spheres of functioning, people do not have direct control over social conditions and institutional practices that affect their everyday lives. Under these circumstances, they rely on socially mediated proxy agency.

In proxy agency, people exert control by influencing others who have the resources, knowledge, and means to act on their behalf. Examples of proxy agency are numerous and diverse in everyday life. Children turn to parents to obtain desired objects. Marital partners turn to their spouses. Citizens appeal to elected representatives. Religious believers, through prayer, appeal to divine agency, especially in times of crisis or physical and emotional distress.

The third form of agency, collective agency, looms large when valued outcomes are beyond the reach of any individual and thus require the coordinated efforts of a group. The outcomes sought by individuals are achievable only through group efforts. Success hinges on collective agency, in which people pool their knowledge, skills, and resources and coordinate their actions to shape their future. In this multiagent model of collective agency, participants achieve unity of effort for common purpose. A key ingredient of collective agency is the shared belief in the collective's power to produce desired results. These collective efficacy beliefs are not a simple sum of the efficacy beliefs of individual members. Groups may be more—or less—than the sum of their parts; for example, collections of talented individuals may perform poorly as a group if members do not function well as a unit. The collective's performance is an emergent group-level phenomenon. Group members commonly are aware of this. Their reflections on the efficacy of their group thus may vary from a simple averaging of their individual self-appraisals.

Causal Processes: Triadic Codetermination

An understanding of human agency requires analysis of causal processes; one must identify personal processes that function as causal determinants of individual development. This need, in turn, raises another. Any analysis of specific causal determinants should occur within a broader, well-specified framework for understanding causal systems. Abstract though such frameworks may be, an overarching conception of causal systems can, in practice, draw attention to significant phenomena that might otherwise be overlooked.

Such causal frameworks have been debated frequently in the past. Many such debates ultimately proved fruitless because the terms of debate were too simple. For example, dispositionalist claims that the causes of human behavior reside in the individual were opposed to situationist claims that causes are found in the environment. The reality of causal systems is more complex.

Today, most theorists adopt an interactionist model of causation. Human functioning is attributed to a mix of personal and environmental influences. However, having said this, one must distinguish among three types of interactionism, two of which subscribe to one-way causation in the link to behavior (Figure 1.1).

In the *Unidirectional model,* persons and situations are treated as independent influences that both contribute to the production of behavior. The major weakness with this casual model is its failure to represent the fact that the personal and environmental influence one another. People create, alter, and destroy environments. The changes they produce in environmental conditions, in turn, affect them personally. This model also is limited by its unidirectional, rather than reciprocal, relations to behavior.

The *Partially bidirectional* model, which is widely adopted, acknowledges that persons and situations affect each other. Yet, the model still treats influences

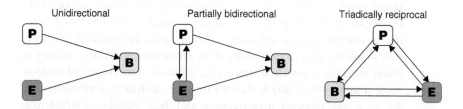

Unidirectional   Partially bidirectional   Triadically reciprocal

Figure 1.1 Schematization of the interplay of constituent determinants in alternative interactional causal models. *P* represents the intrapersonal determinants in the form of cognitive, motivational, affective, and biological events; *B* the behavioral determinants; and E the environmental determinants.

relating to behavior as flowing unidirectionally; the person-situation interchange produces behavior, but that behavior is not recognized as, in turn, affecting the ongoing transaction between the person and the situation. This conceptual model fails to acknowledge that behavior is an interacting determinant of both person-based processes and environmental features.

Research conducted within these frameworks typically evaluates interactions by partitioning the average amount of variance in behavior attributed to persons, environments, and their interaction. "Interaction" thus becomes merely a statistical term; it makes no reference to specified causal processes. But what is needed is a conception of interaction that references identifiable, ongoing dynamic interchanges between person-based processes and environmental forces (Patterson, 1976). Social cognitive theory rejects these first two causal models in in favor of a three-way, interactive conception of causation.

In *triadic reciprocal* causation, shown in the right panel of Figure 1.1, human functioning is a product of the interplay among three classes of influence: intrapersonal factors; the behaviors in which individuals engage; and the environmental forces that impinge on them. The intrapersonal determinants include biological endowment, competencies, aspirations, values, and the like. Social Cognitive Theory's conceptualization of triadic reciprocal causation fosters analyses of each of the variety of causal exchanges:

> – In the reciprocal relation between intrapersonal and behavioral determinants, intrapersonal factors affect how individuals select environments and perceive the ones they encounter. The natural and extrinsic effects of actions, in turn, affect thought processes and affective states.

> – In the reciprocal relation between behavioral and environmental determinants, behavior alters environmental conditions—and, in turn, is then affected by the very conditions it has created.

> – In the reciprocal relation between environmental and intrapersonal determinants, environmental influences such as social modeling, instructional practices, and various modes of social persuasion can affect the development of intrapersonal qualities—which, once developed, function as determinants of subsequent action. In the reciprocal dynamics of this segment, people can affect their environment without saying or doing anything. They elicit stereotypic reactions from the social environment simply by their physical characteristics, such as their ethnicity, gender, race, age, physical attractiveness, and their socially conferred roles and statuses. The social reactions thus elicited, in turn, affect the recipients' conceptions of themselves and others in ways that either strengthen or reduce the environmental stereotype.

The notion of "reciprocal" influence does not imply simultaneity of influence. The determinants in the triadic interplay operate at different time courses rather than simultaneously (Bandura, 1983). The relative causal contribution of one or another factor depends on the nature of the activity and on situational circumstances.

Note that the environment is not a monolithic force acting unidirectionally on individuals. Social Cognitive Theory distinguishes among three types of environments: imposed, selected, and created. The imposed physical and sociocultural environment impinges on people whether they like it or not. They have little control over its presence, but do have some latitude in how they construe it and react to it. However, for the most part, the environment is only a potentiality that does not come into being until it is selected and actualized by the actions that people take. This constitutes the selected lived environment. For example, although college students all inhabit the same campus milieu, they experience different lived environments depending on the courses they select, the major they choose, the extracurricular events they engage in, and the friendships they develop. Within the same potential environment, some people take advantage of the opportunities it provides and the enabling and rewarding features it contains. Others get themselves intricately enmeshed in the environments' debilitating and aversive aspects.

People also construct new physical, technological, and social environments to improve their life conditions. By constructing, to their liking, environments that previously did not exist, people exercise better control over their lives. Life conditions that provide a wide range of options and opportunities for modifying existing environments and creating new ones require increasing levels of personal agency.

The conception of "environment" should not be confined to influences that are physically proximate. For example, an integration of Social Cognitive Theory with social network theory highlights the existence of sources and patterns of social influences that function across broad social networks (Bandura, 2006b). Moreover, as will be addressed more fully in later chapters, technologies that enable instant communication worldwide have transformed the nature, reach, speed, and loci of human influence (Bandura, 2002). People now spend a good share of their waking life in the symbolic environment of the cyberworld.

Social Cognitive Theory's analysis of three distinct yet reciprocally interacting causal factors also is a heuristic for conceptualizing psychology as a whole. Different specialties of psychology address particular segments of the reciprocal interplay.

Triadic Codetermination and Determinism

The exercise of agency raises issues of freedom and determinism. Humans do not simply react to external inputs in a preprogrammed, robotic way. In the triadic causal interplay, intrapersonal determinants are part of the causal mix. Hence, individuals are contributors to the conditions that affect them.

In an informative and complementary analysis of causation, the philosopher Ismael (2006, 2007) builds a strong case that deliberative self-referent thought is key to a variety of intrapersonal influences that can break the chain of determination from environmental influences to action. Her discerning book, "How physics makes us free" (Ismael, 2016) explains how microlaws allow for emergent systems with capabilities for self-governance.

An agentic conception is at odds with the view of physical determinism, which contends that human behavior is completely and inevitably controlled by antecedent, external forces. Murray Gell-Mann, a Nobelist in physics, insightfully acknowledged the causal complexity of human behavior due to the intervention of thought in the causal chain when commenting, "Imagine how hard physics would be if particles could think" (Gruman, 2006). Because intrapersonal influences are part of the determining conditions, freedom is not incompatible with people's actions being determined. Through their contributing influence, people have a hand in shaping events and the courses their lives take.

In triadic codetermination, deliberative thought not only affects a person's reactions to a given environment. Cognitive processes also are a means of creating and altering the physical environments one encounters. When viewed from a social cognitive perspective, freedom is not construed merely as the absence of constraints and coercion in choice of action. Rather, it is viewed proactively as the exercise of self-influence in the service of selected goals and desired futures. For example, people have the freedom to vote, but whether they persuade themselves to vote and the level and form of their political engagement depends, in large part, on the self-influence they bring to bear. Through the social influence of collective action, they change political and other social systems. In addition to regulating their actions, people also live in an intrapsychic environment largely of their own making. In this environment, the self-management of their inner lives frees them from disturbing trains of thought (Bandura, 1997). Because personal influence is an interacting part of determining conditions, people are partial authors of the past conditions that developed them as well as the future course their lives take.

The development of agentic capabilities adds concrete substance to abstract discourses about freedom and determinism. People who develop their competencies, self-regulatory skills, and enabling self-beliefs can create and pursue a wide array of options that expand their freedom of action (Bandura, 1986). They are also more successful in realizing desired futures than those with less-developed agentic capabilities. The development of strategies for exercising control over perturbing and self-debilitating thinking is also intrapsychically liberating. There is no absolute freedom. Paradoxically, to gain freedom, individuals have to negotiate collectively rules of behavior for certain activities that require them to relinquish some autonomy. Without traffic laws, for example, driving would be chaotic, perilous, unpredictable, and uncontrollable for everyone. Sensible traffic rules provide predictability and increased control over getting safely to one's destination and knowing how long it will take.

The exercise of freedom involves not only options and the means to pursue them, but also rights. At the societal level, people institute, by civic action, sanctions against unauthorized forms of societal control. The less institutional jurisdiction there is over given activities, the greater the freedom of action in those domains. Once protective laws are built into social systems, there are certain things that a society may not do to individuals who challenge conventional values or vested interests, however much it might like to. Legal prohibitions against unauthorized societal control create personal freedoms that are realities, not illusory abstractions.

Societies differ in their institutions of freedom and in the number and type of activities that are officially exempted from institutional control. For example, societies that decriminalize dissent and social systems that protect journalists from criminal penalties for criticizing government officials and policies are freer than are societies that allow authoritative power to silence critics or to close down their means of communication. Societies that possess a judiciary that is independent of other branches of government ensure greater social freedom than those that lack this separation of powers.

The Development of Agency

Newborns arrive with no sense of agency or selfhood. Agentic capabilities must be developed. This development is a process of social construction; selfhood develops through transactional experiences with the environment.

Self as Agent

The development of agency proceeds in three phases: from 1) perceiving causal relations between environmental events, through 2) understanding causation by actions, and finally to 3) recognizing oneself as the agent of those actions. Regarding Step 1, infants exhibit sensitivity to causal relations between environmental events even in the first months of life (Lent, 1982; Mandler, 1992a).

They most likely begin to acquire knowledge of causation, Step 2, by seeing the actions of others make things happen. They see inanimate objects remain motionless unless manipulated by others (Mandler, 1992a). Moreover, infants personally experience the effects of actions directed toward them, which highlights the link between actions and their effects.

The recognition of action causation can be enhanced by social factors that enhance the link between infants' actions and their effects. Among these factors are aids that channel infants' attention when there is a temporal lag between their actions and the effects they produce (Millar, 1972; Millar & Schaffer, 1972; Watson, 1979). As infants begin to develop behavioral capabilities, they not only observe, but directly experience that their actions make things happen. With the development of cognitive capabilities, infants learn that *their* actions have remote effects as well—that is, Step 3. Development of a sense of personal agency requires more than simply producing effects by actions. Infants acquire a sense of agency when they recognize that they can make things happen and they regard themselves as agents of those actions. This additional understanding of oneself as the doer extends the perception of agency from action causality to personal causality.

The recognition of oneself as an agent is fueled by sensory feedback from the environment. Touching a hot object produces pain. Feeding oneself brings feelings of comfort. Playing with toys brings enjoyment. Such self-produced effects foster the recognition of personal agency.

One becomes differentiated from others through rudimentary dissimilar experiences. If stubbing one's toe brings pain, but seeing others stub their toe brings no personal pain, one's own activity becomes distinguished from that of other persons.

Agentic capabilities also are fostered by intentional guidance from adults (Heckhausen, 1987; Karniol, 1989). Parents create highly noticeable proximal effects of infants' actions. They also segment activities into manageable subskills, and provide infants with objects within their manipulative capabilities that enable them to produce effects. Adults set challenges for their infants that lie just beyond their existing competencies. They adjust their level of assistance across phases of mastery, offering guidance in earlier phases of skill acquisition but gradually withdrawing aid as infants become more competent in mastering tasks on their own. These types of enabling strategies are highly conducive to the development of agency during the initial years of life.

Construction of Selfhood

In a further phase of agentic development, infants not only come to know themselves as doers, but begin also to recognize themselves as distinctive persons.

This construction of personal identity is not entirely a matter of reflection on one's experiences. There is a social aspect to the process. As infants mature and acquire language, those around them refer to them by personal names and treat them as distinct persons. These social experiences accelerate self-recognition and self-awareness of agency. By about 11 months, infants apply their name to pictures only of themselves (Lewis & Brooks-Gunn, 1979); they thus differentiate themselves from named others.

As children increasingly become aware that they can produce effects by their actions, by about 20 months, they spontaneously describe themselves as agents of their actions and cite their intentions as they engage in activities (Kagan, 1981). Before long, they begin to describe the psychological states accompanying their actions. Based on their growing personal and social experiences, they eventually form a symbolic representation of themselves as a distinct person capable of making things happen.

Social cognitive theory adopts a naturalistic conception of the self (Bandura, 2008). The self is the embodied person, not an immaterial or homuncular overseer that resides in a particular place and does the thinking and managing. The self embodies one's physical and psychosocial makeup with a personal identity and agentic capabilities that operate in concert through a variety of special-purpose biological systems. They include the brain, that is the basis of the mind, as well as sensory and motor systems. Although the brain plays a central role in psychological life, selfhood does not reside solely in the brain, any more than the heart is the sole place of circulation (Schechtman, 1997). For example, the musculature of a gymnast honed through countless hours of practice is part of the self but not solely of the brain. Transplanting the brain of an extraordinary gymnast into an octogenarian's body will not produce a self as a dazzling gymnast as a single organ view would imply.

Self Identity

Identity formation is an important aspect of human agency. Personal identity represents one's individuality as reflected in distinctive characteristics. Most transactions in everyday life are linked to one's identity by name and other identifying characteristics.

The psychological issues of interest in personal identity center on its continuity in the midst of notable physical and adaptational changes over the course of life. The continuity of personal identity resides more in intrapsychic extension and experiential continuity of one's life course than in physical constancy. An amnesic remains the same physically, but has no sense of personal identity. Identity is preserved in memories that give temporal coherence to one's life.

Most theories of personal identity analyze its continuity in terms of autobiographical introspection. In Social Cognitive Theory, people project themselves into the future and shape the courses their lives take. By acting on their beliefs, aspirations, and value commitments, people agentically create continuities over time.

Continuity in personal identity is not solely a product of introspection. Personal identity is partially constructed from one's social identity as reflected in how one is treated by significant others. They perceive, socially label, and treat one as the same person over the course of life despite physical changes. In keeping with the model of triadic codetermination, an enduring sense of continuity is the product of a complex interplay of introspective analysis, agentically constructed continuities, and social judgements of others. Through these psychosocial processes, individuals view themselves as the same person despite changes over time.

Agency in Diverse Cultural Settings

Cultures are diverse. Yet, whatever the culture of interest, a culture is a dynamic social system, not a static monolith. For example, there are generational and socioeconomic variations in communality within collectivistic cultures; younger and more affluent members adopt more individualistic orientations. Analyses across activity domains further reveal that people act communally in some aspects of their lives and individualistically in many other aspects. Not only are cultures not monolithic entities, but also they are no longer insular. Global connectivity is shrinking cross-cultural uniqueness.

Much inquiry in cultural psychology has been based on a territorial culturalism, with nations used as proxies for psychosocial orientations. For example, residents of Japan have been categorized as collectivists, and American citizens as individualists. However, there is substantial diversity among societies that have been placed in the same category. For example, collectivistic systems founded on Confucianism, Buddhism, and Marxism all favor a communal orientation, yet differ in the values, meanings, and customs they promote (Kim, Triandis, Kâitçibasi, Choi, & Yoon, 1994). Nor are so-called individualistic cultures a uniform lot. Americans, Italians, Germans, French, and the British differ in their brands of individualism. There is also diversity across regions within the same country. In the United States, the Northeast brand of individualism differs from Midwestern and Western versions, which differ from that of the Deep South (Vandello & Cohen, 1999). Given the notable diversity, bicultural contrasts in which members of a single collectivist culture are compared with those of a single individualistic one can spawn misleading generalizations.[3]

The differences associated with sociodemographic characteristics are even greater than the differences between cultures (Matsumoto, Kudoh, & Takeuchi, 1996). For example, there are generational and socioeconomic differences in communality in collectivistic cultures. Analyses across activity domains and classes of social relationships further reveal that people behave communally in some aspects of their lives and individualistically in many other aspects (Freeman & Bordia, 2001; Matsumoto et al., 1996). They express their cultural orientations conditionally, depending on incentive conditions, rather than invariantly (Yamagishi, 1988). Measures of cultural traits cast in terms of faceless others and disembodied from domains of activity, social contexts, and incentive conditions mask this diversity. This multifaceted diversity underscores the conceptual and empirical problems of using nations as proxies for culture, and then ascribing global traits to a nation and its members as though they all believed and behaved alike (Gjerde & Onishi, 2000).

Cultures are more dynamic today than in the past because they are less insular. Global connectivity is shrinking cross-cultural uniqueness. Transnational interdependencies and global market forces are restructuring national economies,

---

3 Recent work in cultural psychology has moved beyond the "territorial" nation-based framework critiqued by Bandura. For example, Talhelm et al. (2014) report substantial psychological variations *within* the nation of China that are attributable to a social practice: the growing of rice (whose cultivation requires a uniquely high level of social coordination) as opposed to wheat. In rice-growing regions of the country, people display relatively more interdependent views of self and holistic styles of thinking, as well as higher levels of loyalty to friends. Within Europe, Henrich (2020) documents psychological variations that are attributable to the spread of Protestantism in one versus another region of the continent after the Reformation. Data suggest that Protestantism enhanced people's tendency to engage in diligent self-regulated work and to wait patiently for long-term rewards. Such findings of course are consistent with Bandura's recognition of psychological variations within the same general region of the world. Recent findings also support Bandura's reference to the psychological significance of affluence. For example, the "Big Five" interindividual-difference dimensions, which were first identified in wealthy industrialized nations, are *not* found reliably in survey data from less wealthy nations (Laajaj et al., 2019). The issue is not merely one of broad East-West cultural differences. Failures to replicate occur *within* the West, in its less wealthy nations. For example, the canonical Western personality dimensions do not replicate well in Macedonia—which, of course, borders on Western culture's historical home, Greece. Analyses by Smaldino et al. (2019) suggest that variations in the descriptive structure of inter-individual differences in personality styles result from interactions between persons and environmental contexts; more socioeconomically diverse environments give rise to greater inter-individual diversity, as individuals acquire behavioral styles that fit specific environmental niches. Such person–environment transactions are at the core of Social Cognitive Theory's analysis of personality development.

and shaping the political and social life of societies. The internet disseminates ideas, values, and styles of behavior transnationally at an unprecedented rate. This globally transmitted symbolic environment is altering national cultures and producing intercultural commonalities, resulting in a more extensive globalization of culture. In addition, cultural landscapes are being shaped by mass migrations of people, global mobility of employees in multinational corporations, and the visibility and global social influence of prominent celebrities in music, acting, and athletics. This intermixing creates new hybrid cultural forms, blending elements from different ethnicities. Growing ethnic diversity within societies conveys functional value to bicultural efficacy, that is, the capacity to navigate the demands of both one's ethnic culture and that of the larger society.

These social forces are homogenizing some aspects of life, polarizing others, and fostering considerable cultural hybridization (Holton, 2000). The new realities call for broadening the scope of cross-cultural research to include analyses of how national and global forces interact to shape the nature of cultural life. As globalization reaches ever deeper into people's lives, a strong sense of collective efficacy to make transnational systems work for them becomes critical to furthering their common interests and welfare.

In the study of human agency in cultural contexts, one must distinguish between inherent capacities and how culture shapes these potentialities into diverse forms. Consider observational learning, which figures prominently in Social Cognitive Theory (as is reviewed in the next chapter of this book). Humans have evolved an advanced capacity for observational learning. It is essential for their self-development and functioning regardless of the culture in which they reside. Indeed, in many cultures, the word for "learning" is the word for "show" (Reichard, 1938). Modeling is a universalized human capacity. But what is modeled, how modeling influences are socially structured, and the purposes they serve vary across cultural milieus (Bandura & Walters, 1963). Global applications of Social Cognitive Theory to promote society-wide changes attest to the power of social modeling in diverse cultural milieus (Bandura, 2002a, 2006; Rogers et al., 1999; Vaughan, Rogers, Singhal, & Swalehe, 2000). Such applications are reviewed in Chapter 6 of this volume.

A resilient sense of efficacy has functional benefits whether one resides in an individualistically-oriented or collectivistically-oriented culture (Earley, 1993, 1994; Gibson, 1995). No matter where you are, immobilization by self-doubt has little advantage. But how efficacy beliefs are developed, structured, and exercised, and the purposes to which they are put, vary cross-culturally. In short, there is cultural commonality in basic agentic capacities and mechanisms of operation, but diversity in the culturing of these inherent capacities. In this dual-level analysis, universality is not incompatible with manifest cultural plurality. Kluckhohn and Murray (1948) summarized eloquently the blend of universality, commonality, and uniqueness of human qualities when saying that every person is in certain aspects like all other people, like some other people, and like no other person.

Research testifies to the cross-cultural generalizability of self-efficacy theory. The factor structure of self-efficacy beliefs is essentially the same in different cultural systems (Pastorelli et al., 2001). Not only is the structure of self-efficacy beliefs comparable cross-culturally, but so are their functional properties. Whether the culture is American, Italian, Korean, or Chinese, the stronger the perceived self-efficacy, the higher the performance attainments (Bandura et al., 1996; Bong, 2001; Joo, Bong, & Choi, 2000; Shih & Alexander, 2000). The cross-cultural comparability of function is evident as well in the impact of efficacy beliefs on perceived occupational efficacy and career choice and development (Bandura et al., 2001; R. Lent, Brown, & Larkin, 1987; R. Lent, Brown, Nota, & Soresi, 2003). Even the mechanisms through which self-efficacy beliefs affect performance are replicated cross-culturally (Bandura, 2002b; Cheung & Sun, 2000; R. Lent et al., 2003; Park et al., 2000).

The Growing Primacy of Human Agency in Diverse Spheres of Life

The societies of today are undergoing drastic social, informational, and technological changes. Wrenching societal changes that dislocate populations and restructure lives are not new to human history. However, today's changes occur at a uniquely accelerated rate, thanks primarily to revolutionary advances in communications technologies. Information technologies have transformed the nature, reach, speed, and loci of human influence. These new realities present new challenges, yet also vastly expand people's opportunities to exercise some measure of control over how they live their lives.

The new technologies have created an ever-growing global interconnectedness. Human interactions transcend place, distance, and national borders—and, in so doing, alter our conceptions of them. The majority of the world's 8 billion citizens now have internet access, and thus can communicate instantaneously worldwide. These communications channels are transforming how people educate, relate to each other, and conduct their business and daily affairs. These transformative changes are placing a premium on the exercise of human agency to shape personal destinies and the national life of societies.

Most of our psychological theories were formulated long before these revolutionary changes in communications. They thus could not address the new social realities these technologies have created. Traditional psychological theories focused heavily on behavioral transactions and contingencies operating within people's confined tangible environment—a natural focus given the situational boundedness of most people's lives in earlier eras. The situational transcendence afforded by ready access to vast symbolic environments in the cyberworld has enabled people to take a stronger hand in shaping their lives. Consider some examples of the growing primacy of human agency in virtually every sphere of life.

In education, students can now exercise greater personal control over their own learning. In the past, their educational development was heavily dependent on the quality of the educational resources available at the schools in which they were enrolled. But, today, students have the world's best libraries, museums, and multimedia instruction at their fingertips through the Internet. They can use these resources to educate themselves, independently of time and place. This shift in the locus of initiative requires a major reorientation in students' conception of education. They are agents of their own learning, not just recipients of information. Education for self-directedness is now vital for a productive and innovative society. Proficient self-regulators gain knowledge, skills, and intrinsic interest in academic areas; deficient self-regulators achieve limited self-development (Schunk & Zimmerman, 1994; Zimmerman, 1989). At the student, teacher, and school levels, a sense of efficacy contributes to academic development (Bandura, 1997; Pajares & Schunk, 2001). We are entering a new era in which the construction of knowledge will rely increasingly on electronic inquiry. Students with high perceived efficacy for self-regulated learning make best use of Internet-based instruction (Joo et al., 2000).

Another domain in which the exercise of personal agency is gaining prominence is health. Conceptions of health are changing from a disease model to a health model. It is just as meaningful to speak of levels of vitality and healthfulness as degrees of impairment and debility. Quality of health is heavily influenced by lifestyle habits; thus, people can exercise significant control over their health. Current health practices focus heavily on the medical supply side, and there is growing pressure on health systems to reduce, ration, and delay health services to contain health costs. The social cognitive approach, founded on an agentic model of health promotion, focuses on the demand side (Bandura, 2000b). It promotes effective self-management of habits that keep people healthy, as detailed in Chapter 6.

Increasing applications of the self-regulatory model are enhancing people's health status, improving the quality of their lives, and reducing their risk of disease and need for costly health services (Bandura, 2005; M. Clark et al., 1997; DeBusk et al., 1994; Holman & Lorig, 1992; Lorig & Holman, 2003). This self-regulatory model is being integrated into mainstream health care systems and adopted internationally (N. Clark et al., 2005; Dongbo et al., 2003; Lorig, Hurwicz, Sobel, & Hobbs, 2006). People's beliefs in their self-regulatory efficacy affect every phase in the adoption of healthful practices—whether they even consider changing their health habits, whether they enlist the motivation and perseverance needed to succeed should they choose to do so, and how well they maintain the changes they have achieved (Bandura, 1997, 2004a).

A major part of people's daily life is spent in occupational activities. These pursuits do more than provide income for one's subsistence. They serve as a major source of personal identity, self-evaluation, and social connectedness. Beliefs of personal efficacy play a key role in occupational development and pursuits (Bandura, 1997; R. Lent, Brown, & Hackett, 1994). The capacity for self-renewal is becoming a prominent factor in a satisfying occupational life. In the past, employees learned a given trade and performed it much the same way throughout their lifetime in the same organization. The historic transition from the industrial to the information era calls for advanced cognitive and self-regulatory competencies. With the fast pace of change, knowledge and technical skills are quickly outmoded unless they are updated to fit the new technologies. Employees have to take charge of their self-development to meet the challenges of evolving positions and careers over the full course of their work lives. Those of high self-efficacy influence the course of their occupational self-development, are receptive to innovations, and make their work life more productive and satisfying by restructuring their occupational roles and the processes by which their work is performed (Frese, Teng, & Cees, 1999; Jorde-Bloom & Ford, 1988; McDonald & Siegall, 1992; Speier & Frese, 1997).

Occupational activities increasingly are executed by virtual teams of employees who must coordinate their efforts despite being scattered about Internet locations. Working remotely across time, space, and cultural orientations can be taxing. A high sense of efficacy promotes positive attitudes for remotely conducted collaborative work and enhances group performance (Staples, Hulland, & Higgins, 1998).[4]

Agentic adaptability has become a premium at the organizational level as well. Organizations must continuously innovate to survive and prosper in the rapidly changing global marketplace. They face the paradox of preparing for change at the height of success. Many fall victim to the inertia of success. They get locked into the technologies and products that produced their success and fail to adapt fast enough to the technologies and marketplaces of the future. The development of new business ventures and the renewal of established ones depend heavily on innovativeness and entrepreneurship. Turning visions into realities entails heavy investment of time, effort, and resources in ventures strewn with many difficulties, unmerciful impediments, and uncertainties. A resilient sense of efficacy provides the necessary staying power in the torturous pursuit of innovations. Indeed, perceived self-efficacy predicts entrepreneurship and which patent inventors are likely to start new business ventures (Baron & Markman, 2003; Chen, Greene, & Crick, 1998). It is the organizations with a high sense of collective efficacy that create innovative changes that fit evolving technologies and global marketplaces (Bandura, 2000a).

---

4 Research on this topic has expanded considerably in recent years; see, for example, Adamovic et al. (2001); Richter et al. (2021).

Hard-driving competitiveness, however, raises value issues concerning the purposes to which human talent, advanced technologies, and resources are put. Some intense market activities promote lavish consumption that neither uses our finite resources wisely nor leads to a better quality of life. Many of these practices may be profitable in the short run, but, as previously noted, they are environmentally unsustainable in the long run.

The revolutionary advances in communications technology also magnify people's potential to influence political affairs at local, national, and even global levels. The Internet enables sociopolitical speech that is relatively free of the centralized institutional controls and gatekeepers who reign over the mass media. People can make their voice heard across local and national borders. The Internet functions not only as a "mouthpiece" for individual expression, but also as a tool for building social networks that connect disparate individuals and groups in pursuit of common cause. By coordinating and mobilizing decentralized self-organizing groups, people can meld local networks with different self-interests into a vast collectivity for unified action for common purpose (Shapiro, 2003).

The Internet is a double-edged tool; it does not come with a built-in value system. Internet freelancers can use unfiltered and unfettered forums to propagate hate and to mobilize support for detrimental social practices.

Growing Primacy of Human Agency in the Process of Coevolution

Dobzhansky (1972) reminded us that humans are a generalist species that was selected for learnability and plasticity of behavior, not behavioral fixedness. Although not limitless, malleability and agentic capability are the hallmark of human nature. Because of limited innate programming, humans require a prolonged period of development to master essential competencies. Moreover, different periods of life present variant competency demands requiring self-renewal over the life course if the challenges of changing life circumstances are to be met. Adding to the necessity of changeability, the eras in which people live usher in technological innovations, shifts in socioeconomic conditions, cultural upheavals, and political changes that make life markedly different and call for new advantageous adaptations (Elder, 1994). These diverse adaptational changes are cultivated by psychosocial means.

People are not just reactive products of selection pressures served up by a one-sided evolutionism. They are prime players in the coevolution process. Social Cognitive Theory does not question the contribution of genetic endowment. Indeed, this endowment provides the very neuronal structures and mechanisms for the agentic attributes that are distinctly human. These include generative thought, symbolic communication, forethought, self-regulation, and reflective self-consciousness. The uniqueness of humans resides in these self-directing and self-transforming capacities.

Other species are heavily innately programmed as specialists for stereotypic survival in a particular habitat. In contrast, through agentic action, people devise ways of adapting flexibly to remarkably diverse geographic, climatic, and social environments. They transcend biological limitations. For example, humans have not evolved morphologically to fly, yet soar through the atmosphere and beyond. Agentic inventiveness trumps biological design.

People use their ingenuity to circumvent and insulate themselves from selection pressures. They invent devices that compensate for their sensory and physical limitations, and construct artificial environments that match their desires—many of which are themselves socially constructed fads and fashions. People create intricate styles of behavior necessary to thrive in complex social systems, and pass these behavioral styles on to subsequent generations through social modeling and other forms of social guidance.

Through contraceptive ingenuity that disconnected sex from procreation, humans have outwitted and taken control over their evolved reproductive system. They seek sex without reproductive outcomes, rather than as a means to propagate the species. Reproductive technologies even separate sex from fertilization. Through genetic engineering, humans are creating biological natures, for better or for worse, rather than waiting for the slow process of natural evolution. They are now changing the genetic makeup of plants and animals. Unique native plants that have evolved over eons are disappearing as commercial horticulturalists are supplanting them with genetically uniform hybrids and clones. Not only are humans cutting and splicing nature's genetic material, but, through synthetic biology, they are also creating new types of genomes. Humans are even toying with the prospect of fashioning some aspects of their own biological nature by genetic design.

Accounts of human behavior grounded in evolutionarily-based psychology generally downplay the creative power of human agency. This is especially true in the more biologically deterministic views propounded in psychological evolutionism.[5] Given the growing human modifications of evolved heritages and creative circumventing of endowed limitations, the common notion that biological

---

5 Discussions in Bussey and Bandura (1999, p. 679) clarify the theoretical positions being critiqued here: "Psychological evolutionists often take a more extreme deterministic stance regarding the rule of nature (Archer, 1996; Buss, 1995) . . . [they] invoke evolved behavioral traits as cultural universals, whereas biological evolutionists emphasize functional relations between organism and situated environment that underscores the diversifying selection influence of variant ecological contexts (Caporael, 1997)."

evolution provides the potential and culture can do only so much with it alleges greater physical constraints than does evidence from the extraordinary human achievements of inventive agency.

The diverse biobehavioral technologies reviewed above indicate that the psychosocial side of coevolution is gaining ascendancy. Through their agentic power, humans transform their environments, their own biology, and thus what they themselves become. We are an agentic species—unique among species in our capacity to alter evolutionary heritages and thus shape our future. What is technologically possible is likely to be attempted by someone. We face the prospect of increasing effort directed toward social construction of our biological nature through genetic design. These developments present an enormous challenge regarding how to bridle unbounded genetic manipulation (Baylis & Robert, 2004). The values to which people subscribe, and the social systems they devise to oversee the uses to which their technological power is put, will play a vital role in what people become and how they shape their destiny.

Were Darwin writing today, he would be documenting the overwhelming human domination of the environment. Many of the species in our degrading planet have no evolutionary future. We are wiping out species and the ecosystems that support life at an accelerating pace. Unlike former mass extinctions by meteoric disasters, the current mass extinction of species is the product of human behavior. As the unrivaled ruling species atop the food chain, we are drafting the requiem for biodiversity. By wielding powerful technologies that amplify control over the environment, humans are producing hazardous global changes of huge magnitude—deforestation, desertification, global warming, topsoil erosion and sinking of water tables in the major food-producing regions, depletion of fisheries, and degradation of other aspects of the earth's life-support systems. Expanding economies fueling consumptive growth by billions of people will intensify competition for the earth's vital resources and overwhelm efforts to secure an environmentally and economically sustainable future. Such a future might be achieved by sustainable ecodevelopment that fosters economic growth while preserving the environment on which that growth depends. But myriad parochial interests impede the implementation of eco-environmental policies that would best promote long-term global welfare. Through collective practices driven by a foreshortened perspective, humans may be well on the road to outsmarting themselves into irreversible ecological crises.

The global ecosystem cannot sustain soaring population growth and high consumption of finite resources. Some of the global applications of Social Cognitive Theory, reviewed in Chapter 6, aim to abate this most urgent global problem, especially in less developed nations that have experienced high fertility rates and a doubling of populations over a short period (Bandura, 2002a; Rogers et al., 1999).

Human Agency and the Field of Psychology

The field of psychology is not merely an ancillary branch of some more fundamental physicalistic theoretical system. The discipline of psychology uniquely encompasses the complex interplay among biological, intrapersonal, interpersonal, and sociostructural determinants of human functioning. As a core discipline, it is especially well suited to advance understanding of the integrated biopsychosocial nature of humans and their agentic capacity to shape the world around them.

As we have reviewed, today's informational and communicative technologies provide much of the world's population with expanded opportunities to affect the events that, in turn, affect their lives. Individual and collective agency increasingly influences virtually every sphere of life. Recognition of this fact raises two challenges for psychological theory and research. One is to understand basic psychological mechanisms of human agency. The other is to put basic scientific knowledge into action; one must identify ways to enlist agentic human capabilities in ways that shape a better, sustainable future for our world's citizens.

These challenges are addressed in the remainder of this book. Its chapters review the multifaceted ways in which Social Cognitive Theory illuminates basic mechanisms of human agency and puts this knowledge to work for human betterment.

2

Social Modeling and Psychological Processes of Observational Learning

Chapter 1 identified three psychological functions that are key to human agency: forethought, self-reactiveness, and self-reflection. Yet, in and of themselves, these three processes are insufficient for *effective* agency. People who boldly endeavor to fix a car, argue a legal case, or manage a business will not be effective if they lack the required mechanical, legal, and business skills. Thus, before focusing on agentic mechanisms of motivation and self-regulation in subsequent chapters, this chapter examines the processes through which people acquire the skills needed to be effective agents.

These processes fall under the general header of "learning"—a phenomenon that has occupied a central position across the history of psychology. The present chapter examines the processes through which people learn by exposure to social models. Social Cognitive Theory distinguishes among a variety of distinct social modeling phenomena. As will be reviewed, observers learn patterns of behavior, standards for evaluating those behaviors, external outcomes that may follow a given course of behavior, as well as emotional reactions by observing psychological models in the social world.

For much of psychology's history, the power of observational learning was overlooked. Researchers were keenly interested in learning, but focused most of their attention on the process of learning by direct experience. Yet, it is evident from informal observation that human behavior is transmitted, whether deliberately or inadvertently, largely through exposure to social models. Indeed, as noted in Chapter 1, in many languages "the word for 'learning' is the same as the word for 'show'." It is difficult to imagine a culture in which language, mores, vocational activities, familial customs, and educational, religious, and political practices are gradually shaped in each new member merely by direct consequences of their trial-and-error performances, without benefit of models who display the cultural patterns in their own actions.

Social Cognitive Theory: An Agentic Perspective on Human Nature, First Edition. Albert Bandura.
© 2023 John Wiley & Sons, Inc. Published 2023 by John Wiley & Sons, Inc.

Although much social learning is fostered through observation of models who are physically present in one's environment, advances in communication have increased people's reliance upon symbolic models. People commonly pattern their behavior after models they observe in verbal or pictorial form, in print media or electronically. Without the guidance of handbooks or videos that display effective behaviors in particular situations, members of technologically advanced societies would spend much of their time groping for effective ways of handling recurring challenges of modern life. Given that the influence of modeled examples in the development and regulation of human behavior is self-evident, it is surprising that traditional accounts of learning contained such little mention of modeling processes. If peripatetic Martians had visited Earth, observed humans, and scrutinized texts on the psychology of learning during the first two-thirds of the 20th century, they would have been puzzled. The texts would explain that humans learn through two basic modes: Conditioning of behavior by contingent rewards and punishments, and conditioning of emotional responses by close association of neutral and evocative stimuli. But observations of human life and culture would reveal that people can perform complex skills: flying planes, building skyscrapers, performing surgeries. How, our Martian visitors would wonder, could the individual humans have acquired these skillful capabilities solely through laborious trial-and-error learning processes?

The discrepancy between textbook characterizations and social reality is attributable largely to the fact that certain critical features of natural environments were rarely, if ever, incorporated into laboratory paradigms. In laboratory investigations of learning, experimenters arranged environments that were comparatively benign. Errors did not create fatal consequences for organisms. By contrast, natural environments are loaded with potentially lethal consequences for hazardous acts. It would be exceedingly injudicious to rely on differential reinforcement of trial-and-error performances in teaching children to swim, adolescents to drive automobiles, or medical students to conduct surgical operations. Had experimental situations been made more realistic so that animals pressing levers or running mazes were drowned, electrocuted, dismembered, or extensively bruised for the errors that invariably occur during early phases of unguided learning, the limitations of instrumental conditioning would have been forcefully revealed.[1]

---

1 Bandura's present discussion would appear to raise the question of how, exactly, animals managed to survive the environment's "lethal consequences" if they lack the human capacity for observational learning. Bandura notes later in this chapter that animals do have the capacity to learn new behavior patterns observationally (also see Bandura, 1986, Chapter 2). Mechanisms underlying observational learning in animals have been explored in comparative psychology

There are several reasons why modeling influences are heavily favored in promoting everyday learning. When mistakes are highly costly, modeling enables learners to acquire skillful performances without experiencing the costs; learners can acquire, in one step, behavioral patterns that are displayed by competent models. Some complex behaviors only can be produced through the influence of models. For example, if children had no opportunity to hear speech, it would be virtually impossible to teach them the linguistic skills that constitute a language. It is doubtful whether one could ever shape the vocalization of individual words, let alone grammatical utterances, by selective reinforcement of random vocalizations. Where desired forms of behavior can be conveyed only by social cues, modeling is indispensable to learning. Even in instances where new response patterns can be established through other means, the process of acquisition can be considerably shortened by providing appropriate models (Bandura & McDonald, 1963; John, Chesler, Bartlett, & Victor, 1968; Luchins & Luchins, 1966).

Differentiation of Modeling Phenomena

When 20th-century psychologists did turn their attention to modeling phenomena, they introduced a potentially bewildering collection of terms. The matching of personal behavior to others' previously observed actions was variously referred to as "imitation," "modeling," "observational learning," "identification," "internalization," "introjection," "incorporation," "copying," "social facilitation," "contagion," and "roletaking." Much time was spent debating these arbitrary classifications.

"Imitation" and "Identification"

Much of this debate centered on the concepts of "imitation" and "identification." In theoretical discussions, imitation was most frequently differentiated from identification on the basis of the content of the changes resulting from exposure to modeling influences. Imitation generally was defined as the reproduction of discrete responses. Identification had no consensually accepted definition, with different writers using the term to reference the adoption of diverse behavioral

---

and neuroscience (Yamada & Sakurai, 2018; Zentall, 2012). In addition, organisms respond innately to stimuli that predict threat; for example, in rodents, an organic compound that corresponds to an odor that signals the presence of foxes (a predator) triggers a fear response (Rosen, Asok, & Chakraborty, 2015). Yet, even innate neural circuits do not produce fixed, inflexible patterns of behavior. Animal social behavior is responsive to social cues, the balancing of multiple organismic needs, and the successfulness of recent past behavior (Rutte, Taborsky, & Brinkhof, 2006; Wei, Talwar, & Lin, 2021).

patterns (Kohlberg, 1963b; Parsons, 1955; Stoke, 1950), symbolic representations of the model (Emmerich, 1959), or similarity in meaning systems (Lazowick, 1955) or motives, values, ideals, and conscience (Gewirtz & Stingle, 1968).

Distinctions sometimes were based on the conditions assumed to produce and maintain matching behavior, as illustrated by Parsons's (1951) view that a generalized "cathectic" attachment is required for identification, but not imitation. Kohlberg (1963b) reserved the term identification for matching behavior that is presumed to be maintained by intrinsic satisfactions derived from perceived similarity, and applied the label imitation to instrumental matching responses supported by extrinsic rewards. Others defined imitation as matching behavior occurring in the presence of the model, and identification as performance of the model's behavior in his absence (Kohlberg, 1963b; Mowrer, 1950). Not only was consensus about differentiation criteria lacking, but some theorists presumed that imitation produces identification, whereas others posited the reverse.

Unless it can be shown that modeling of different forms of behavior is governed by separate determinants, distinctions involving the content of what is emulated not only are gratuitous, but potentially confusing. Arbitrary, unsupported proposals that different processes are involved in the acquisition of one versus another form of social behavior could impede understanding of learning processes. Results of numerous studies reviewed in detail elsewhere (Bandura, 1969a, 1996b, 1986) reveal that the same determinants influence acquisition of isolated matching responses and of entire behavioral repertoires in identical ways. Moreover, retention and delayed reproduction of even discrete matching responses require symbolic representation of previously modeled events, especially in early stages of learning.

There is also little reason to suppose that the principles and processes involved in the acquisition of modeled behaviors later performed in the presence of models differ from those performed in their absence. Several experiments (Bandura, Blanchard, & Ritter, 1969; Blanchard, 1970; Perloff, 1970) have demonstrated that exposure to the same modeling influence simultaneously produces in observers analogous changes in specific behavior, emotional responsiveness, valuation of objects involved in the modeled activities, and in self-evaluation. It may be questioned whether any conceptual benefits accrue from arbitrarily designating some of these changes as identification and others as imitation.

Modeling

In Social Cognitive Theory, phenomena previously subsumed under the labels imitation and identification are designated as modeling. This term was adopted because modeling influences have much broader psychological effects than the simple response mimicry implied by the term imitation, and because the distinguishing properties of identification were too diffuse, arbitrary, and empirically questionable.

Research conducted within the social-cognitive framework has revealed that modeling influences can produce three separable types of effects depending on the different processes involved. These distinctions among qualitatively distinct functional effects yield a non-arbitrary classification of the pertinent phenomena.

Observational Learning. The first effect is the learning of new behavioral capabilities. In observational learning, people acquire new patterns of behavior by watching the performances of others. This effect is demonstrated most clearly when models exhibit novel responses which observers have not previously learned. The capacity of observers subsequently to reproduce the observed acts in substantially identical form is the evidence of learning by observation.

Such evidence initially derived from the Bobo Doll experiments (e.g., Bandura, Ross, & Ross, 1961). In this research, nursery school children observed filmed displays in which an adult acted aggressively toward an inflated clown doll. Specifically, the adult engaged in designated acts: pummeling the doll with a mallet; kicking it; aggressively hurling it; and sitting on it while beating its face. The actions were accompanied by scripted expressions (e.g., "*sockeroo*"). Subsequently, children's behavior was observed while they were in a playroom that featured a wide variety of toys—including a Bobo Doll. The mallet that, on film, had been used to pummel the Bobo Doll was placed next to a pegboard as a regular part of that toy; to use the mallet as a tool for aggression thus was a marked departure from its normal use, to hammer pegs. Children were alone in the room to remove any possible social influences. In the research design, children were blocked on levels of aggression based on teachers' ratings of the children's everyday aggressiveness and were assigned randomly from each block to aggressive modeling or a control condition that had no exposure to aggressive modeling. Children who had observed the modeled aggression readily adopted the filmed aggressive acts and verbalizations in interaction with the Bobo Doll.[2]

The results were significant not merely because they demonstrated people's capacity to learn rapidly by observation, rather than learning only slowly through trial-and-error reinforcement processes. The findings also contradicted psychodynamic theory, which contended that observation of aggression at any given Time 1 would *reduce* aggression at Time 2 as a result of an alleged cathartic release of aggressive energy. The role of modeling in the social acquisition of aggressive conduct is reviewed in greater detail later in this chapter. The use of modeling principles in applications to foster widespread beneficial social change is reviewed in Chapter 6.

Models need not be physically present in one's environment for observational learning to occur. Findings have long demonstrated that matching performances

---

2 The Editor notes that the Bobo Doll survived these assaults and, today, resides happily in the National Museum of Psychology, Cummings Center for the History of Psychology, The University of Akron, Akron, Ohio, USA.

readily can be achieved without the physical presence of a model, as long as the essential features of behavior are depicted accurately either pictorially or verbally (Bandura & Mischel, 1965; Bandura, Ross, & Ross, 1963a). To the extent that live and symbolic modeling convey the same amount of response information and are equally effective in commanding attention, they are likely to produce comparable levels of imitative behavior. Different forms of modeling, however, are not always equally efficacious. Performances that entail strong inhibitions may be more easily established through live demonstrations than by filmed presentations (Bandura & Menlove, 1968).

Modification of Behavioral Inhibitions. A second functional effect involves the strengthening or weakening of inhibitions on behaviors that observers already know how to perform. These effects, which can be either inhibitory or disinhibitory, are primarily determined by observed response consequences to the model.

First, consider inhibitory effects, that is, reductions in the performance of the modeled class of behavior or a general reduction of responsiveness. Inhibitory effects tend to occur when observers view modeled behavior that is followed by punishing consequences. In the early years of modeling research, observed punishments were found to reduce exploratory behavior (Crooks, 1967), aggression (Bandura, 1965b; Wheeler, 1966a, 1996b), and transgressive behavior (Walters & Parke, 1964; Walters, Parke, & Cane, 1965). Comparable reductions in performance were observed when models responded self-punitively to their own behavior (Bandura, 1971a; Benton, 1967).

*Dis*inhibitory effects, in which observers become more likely to display behavior that was formerly inhibited, primarily occur when people observe models who engage in activities without experiencing adverse consequences. Observing the absence of negative consequences disinhibits the observer's behavior. Modeling treatments for phobias strikingly illustrate disinhibitory effects (Bandura, 1971b). Initially, people with phobic conditions strongly inhibit any responses that bring them near feared objects. In the treatment, they observe models who interact with the feared objects with no untoward consequences. As a result, observers frequently interact in a much less inhibited manner with those same objects.[3]

Social Facilitation. In the third class of modeling effects, others' behavior functions as a cue that facilitates performance of existing responses in the same general class. People applaud when others clap, look up when they see others gaze skyward, and in countless other situations enact behaviors that are prompted by the actions of others. These response facilitation effects are distinct from observational learning because no new responses are acquired. They also are distinct from (dis)inhibitory processes because no social sanctions or personal inhibitions govern the behavior in question.

---

3 For a more recent overview of the efficacy of such methods, see Davis III, Ollendick, and Öst (2019), who review findings documenting the efficacy of a one-session treatment for specific phobias in which modeling methods are a central tool for fear reduction and skill building.

Prior Explanatory Accounts of Modeling Phenomena

When seeking to explain modeling phenomena, one must recall the above distinctions among observational learning, modification of behavioral inhibitions, and social facilitation. Different conditions are required to produce one versus the other phenomenon. Any theorist who crafts an explanation of modeling phenomena thus must acknowledge the distinctions.

In years past, theorists offered diverse theoretical explanations. The earliest ones (McDougall, 1908; Morgan, 1896; Tarde, 1903) regarded modeling as instinctual: People reproduce the behavior of others due to their innate propensity to imitate. Subsequently, as psychologists became critical of instinct explanations, writers proposed that imitativeness is acquired through some type of learning mechanism—although they differed, one from another, in their beliefs about what is learned and the factors essential for imitation to occur.

Humphrey (1921), Allport (1924), Holt (1931), and Guthrie (1952) portrayed modeling in terms of associative principles. Associative learning was believed to be achieved most rapidly through initial reverse imitation; for example, in Holt's conceptualization, when an adult copies the response of a child, the latter tends to repeat the behavior, which begins a circular associative sequence in which the adult's behavior becomes an increasingly effective stimulus for the child's responses. If, during this spontaneous mutual imitation, adults perform responses that are novel for children, they will copy them. Piaget (1951) likewise cited imitations at early stages of development in which the child's spontaneous behaviors serve initially as stimuli for matching responses by the model in alternating imitative sequences (as is discussed in greater detail below). A serious limitation of associative theories, however, is their failure to explain precisely how novel responses are learned. What is needed is a theoretical explanation of how an observer is able to "copy" or "match" a behavior in the first place.

With the advent of reinforcement principles, theorists began to propose that observational learning occurs through the reinforcement of imitative behavior. The foremost proponents of behaviorism, Watson (1908) and Thorndike (1898), dismissed the existence of observational learning on the basis of disappointing results from studies with animals. Since the theories in vogue at the time assumed that learning required performance of responses, the notion of learning by observation alone was perhaps too divergent to be given serious consideration. In later operant conditioning analyses of modeling phenomena (Baer & Sherman, 1964; Skinner, 1953), reinforcement was seen as a necessary condition for modeling processes. Observational learning was said to occur through a process of differential reinforcement: When imitative behavior has been positively reinforced and divergent responses either not rewarded or punished, other's behaviors function as discriminative stimuli for matching responses.

An advance in understanding modeling processes did occur in the publication of Miller and Dollard's (1941) classic text, *Social Learning and Imitation*. These authors advanced the view that in order for imitative learning to occur, a number of conditions must be met: observers must be motivated to act; modeling cues for the requisite behavior must be provided; observers must perform matching responses; and those responses must be positively reinforced. It was further assumed that if imitative behavior is repeatedly rewarded, imitation itself becomes a secondary drive that presumably is reduced by acting like the model. Experiments conducted by Miller and Dollard demonstrated that when people consistently are rewarded for imitating the choice responses of a model in two-choice discrimination problems, they show a marked increase in imitativeness, but cease imitating the model if they are never rewarded for making the same choices. Moreover, participants generalized copying responses to new models and to different motivational states. In this work, however, no attempt was made to test whether imitation functions as a drive, which presumably should be altered in strength by deprivation or satiation of matching behavior.

These experiments were widely accepted as demonstrations of imitative learning, although they actually represented only a special form of discrimination place-learning in which social rather than environmental cues serve as stimuli for choice responses that already exist in the subject's behavioral repertoire. Indeed, had a light or some other distinctive cue been used to signify the outcomes of choices, the behavior of models would have been irrelevant, perhaps even a hindrance, to efficient performance. By contrast, most forms of imitation involve response rather than place-learning, in which observers organize behavioral elements into new compound responses solely by observing modeled performances. Since Miller and Dollard's theory requires a person to perform imitative responses before he can learn them, it accounts more adequately for the expression of previously established matching responses than for their acquisition. It is perhaps for this reason that the publication of *Social Learning and Imitation*, which contained many provocative ideas, stimulated little new research, and modeling processes continued to be treated in a cursory fashion or ignored entirely in accounts of learning.

Social Cognitive Theory of Observational Learning

Social cognitive theory recognizes that observational learning is fundamentally a cognitive activity. Modeled actions provide information. Humans have the cognitive capacity to mentally represent that information and then to draw on those mental representations to guide future actions. This capacity expands human agency. People can acquire a vast repertoire of knowledge and behavioral skills merely by observing the behavior of others. They then, in turn, can draw on these socially acquired capabilities to meet a range of future challenges.

A cognitive perspective naturally draws attention to the possibility that the overall phenomenon of observational learning can be understood by identifying its constituent subsystems. Social Cognitive Theory identifies four subsystems of observational learning: attentional, retentional, motivational, and production processes through which exposure to models results in the performance of newly learned behaviors (Figure 2.1).

Attentional Processes

One cannot learn from a modeled behavior unless one attends to it. Simply exposing persons to modeled responses does not guarantee that they will attend closely to those actions and detect the most relevant aspects of the action sequence. Observers will, of course, be unable to acquire behavior that matches that of a model if they fail to attend to the distinctive features of the model's responses. Attentional processes constitute the first subsystem of observational learning.

A number of factors differentiate models that are closely observed from those who are largely ignored. The incentives provided for learning modeled behavior, the motivational and psychological characteristics of the observer, and the physical and acquired distinctiveness of models, as well as their power and interpersonal attractiveness are some of the many qualities that exert selective control over the attention people pay to the variety of modeled activities they encounter in their everyday life. The people with whom one regularly associates delimit the types of behavior that one will repeatedly observe and hence learn most thoroughly.[4]

---

4 Contemporary research on "selective social learning" (Poulin-Dubois & Brosseau-Liard, 2016) adds to Bandura's discussion of attentional processes in observational learning. An interesting recent finding is that even young children (under age 2) have meta-cognitive awareness that guides their attention to modeling cues; findings suggest, for example, that children follow a *"copy when uncertain* social learning rule" (Kuzyk et al., 2020, p. 9). Such findings expand the theme of human agency Bandura advances in this book. Once learners' self-reflective capacities influence their attentional processes, the learners become active agents who contribute to the attentional processes that constitute the first stage of observational learning.

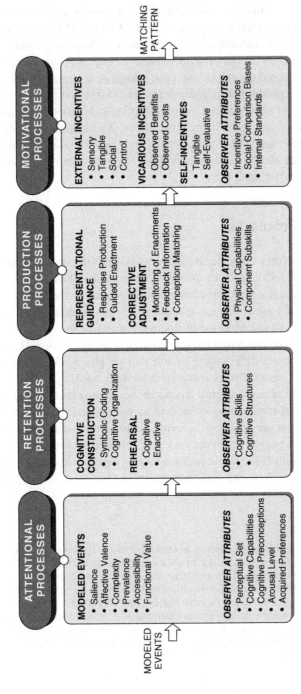

Figure 2.1 Four subprocesses governing observational learning. From Bandura (1986). Copyright 1986 by Prentice-Hall. Reprinted by permission.

Retention Processes

The second cognitive process in observational learning is retention. To reproduce a previously observed behavior, the observer must retain information about the original observational inputs in some symbolic form. Observers cannot retain all the information in a modeled display—nor should they; most modeling activities contain extraneous movements that are inconsequential to the overall purpose of a given act. By transforming modeled actions into symbolic representations of key aspects of the behavior that was observed, learners can retain an efficient record of observed acts that, in turn, can guide their future behavior.

The retention component of observational learning involves two representational systems: imaginal and verbal. Some activities (e.g., a golf swing, a dance movement) are more easily portrayed than described. The retention of visual information corresponding to the displayed action thus is an efficient means of retaining knowledge. The second representational system, which probably accounts for the notable speed of observational learning and long-term retention of modeled contents by humans, involves verbal coding of observed events. Most of the cognitive processes that regulate behavior are primarily verbal rather than visual. To take a simple example, the route traversed by a model can be acquired, retained, and later reproduced more accurately by verbal coding of the visual information into a sequence of right-left turns (RRLRR) than by reliance upon visual imagery of the itinerary. Observational learning and retention are facilitated by such codes because they carry a great deal of information in an easily stored form. After modeled responses have been transformed into images and readily utilizable verbal symbols, these memory codes serve as guides for subsequent reproduction of matching responses. In creating these codes, observers often abstract common features from a variety of modeled responses and construct higher-order codes that have wide generality.

The verbal and imaginal systems functionally are closely related. The mere verbal mention of a person, place, or activity often immediately elicits vivid imaginal representations of the entity.

Findings from several studies in the early years of research on observational learning revealed the role of symbolic representation. In one experiment (Bandura, Grusec, & Menlove, 1966), children observed several complex sequences of behavior modeled on film. During exposure the children either watched attentively, coded the novel responses into their verbal equivalents as they were performed by the model, or counted rapidly while watching the film to prevent implicit verbal coding of modeling stimuli. A subsequent test of observational learning disclosed that children who verbally coded the modeled patterns reproduced significantly more matching responses than those in the viewing-along condition, who in turn showed a higher level of acquisition than children who engaged in competing symbolization. Children within the verbalizing condition reproduced a high proportion (60%) of the modeled responses that they had coded into words, whereas they retrieved a low proportion (25%) of the responses they failed to code.

Coates and Hartup (1969) investigated developmental changes in the role of verbal coding of modeling stimuli in observational learning within the context of the production deficiency hypothesis. According to this hypothesis, originally proposed by Keeney, Cannizzo, and Flavell (1967), young children are capable of, but do not utilize symbolic activities that would facilitate performance, whereas older children spontaneously produce and employ verbal mediators and therefore do not benefit from further prompts to engage in symbolic activities. Consistent with this view, Coates and Hartup found that induced verbal labeling of modeling stimuli enhanced observational learning in young children but had no effect on older subjects. Additional evidence indicated that induced verbal coding can facilitate observational learning in both older children (Bandura, Grusec, & Menlove, 1966) and adults (Bandura & Jeffery, 1971; Gerst, 1971). Moreover, van Hekken (1969) found that it was the older children who spontaneously used symbolic skills in other learning tasks rather than the "nonmediators" who achieved increases in observational learning through induced verbal coding of modeling stimuli.

Additional evidence for the influence of symbolic coding operations in the acquisition and retention of modeled responses came from research by Gerst (1971). College students observed a filmed model perform complex motor responses composed of intricate movements taken from the alphabet of the deaf. Immediately after observing each modeled response, participants engaged in one of four symbolic activities for a period of one minute. One group reinstated the response through vivid imagery; a second coded the modeling stimuli into concrete verbal terms by describing the specific response elements and their movements; the third group generated concise labels that incorporated the essential ingredients of the responses (e.g., a pretzel-shaped response might be labeled as an orchestra conductor moving his baton in a symphonic finale). Finally, participants assigned to the control group performed mental calculations to impede symbolic coding of the depicted events. Participants reproduced the modeled responses immediately after coding, and following a 15-minute period during which they performed a distracting task designed to prevent symbolic rehearsal of modeled responses.

All three coding operations enhanced observational learning. Concise labeling and imaginal codes were equally effective in aiding immediate reproduction of modeled responses, both being superior to the concrete verbal form. The delayed test for retention of matching responses showed concise labeling to be the best coding system for memory representation. Participants in this condition retained significantly more matching responses than those who relied upon imagery and concrete verbalizations.

The results reported by Gerst (1971) indicate that modeled behavior is most effectively acquired and retained when modeled configurations are likened to events that are familiar and meaningful to the observer. These findings accord with the common observation that learning through modeling is often enhanced when required performances are represented as resembling familiar activities. The members of a ski class that could not learn to transfer their weight to the downhill ski despite several demonstrations by the instructor were observed to promptly master the maneuver when asked to ski as though they were pointing a serving tray downhill throughout the turns and traverses.

Another means of stabilizing and strengthening acquired responses is rehearsal operations. The level of observational learning can be considerably enhanced through practice or overt rehearsal of modeled response sequences, particularly if the rehearsal is interposed after natural segments of a larger modeled pattern. Of greater import is evidence that covert rehearsal, which can be readily engaged in when overt participation is either impeded or impracticable, may likewise increase retention of acquired matching behavior (Bandura & Jeffery, 1971; Michael & Maccoby, 1961). Like coding, rehearsal involves active processes. There is reason to believe that the benefits accruing from rehearsal result from an individual's reorganization and recoding of input events rather than from sheer repetition.

The role of active cognitive processing in the retention of information means that observers function as active agents. They transform, classify, and organize modeling stimuli into easily remembered schemes rather than storing isomorphic representations of modeled events as if they, the observers, were passive cameras or tape recorders.

Theories of imitation that disregard cognitive functioning cannot adequately account for variations in matching performances that result when symbolic cognitive activities vary while external stimuli remain the same (Bandura & Jeffery 1971; Gerst, 1971). The limitations of conceptual schemes that depict matching behavior as controlled solely by external stimuli and reinforcing consequences are also readily apparent in instances of repeated presentation of modeling stimuli under favorable reinforcement conditions that fail to produce matching responses.

Social Cognitive Theory proposes that that behavior is learned and organized chiefly through central integrative mechanisms prior to motor execution. When viewing models of desired behavior, observers form an idea of how response components must be combined and temporally sequenced to produce new behavioral configurations. Subsequent patterned behavior is largely guided by these symbolic representations, rather than being created directly through reinforced motor movements. The implication—abundantly documented in research conducted in the 1960's—is that observers can learn behaviors without performing them. Observational learning without performance was revealed in modeling studies using a nonresponse acquisition procedure (Bandura, 1965a; Flanders, 1968); after observing modeled acts, observers accurately could describe entire patterns of action and often could errorlessly reproduce behaviors on the first trial. These findings indicated that modeled behavior is learned as a whole in symbolic form before behavioral enactment.

Motoric Reproduction Processes

Even when clear mental representation of modeled activities are developed and retained, behavioral enactment may be faulty because individuals do not have the requisite physical capabilities. One can carefully observe a difficult juggling routine, form a mental representation of the necessary actions, yet remain completely unable to keep the balls in the air oneself. The third component of observational learning modeling phenomena is a motoric reproduction process.

In motoric reproduction, people utilize symbolic representations of past modeled action to guide their current performances. This process of motor production based on mental representations of actions observed in the past is analogous to basing one's actions on an externally depicted pattern or a series of instructions in the present environment that are designed to guide novel response sequences. In these latter cases, performance is guided by external cues, whereas in delayed modeling, behavioral reproduction is guided by mental representations of stimuli encountered previously.

The psychological mechanisms through which people motorically reproduce past behavior can be understood in terms of a conception-matching process (Carroll & Bandura, 1987). As people observe their own actions, they compare their current behavior to a mental representation of a model's past action and modify ongoing behavior to match the conception. Appropriately timed visual cues provided to learners enhance the accuracy with which they can match current performances to past models (Carroll & Bandura, 1985, 1987).

The rate and level of observational learning will be partly governed, at the motoric level, by the availability of essential component responses. Complex modes of behavior are produced by combinations of previously learned components which may, in themselves, be relatively complicated compounds. In instances where observers lack some of the necessary components, the constituent elements may be modeled first; then in stepwise fashion, increasingly intricate compounds can be developed imitatively. In most everyday learning, people achieve rough approximations of desired behavior by observation. Initial behavioral enactments are then refined through self-corrective adjustments based on informative feedback from performance.

In cases of complex motor skills, the problem of behavioral reproduction is complicated by the fact that actors generally cannot observe the movements they are making. For example, an athlete seeking to develop her motor skills commonly must, when competing, concentrate on some external target (e.g., a goal toward which one is aiming) rather than her own motor movements. It is exceedingly difficult to guide and correct actions that one cannot observe. To facilitate development of motor skills, delayed self-observation through videotape procedures may be employed. Dowrick (1999) reviews "self-modeling" studies in which video images of a learner are employed not only to enhance the development of skills, but also to boost perceptions of self-efficacy for skilled performance.

Motivational Processes

The final component function concerns motivational processes. A person may acquire the capability to execute a modeled behavior, but choose not to do so. Motivational processes are the determinants of whether people enact behaviors that they have learned.

The significance of motivational processes indicates that, in the study of learning, one must distinguish learning from performance. People may learn a pattern of behavior (that is, acquire the potential to perform the action) without being motivated to perform it.

Learning will rarely be translated into overt performance if negative sanctions or unfavorable incentive conditions inhibit the learned behavior. In such circumstances, the introduction of positive incentives promptly converts observational learning into action (Bandura, 1965b). Incentives influence not only the overt expression of matching behavior, but also the types of modeled events to which people attend. Furthermore, incentives facilitate selective retention by activating deliberate coding and rehearsal of modeled behaviors that have functional value.

The constituent processes of observational learning are functionally interrelated. For example, anticipated rewards, which are motivational, can influence what is observed and what goes unnoticed. Knowledge that performance of matching behavior produces valued rewards or averts punishment is likely to increase attentiveness to models whose behavior has functional value. Thus, anticipated rewards may indirectly affect the course of imitative learning by enhancing and focusing observing responses. Moreover, anticipated consequences can strengthen retention of what has been learned observationally by motivating people to code and to rehearse modeled responses that have utilitarian value.

Social Cognitive Theory's recognition of the motivational properties of rewards sometimes has caused observers to conflate social cognitive and operant conditioning accounts. In reality, these two frameworks differ fundamentally. In operant conditioning, human behavior is controlled by its response consequences. In Social Cognitive Theory, human behavior is controlled by humans: agentic persons who acquire knowledge of past response contingencies, anticipate future contingencies, and select activities and regulate their actions based in part on these anticipations. They acquire this information about response consequences in part from direct experience—but only in part; much of this learning occurs vicariously, from the observation of models. In everyday life, people continually observe the actions of others and the occasions on which they are rewarded, ignored, or punished. The maintenance of behavior can best be understood by considering the interactive effects of personal and vicarious experience.

The distinction between conditioning accounts and Social Cognitive Theory can be illustrated in the case of vicarious reinforcement. In everyday life, observers view not only modeled performances but also outcomes that are experienced by the model. The term *vicarious reinforcement* describes changes in the behavior of observers that result from witnessing a model's actions being rewarded or punished. This phenomenon, pervasive in human social behavior, was almost entirely overlooked in operant and classical conditioning accounts, which focused so heavily on consequences that animal or human learners experienced directly. Social Cognitive Theory recognizes that observed consequences serve an informative function. When observing consequences to models, observers learn the types of behavior that are likely to meet with approval or disapproval. Unlike the operant conditioning interpretation, Social Cognitive Theory assumes that imitative behavior is regulated by observers' judgments of probable consequences for prospective actions rather than being directly controlled by external stimuli. Findings have long shown that erroneous judgments about likely response consequences may be more powerful in controlling imitative behavior, at least for a time, than discriminative stimuli and the actual effects the responses produce (Bandura & Barab, 1971). Reinforcement schedules that people believe to be in effect can outweigh the influence of actual external reinforcement contingencies (Kaufman, Baron, & Kopp, 1966).

In addition to their aforementioned effects, vicarious rewards can convey social status on observed performers and the style of behavior that they modeled. Punishment tends to devalue models and their behavior, whereas praise and other rewards enhance status (Bandura, Ross, & Ross, 1963b; Hastorf, 1965). Modification of model status, in turn, influences the degree to which observers attend to, and pattern their own actions after, behavior exemplified by different models. This process of course illustrates the principle of reciprocal causation outlined in Chapter 1. Rewards to a model (an environmental factor) influence a person-based process (the observer's deployment of attention) which, in turn, affects another person-based process (the information and skills acquired by the observer), which then influence the observers' subsequent behavior.

Theoretical Contrasts

As noted above, initial findings on observational learning revealed substantial limitations in two frameworks for understanding human nature that were greatly popular at the time. Behavioristic accounts of trial-and-error learning had overlooked a major means through which humans learn: by observing other humans. Psychodynamic predictions of a cathartic release of aggressive energy were flatly contradicted by the empirical results.[5]

Given the broad influence of Piagetian theory on 20th-century developmental psychology (Flavell, 1996), another contrast to consider is the relation between Piaget's account of imitation and the Social Cognitive Theory analysis of modeling processes. Piaget (1951) presented a developmental account of imitation in which symbolic representation assumes an important function, especially in higher forms of modeling. He proposed that, at the earlier sensorimotor stages of development, imitative responding can be evoked only by having the model repeat the child's immediately preceding responses in alternating imitative sequences. During this period, according to Piaget, the child is unable to imitate responses that he has not previously performed spontaneously because actions cannot be assimilated unless they correspond to already existing schemas. Piaget reports that when models introduce new behavioral elements or even familiar responses that children have acquired but are not exhibiting at the moment, they do not respond imitatively. Imitation is thus restricted to reproduction of activities that children have already developed, that they can see themselves make, and that they have performed immediately before the model's reiteration.

If the above observations based on Piaget's longitudinal study of his own three children are replicable, then young children have weaker capabilities for observational learning than subhuman species. Animals (Adler & Adler, 1968) and birds

---

5 Limitations of the cathartic-release hypothesis of psychodynamic theory also were revealed in research by Bandura's Stanford University colleague Walter Mischel. Psychodynamic accounts would predict that, in Mischel's delay of gratification paradigm—in which children must wait to obtain a delayed reward—delay abilities would be enhanced by attention to the reward; the visual attention supposedly would foster a cathartic release of mental energies. As Mischel (1981) explained, the actual empirical results were the exact opposite of the psychodynamic prediction. Delay-of-reward and modeling are related in that exposure to models who display delayed-reward tendencies influences the delay behavior of observers (Bandura & Mischel, 1965). The implications of these social-cognitive research programs for classical psychodynamic theory are discussed also in Cervone & Pervin (2023).

(Foss, 1964) can learn new patterns of behavior observationally, and modeling stimuli can acquire the capacity to evoke existing matching responses even though the organism was not performing them beforehand. It is assumed by Piaget that during initial stages children do not distinguish between self-imitation and imitation of the actions of others. If this is the case, then the theory must explain why a child's own behavior can originally induce matching responses but identical actions initiated by others cannot.

In Piaget's view, schemas, which refer to schematic outlines of activities, determine what behaviors can or cannot be imitated. Unfortunately, the descriptive account does not specify in any detail the extent to which schemas are learned or furnished innately and, if learned, the process whereby general features of an activity are abstracted from otherwise different instances. From the perspective of the multiprocess theory of modeling, deficiencies in imitative performance, which are typically attributed by Piaget to insufficiently differentiated schemas, may likewise result from inadequate observation of modeling stimuli, from motoric difficulties in executing learned patterns, or from faulty reinforcement. The latter factor deserves further comment because of its important bearing on evaluation of findings from naturalistic studies of modeling.

Observational data must be accepted with reservation when the model's reactions to the child's performances are not reported. Young children's imitative acts are precise when they are rewarded only for exact matches, but deteriorate rapidly if they are rewarded without regard to the quality of their reproduction (Lovaas, 1967). If researchers were to record only a child's responses, they would overlook the possibility that imitative deficiencies arise from external reward structures rather than from the child's capacity to learn by observation. Since observational studies of the type conducted by Piaget involve a two-way influence process, imitative performances reflect not only the competency of the child but the reactions of the participating model to accurate and inadequate matches. If models respond alike to performances that differ widely in quality, children will tend to disregard modeling stimuli, whereas they reproduce accurately any activities within their capacity if models respond discriminately.

The discussion thus far has been concerned with early stages in the development of imitation as depicted by Piaget. As children's intellectual development progresses, they become capable of delayed imitation of modeled events which they previously could not make. These changes presumably come about through coordination of visual and sensorimotor schemas, and differentiation of the child's own actions from those of others. After learning from a model, the child can begin a systematic trial-and-error performance until achieving a good match of the modeled action.

At the final stages of development, which generally begin in the second year of life, children attain representative imitation. Schemas are coordinated internally to form new and complex patterns of modeled behavior without requiring overt provisional trials of actions. This covert imitation occurs through imaginal representation of modeled performances, which also serves as the basis for reproducing matching behavior when models are no longer present. Had Piaget extended his studies of imitation into later childhood years, it is likely that verbal representation would also have emerged as an important functional mediator in delayed modeling.

A comprehensive theory of modeling must explain not only how patterned behavior is acquired observationally, but also when and how frequently imitative behavior will be performed, the persons toward whom it will be expressed, and the social settings in which it is most likely to be exhibited. Piaget's account of imitation contains only a few passing remarks about the motivational factors regulating performance of matching behavior. Imitation is variously attributed to an intrinsic need for acting and knowing, to a desire to reproduce actions that differ partially from existing schemas, and to the esteem in which the model is held. These factors are too general to account satisfactorily for the highly discriminative character of imitative responding. In view of the abundant evidence that imitative performances can be strongly controlled by their external consequences, the role of reward contingencies must be considered in explanatory schemes, whatever their orientation.

Scope of Modeling Influences

One should not assume that modeling produces mere mimicry of observed responses. Research involving relatively complex forms of learning has revealed that modeling influences have a broader scope (Bandura & Harris, 1966; Bandura & McDonald, 1963; Bandura & Mischel, 1965).

In the paradigm employed in these studies, participants observed models who responded according to pre-selected rules, to which they adhered across diverse stimuli. To explore the effects of exposure to these models, participants' subsequent actions were recorded as they interacted in different social contexts, with the models absent, and with different stimulus items. We found that observers' response styles were consistent with the models' displayed rules, even though the models had not interacted with the stimuli that the observers encountered. In this higher-order form of modeling, modeled actions convey information about the characteristics of appropriate responses. Observers abstract common attributes exemplified in diverse modeled responses and formulate a rule for generating similar patterns of behavior. Responses performed by subjects that embody the observationally derived rule are likely to resemble the behavior that the model would be inclined to exhibit under similar circumstances, even though subjects had never witnessed the model's behavior in these new situations.

Broad effects of modeling influences occur when individuals are exposed to a variety of models. Rarely do they confine their imitation to a single source. Even when they do focus on one model, they rarely reproduce all of the characteristics of the preferred individual. Observers commonly exhibit relatively novel responses representing amalgams of the behavior of different models. The human capacity for conscious reflection and deliberate selection of modeling influences thus makes observational learning an agentic capacity.

Language Acquisition

Evidence that response-generative rules can be acquired observationally has interesting implications for language learning. Because of the highly generative character of linguistic behavior, some psycholinguists have assumed that imitation cannot play much part in language development and production (Brown & Bellugi, 1964; Ervin, 1964; Menyuk, 1964). This conclusion reflected the mistaken assumption that one can learn, observationally, only the concrete features of behavior, not its abstract properties. Obviously, children are able to construct an almost infinite variety of sentences that they have never heard. Therefore, rather than acquiring specific utterances through imitation, children must learn sets of rules on the basis of which they can generate an unlimited number of novel grammatical sentences. The importance of imitative learning in language development was further discounted on the grounds that children often display only crude approximations of adult verbalizations (Brown & Bellugi, 1964), and they can acquire linguistic rules without engaging in any motor speech (Lenneberg, 1967).

The above criticisms have validity when applied to theories of imitation that emphasize verbatim repetition of modeled responses and that assume matching responses must be performed and reinforced in order to be learned. It is evident from the material already discussed at length that the social learning interpretation of modeling processes is compatible with rule-learning theories advanced by psycholinguists. Both points of view assign special importance to the abstraction of productive rules from diverse modeled examples. The differentiation made by psycholinguists between language competence and language performance corresponds to the distinction made between learning and performance in Social Cognitive Theory.[6] Another point of similarity is that neither approach assumes that observational learning necessitates performance. Finally, the basic rules, or

---

6 An interesting aspect of 20th century intellectual history is that, working independently, Bandura (1965) and Chomsky (1965) essentially simultaneously drew this distinction between learning (competence) and performance. The distinction seems self-evident in historical retrospect; yet, prior behavioristic frameworks had not drawn this distinction with sufficient clarity.

prototypes, that guide production of grammatical utterances are presumed to be extracted from individual modeled instances rather than innately programmed. People are innately equipped with information-processing capacities, not with response-productive rules.

Rules about grammatical relations between words cannot be learned unless they are exemplified in the verbal behavior of models. A number of experiments have been conducted to discover conditions that facilitate abstraction of rules from verbal modeling cues. The principle underlying a model's varied responses can be most readily discerned if its identifying characteristics are distinctly repeated in responses which differ in other aspects. If, for example, one were to place a series of objects first on tables, then on chairs, boxes, and other things, simultaneously verbalizing the common prepositional relationship between these different objects, a child would eventually discern the grammatical principle. The child then easily could generate a novel grammatical sentence if a toy hippopotamus were placed on a xylophone and the child were asked to describe the stimulus event enacted.

The influential role of both modeling and discrimination processes in language development was revealed in an experiment designed to alter the syntactic style of young children who had no formal grammatical knowledge of the linguistic features selected for modification (Bandura & Harris, 1966). Children increased grammatical constructions in accord with the rules guiding the modeled utterances when verbal modeling influences were combined with attention-directing and reinforcement procedures designed to increase syntactic discriminability. This finding was replicated by Odom, Liebert, and Hill (1968) and extended by Rosenthal and his associates (Carroll, Rosenthal, & Brysh, 1969; Rosenthal & Whitebook, 1970), who demonstrated that exposure to verbal modeling altered structural and tense components of children's linguistic behavior congruent with the model's sentence rules.

The studies cited above were principally devoted to the modification of linguistic features with which the children had some familiarity. Liebert, Odom, Hill, and Huff (1969) showed that children can acquire, through modeling, an arbitrary ungrammatical rule, which they use to generate peculiar sentences.

Further evidence for the influential role of modeling processes in language acquisition came from naturalistic studies employing sequential analyses of children's verbalizations and the immediately following parental responses. They revealed that young children's speech is at best semi-grammatical; in approximately 30 percent of instances, adults repeat children's verbalizations in a grammatically more complex form, accenting the elements that may have been omitted and inaccurately employed (Brown & Bellugi, 1964); and children often reproduce the more complicated grammatical reconstructions modeled by adults (Slobin, 1968).

Moral Judgment

Another domain in which modeling influences convey rules for action, rather than merely response sequences to "mimic," is that of moral judgment. Findings reveal that modeling can transmit behavior-guiding principles that modify observers' moral judgmental orientations (Bandura & McDonald, 1963; Cowan, Langer, Heavenrich, & Nathanson, 1969; Le Furgy & Woloshin, 1969). Modeling cues also can alter delay of gratification patterns (Bandura & Mischel, 1965; Stumphauzer, 1969) and styles of information-seeking (Rosenthal & Zimmerman, 1970).

Additional findings have shown how modeling influences alter cognitive functioning of the type described by Piaget and his followers. Some of these studies are concerned with the principle of conservation, which reflects a child's ability to recognize that a given property remains invariant despite external changes that make it look different (as when the same amount of liquid is poured into different shaped containers). Young children who do not conserve are able to do so consistently after observing a model's conservation judgments and supporting explanations (Rosenthal & Zimmerman, 1970). Conservation judgments induced through modeling generalize to new characteristics, endure over time, and they do not differ from conservation concepts acquired by children in the course of everyday experiences (Sullivan, 1967).

Gender Development

Modeling also is significant to gender development and differentiation.[7] From the early days of life, children are exposed to gender-linked modeling cues. Although this has been true throughout human history, these cues are even more prevalent in a contemporary world in which gender-linked modeling displays appear so commonly in broadcast and internet media.

Within a given family even same-sex siblings may thus develop unlike personality characteristics as a result of imitating different combinations of parental and sibling attributes. A succession of modeling influences in which observers later became sources of behavior for new members would most likely produce a gradual imitative evolution of novel patterns bearing little resemblance to those exhibited by the original models.

The degree of behavioral innovation that results from modeling will depend on the diversity of modeled patterns to which one is exposed. In homogeneous cultures in which all models display similar modes of response, imitative behavior

---

7 A detailed account of the Social Cognitive Theory view of gender development and differentiation can be found in Bussey and Bandura (1999).

may undergo little or no change across successive models, but model dissimilarity is apt to foster new divergent patterns. The evidence accumulated to date suggests that, depending on their complexity and diversity, modeling influences can produce, in addition to mimicry of specific responses, behavior that is generative and innovative in character.

Aggression

Finally, let us return to the phenomenon with which we started: aggression, the class of behavior examined in the Bobo Doll studies. Aggression is a multifaceted phenomenon; it has many determinants and serves diverse purposes in different sociocultural settings. A comprehensive theoretical account thus must be broad in scope. It must encompass a large set of variables governing diverse facets of aggression, whether individual or collective, personal or institutionally sanctioned. A complete theory of aggression must explain how aggressive patterns are developed, what provokes people to behave aggressively, and what sustains such actions after they have been initiated. Theoretical formulations couched in terms of singular variables (e.g., frustrating instigators) have limited power.

Aggressive action has social foundations. People do not inherit preformed repertoires of aggressive behavior. They must learn aggressive acts. Much of this learning occurs vicariously, by observing others' aggressive behavior and the consequences that follow it.

In contemporary society, aggressive styles of behavior may be learned from three principal sources. One is aggression modeled and rewarded by family members. Studies of familial determinants of aggression show that parents who favor aggressive solutions to problems tend to produce children who tend to use similar aggressive tactics in dealing with others (Bandura & Walters, 1959). The subculture in which people reside, and with which they have repeated contact, is a second source. Not surprisingly, the highest incidence of aggression is found in communities in which aggressive models abound and fighting prowess is valued (Short, 1968). The third source of aggressive conduct is the abundant symbolic modeling available in mass media and the internet. In the 20th century, the advent of television greatly expanded the range of models—including aggressive models—available to the growing child. For decades, children and adults have had unlimited opportunities to learn the whole gamut of violent conduct from the comfort of their homes.

Social diffusion of aggressive styles and tactics conforms to the generalized pattern of most other contagious activities. New behavior is introduced by a salient example, spreads rapidly in a contagious fashion, and then either stabilizes or is discarded depending on its functional value.

Several characteristics of televised presentations tend to weaken people's restraints over behaving aggressively. Physical aggression is portrayed as a preferred solution to interpersonal conflicts; it appears acceptable, unsullied, and relatively successful. Much of the killing is done by fictional heroes. When good triumphs violently over evil, viewers are more strongly influenced than when the aggression that is witnessed is not sanctioned by prestigeful figures.

Repeated exposure to violence fosters desensitization and habituation that is reflected in decreased physiological reactions to violent displays. Heavy viewers of television respond with less emotion to violence than do light viewers (Cline et al., 1973). In addition to emotional desensitization, violence viewing can create behavioral indifference to human aggression. In studies that demonstrated the habituation effect, children who had prior exposure to interpersonal violence were less likely to intervene in escalating aggression between children they were overseeing.

To account for the broad range of aggressive conduct both—impulsive and principled—that occurs in contemporary society, one must address a broad range of causal factors. Psychologists since the psychodynamic era have concentrated their attention primarily on one class of causes: a breakdown of self-control (or "ego") functions that results in impulsive aggression. But violent activities commonly result not from impaired self-control but from the deployment of cognitive skills, specifically, the skills of moral justification and self-exoneration. People engage in destructive acts for what they claim are principled, valid reasons. Indeed, massive threats to human welfare generally stem from deliberate acts of principle rather than unrestrained acts of impulse. Such principled acts of aggression are of the greatest social concern, yet have commonly been ignored in psychological theorizing and research.[8]

---

8 Bandura's definitive analysis of the social origins of aggressive conduct is Bandura (1973). Although not addressed in detail in the passages prepared for this book, Bandura's famed Bobo Doll studies raise the question of whether exposure to media violence enduringly affects the behavioral tendencies of developing children. A late-20th century review of this literature is that of Liebert and Sprafkin (1988). More recently, an empirical review by a large workgroup of scholars confirms the short- and long-term effects of exposure to media violence; as they write, "Since Albert Bandura's classic Bobo doll study, which illustrated that children will imitate physical attacks on inanimate objects that they view on television, social learning theories have provided a convincing theoretical framework to understand violent media effects. A large body of evidence reveals that violent media can increase aggression. Indeed, the effects of screen violence on increased aggressive behavior have been reviewed and affirmed by numerous major scientific organizations, including the American Academy of Pediatrics, the American Academy of Child and Adolescent Psychiatry, the American Medical Association, the American Psychiatric Association, the American Psychological Association, the US Surgeon General, the Society for the Psychological Study of Social Issues, and the International Society for Research on Aggression" (Anderson et al., 2017, S143).

Vicarious Affective Learning

This chapter has focused on the observational learning of patterns of overt behavior. But observers also learn by observing a model's emotional responses. We conclude this chapter by reviewing processes of vicarious affective learning.

Vicarious affective learning occurs readily. Both adults and children are easily aroused by the emotions that are displayed by others (Bandura & Rosenthal, 1966 [also see Cao et al., 2020; Morelli et al., 2015 for research that begins to identify neural systems underlying the capacity for vicarious affective response]). In addition to influencing emotional experience at the time of the modeled display, modeled emotions also can affect observer's future emotional tendencies. Observers may associate modeled emotions either with the models themselves or with the environmental contexts that appear to have elicited the model's affective response (Bandura & Rosenthal, 1966). Once this occurs, the observer may re-experience the observed emotion in the presence of the previously encountered stimuli.

Emotional arousal and behavioral inhibitions can also be extinguished by having fearful observers watch performers engage in threatening activities in the absence of aversive consequences. Because this aspect of vicarious affective learning is substantially mediated by changes in self-efficacy beliefs, it is reviewed in the next chapter of this text.

Although people are endowed with receptive and expressive capacities for vicarious arousal, the exact level and pattern of emotion that occurs at any given time is substantially determined by social experience. These social mechanisms inherently involve reciprocal processes. When individuals are in good spirits they tend to treat others amiably, which produces positive affect in others, thus creating an environment that, in part, is determined by personal factors. Conversely, when individuals are dejected, distressed, or angry, people around them are likely to suffer as well. Research confirms this correlated feature of interpersonal emotions (Miller, Caul, & Mirsky, 1967; Church, 1959; Englis, Vaughan & Lanzetta, 1982).

The capacity for vicarious affective experience operates substantially through self-processes. When people see others react emotionally to instigating conditions, they themselves tend to engage in emotion-arousing thoughts and imagery. Developmental analyses indicate that, as children develop their capacity for cognitive self-arousal, they become able to generate emotional reactions to cues that merely are suggestive of a model's emotional experiences (Wilson & Cantor, 1985). They also become able to lessen the emotional impact of modeled distress through thoughts that transform threatening into nonthreatening situations (Cantor & Wilson, 1987; Dysinger & Ruckmick, 1933).

Vicarious affective influence is particularly significant because its effects can be enduring. Observers can acquire long-lasting attitudes and emotional reactions toward persons, places, or things that they have not encountered themselves, but for which they have observed model's emotional responses (Bandura, 1988b; Duncker, 1938; Mineka, 1987). Fears and phobias are ameliorated by models whose actions convey information about ways of coping with feared encounters (Bandura, 1982). Values can similarly be developed and altered vicariously by repeated exposure to modeled preferences.

As noted a number of times in this chapter, modeling effects commonly are mediated by self-referent thoughts. Observations of others' actions and experiences alters people's thoughts about themselves. Our next chapter addresses a self-referent thinking process that is a core foundation of human agency.

3

Perceived Self-Efficacy as a Foundation of Agency

Social Cognitive Theory subscribes to a model of human agency that is interactive (Bandura, 1986). Persons are not autonomous agents who exert an inner "willpower" that stands apart from the social world in which they develop and live. Nor are they merely collections of reflexive mechanisms that animate environmental influences. Rather, people make causal contributions to their own motivation and action as they interact with their environments and reflect on their own behaviors, as was discussed in Chapter 1. Within the social cognitive model of triadic reciprocal causation, three classes of influences—actions; cognitive, affective and other personal factors; and environmental events—are mutually interacting determinants.

Within this causal interplay, a diverse range of the personal factors contributes to human agency, as the chapters of this book explain. Yet, among them, one stands out. No psychological mechanism is more central or pervasive than people's beliefs about their capabilities to exercise control over events that affect their lives. The present chapter analyzes these beliefs in self-efficacy.

Exercise of Agency Through Self-Belief of Efficacy

Self-efficacy beliefs are an aspect of thinking; specifically, they are a class of judgments. When people contemplate challenging activities, they commonly judge the effectiveness with which they can take actions to meet the challenges and attain a given level of success. Perceptions of self-efficacy are defined as people's judgments of their capabilities to execute courses of action that are required to attain designated types of performances (Bandura, 1986). Self-efficacy beliefs are judgments of what one *can* do in a current or prospective situation, not statements of intentions of what one will do (Bandura, 2006a–c).

Social Cognitive Theory: An Agentic Perspective on Human Nature, First Edition. Albert Bandura.
© 2023 John Wiley & Sons, Inc. Published 2023 by John Wiley & Sons, Inc.

The Social Cognitive Theory program of theory and research on self-efficacy beliefs originated in studies of phobic behavior change (Bandura, 1976). The therapy findings showed that severe snake phobics benefitted rapidly from an intervention in which, with a therapist's guide, they directly interacted with the object they fear (Bandura, Blanchard, & Ritter, 1969; Bandura, Jeffery, & Gajdos, 1975; also see Biran & Wilson, 1981; Thase & Moss, 1976). These guided mastery experiences demonstrate to phobics that stimuli are safer, and that their capacity to exercise control over threats is greater, than they previously had thought.

In follow-up assessments, participants reported psychological changes that went beyond the specific behavioral treatment targets. Former phobics no longer were plagued by dreams of dreaded objects. Their social and recreational lives no longer were disrupted by ruminative fears of snakes. Such participant reports suggested that the effects of mastery therapy extended beyond changes in the target behavior. Mastery therapy appeared to have altered a belief system with widespread consequences for personal well-being. This system of beliefs—self-efficacy beliefs—became a target of study for Social Cognitive Theory (Bandura, 1977).

Thanks to the work of numerous investigators (reviewed in Bandura, 1997), the scope of self-efficacy theory rapidly expanded beyond the question of phobic behavior change. Self-efficacy beliefs are of particular significance because they contribute causally to a wide range of psychological processes. We review these below, after some additional words about the conceptualization of self-efficacy beliefs in Social Cognitive Theory.

Concepualizing Self-Efficacy Beliefs

The reader can best understand the exact nature of self-efficacy beliefs by considering not only what they are (see definition above) but what they are not. A number of distinctions clarify the nature of self-efficacy beliefs.

Self-efficacy beliefs are not abstract conceptions of one's "skills." Consider cases such as a world-class athlete coping with injuries or a musical soloist who has received a new composition but has insufficient time to practice it. In both cases, the individuals may have no doubts whatsoever about their absolute level of skill. Yet, they may harbor doubts about their efficacy for attaining high levels of performance in an upcoming game or concert.

Self-efficacy beliefs are not feelings of self-worth. People may possess robust self-efficacy beliefs for executing activities that contribute little or nothing to their sense of personal esteem. Such would be the case for someone who has mastered the skills of a boring job that they hope soon to quit.

Beliefs in self-efficacy for performance attainments differ qualitatively from expectations about the outcomes that may follow upon those attainments.

The distinction is particularly significant for members of groups that have been subjected to societal discrimination. Such individuals may have unquestioned confidence in their own capabilities while simultaneously questioning whether institutions will give them a fair opportunity to capitalize on their skills.

These conceptual distinctions have practical implications. They must be kept in mind when one designs measures to assess self-efficacy beliefs—a methodological challenge discussed later in this chapter.

A final conceptual point before we turn to the processes through which self-efficacy beliefs contribute to achievement concerns the role of self-efficacy processes within Social Cognitive Theory as a whole. Self-efficacy has received such attention that writers have sometimes appeared to conflate the study of self-efficacy beliefs with the entire social cognitive framework. This is a mistake. One must distinguish Social Cognitive Theory as a whole from its self-efficacy component. As is evident from other chapters of this book (and see Bandura, 1986), Social Cognitive Theory encompasses a large set of motivators and regulators of human behavior. Self-efficacy is but one. It is a pivotal one because self-efficacy judgments partly determine the other classes of determinants, such as goal setting, outcome expectations, and quality of analytic thinking (see Chapter 4). Nonetheless, in Social Cognitive Theory, self-efficacy processes operate in concert with other determinants; they are a partner rather than an independent player in the determination of motivation, affect, and the regulation of action.

From Self-Efficacy to Action: A Multiprocess Analysis

Robust beliefs in personal efficacy foster success. Self-doubts impair achievement. But these relations between self-efficacy beliefs and performance outcomes are not direct or automatic; self-efficacy is not a "magic wand" that simply conjures a brighter future. In Social Cognitive Theory, self-efficacy judgments function as one proximal determinant of four classes of psychological processes: Selection Processes (that is, choices of environments), Cognitive Processes, Motivational Processes, and Affective Processes. These four processes, in turn, are consequential to human achievement and well-being in a very wide range of social contexts. We review each of the four processes now.

Selection Processes

People can exert some influence over their life course by selecting the environments they encounter and the activities they pursue. These choices rest, in part, on subjective beliefs about personal efficacy. People appraise their capability to execute the actions that they expect to arise in prospective environments. These self-efficacy appraisals are one determinant of the environments that they select. People tend to avoid activities and situations they believe exceed their coping capabilities, and to undertake even challenging activities that they judge themselves capable of handling.

Selection processes have a multiplicity of effects, both immediate and long-term. Regarding the enduring effects, once one encounters the selected environment, its features promote certain competencies, values, and interests. These effects of environmental experiences may last long after the original selection of environments was made. Thus, seemingly inconsequential determinants can initiate selective associations that produce major and enduring personal changes (Bandura, 1986; Snyder, 1980). Choices of environments thus can profoundly affect the direction of one's personal development.

The power of self-efficacy beliefs to affect the course of life paths through selection processes is revealed clearly in studies of career decision-making (Betz & Hackett, 1986; Lent & Hackett, 1987). The more efficacious people judge themselves to be, the wider the range of career options they consider appropriate for themselves and the better they prepare themselves educationally for such pursuits. People who doubt their efficacy can self-limit their career development. Self-doubts may cause people to avoid activities with the potential to enhance career interests and competencies. When this happens, self-doubt becomes self-validating.[1]

---

1 A significant implication of selection effects—one that is not explicitly discussed in Bandura's present writing, but is implicit—is the following. Meta-analyses document robust effects of self-efficacy beliefs on performance outcomes (e.g., Livinti et al., 2021; Rottinghaus et al., 2003; Stajkovic & Luthans, 1998). Yet, the meta-analytic estimates may *underestimate* naturally-occurring self-efficacy effects. In the typical research paradigm, investigators relate variations in self-efficacy beliefs to variations in performance outcomes among people who are engaged in a given pursuit (e.g., a business, a profession, a college). The research strategy inherently disregards a significant group of people: Those who, due to low self-efficacy beliefs, choose not to engage in the pursuit in the first place. Consider a valuable research report by Livinti et al. (2021). In a sample consisting primarily of doctoral students and faculty engaged in research-related careers, higher levels of subjective beliefs in one's efficacy to carry out research activities predicted greater interest in research and greater research productivity, with effect sizes of .47 and .36, respectively. These effects, substantial though they are, do not include the impact of self-efficacy processes among those individuals who selected themselves out of research training and careers, and thus never ended up in the study samples. A second significant aspect of the research Bandura reviews here is that the impact of self-efficacy beliefs is evident even among samples that are equated for tested intellectual ability. For example, in a seminal research report, Betz and Hackett (1981) documented gender differences in self-efficacy beliefs and perceived career options in a college student sample in which men and women did not differ in ACT math or English scores. Social factors, such as the availability of role models, can create disparate subjective beliefs among individuals with similar abilities; for example, Gillooly et al. (2021) report complex effects of role models on self-efficacy beliefs among a sample of nearly 300 PhD students.

Efficacy beliefs, such as those that contribute to selection processes, exhibit a gradient of strength as a function of temporal and physical proximity to the relevant activity. One must consider the height and slope of the efficacy gradient and the threshold strength for acting on one's self-belief. These characteristics of the self-belief system are affected by the authenticity of the efficacy information on which they are based. Self-efficacy beliefs that are firmly established are likely to remain strong regardless of whether one is far removed from the taxing or threatening activities or is about to perform them. Such beliefs are resilient to adversity. In contrast, when self-efficacy beliefs are weak, they are highly vulnerable to change, with self-doubts mounting the nearer one gets to the taxing activities (Kent, 1987; Kent & Gibbons, 1987) and negative experiences readily reinstating disbelief in one's capabilities.

Cognitive Processes

Self-efficacy beliefs affect thought patterns. Once activated, these patterns of thinking, in turn, may aid or hinder one's future efforts. Cognitive processes that are shaped by self-efficacy beliefs thus are a second mechanism through which self-efficacy belief affects achievement.

A major function of thought is to enable people to predict the occurrence of events and to create the means for exercising control over those that affect their daily lives. Many activities involve inferential judgments about conditional relations between events in probabilistic environments. Discernment of predictive rules requires cognitive processing of multidimensional information that contains many ambiguities and uncertainties. In ferreting out predictive rules people must draw on their state of knowledge to generate hypotheses about predictive factors, to weight and integrate them into composite rules, to test their judgments against outcome information, and to remember which notions they had tested and how well they had worked. It requires a strong sense of efficacy to remain task oriented in the face of judgmental failures. Indeed, people who believe strongly in their problem-solving capabilities remain highly efficient in their analytic thinking in complex decision-making situations, whereas those who are plagued by self-doubts are erratic in their analytic thinking (Bandura & Wood, 1989; Wood & Bandura, 1989a). Quality of analytic thinking, in turn, affects performance accomplishments.

Perceptions of their efficacy influence the types of anticipatory scenarios people construct and dwell upon. Those who have a high sense of efficacy visualize success scenarios that provide positive guides for performance. Those who judge themselves as inefficacious are more inclined to visualize failure scenarios which undermine performance by dwelling on how things will go wrong. Cognitive simulations in which individuals visualize themselves executing activities skillfully enhance subsequent performance (Bandura, 1986; Corbin, 1972; Feltz & Landers, 1983; Kazdin, 1978; Markus, Cross, & Wurf, 1990). Perceived self-efficacy and cognitive simulation affect each other bidirectionally. A high sense of efficacy fosters cognitive constructions of effective actions and cognitive reiteration of efficacious courses of action strengthens self-percepts of efficacy (Bandura & Adams, 1977; Kazdin, 1979).

Self-efficacy beliefs usually affect cognitive functioning through the joint influence of motivational and information-processing operations. This dual influence is illustrated in studies of different sources of variation in memory performance. The stronger people's beliefs in their memory capacities, the more effort they devote to cognitive processing of memory tasks which, in turn, enhances their memory performances (Berry, 1987).

Another set of cognitive processes that are partly shaped by self-efficacy beliefs are those thoughts through which people regulate ongoing actions (discussed in more detail in Chapter 4). Much human behavior is regulated by forethought embodying cognized goals. Personal goal setting is influenced by self-appraisal of capabilities. The stronger the perceived self-efficacy, the higher the goals people set for themselves and the firmer their commitment to them (Locke, Frederick, Lee, & Bobko, 1984; Taylor, Locke, Lee, & Gist, 1984; Wood & Bandura, 1989b).

Motivational Processes

People's self-efficacy beliefs determine their level of motivation, as reflected in how much effort they will exert in an endeavor, and how long they will persevere in the face of obstacles. The stronger the belief in their capabilities, the greater and more persistent are their efforts. When faced with difficulties, people who are beset by self-doubts about their capabilities slacken their efforts or abort their attempts prematurely and quickly settle for mediocre solutions, whereas those who have a strong belief in their capabilities exert greater effort to master the challenge (Bandura & Cervone, 1983, 1986; Cervone & Peake, 1986; Jacobs, Prentice-Dunn, & Rogers, 1984; Weinberg, Gould, & Jackson, 1979). Strong perseverance usually pays off in performance accomplishments.

Substantial evidence indicates that attainments and well-being require an optimistic sense of personal efficacy (Bandura, 1986). Social realities are strewn with difficulties. People experience impediments, failures, adversities, setbacks, frustrations, and inequities. A robust sense of personal efficacy is needed to sustain perseverant effort in the face of obstacles. Self-doubts can set in fast after some failures or reverses. The important matter is not the sheer existence of self-doubt—a natural immediate reaction to difficulty—but the speed of recovery of strong self-efficacy beliefs. Some quickly recover their self-assurance, whereas others enduringly lose faith in their capabilities. Because skill development requires sustained effort and occasional setbacks are inevitable, it is resiliency of self-belief that counts.

John White's *Rejection* (1982) provides vivid testimony that the striking characteristics of people who achieve eminence in their field are an inextinguishable sense of efficacy and a firm belief in the worth of their pursuit. This resilient self-belief system provides the needed staying power that enables people to override early rejections of their work. Many literary classics came to publication only after such rejection. The novelist, Saroyan, accumulated several thousand rejections before he had his first literary piece published. Gertrude Stein continued to submit poems to editors for about 20 years before one was finally accepted. James Joyce's *Dubliners* was rejected by 22 publishers. Such extraordinary persistence in the face of massive unremitting rejection defies explanation in terms of either reinforcement theory or utility theory. Over a dozen publishers rejected a manuscript by e. e. cummings. When his mother finally published it the dedication, printed in upper case, read: *With no thanks to . . .* followed by the long list of publishers who had rejected his offering.

Early rejection is the rule, rather than the exception, in other creative endeavors, too. The Impressionists had to arrange their own art exhibitions because their works were routinely rejected by the Paris Salon. Van Gogh sold only one painting during his lifetime. Rodin was repeatedly rejected by the École des Beaux-Arts. The musical works of most renowned composers were initially greeted with derision. For example, Stravinsky was run out of Paris by an enraged audience and critics when he first served them the *Rite of Spring*. In architecture, designs of the brilliant Frank Lloyd Wright commonly were rejected.

The entertainment industry provides more examples. Hollywood initially rejected the incomparable Fred Astaire for being only "a balding, skinny actor who can dance a little." Decca Records turned down a recording contract with the Beatles with the nonprophetic evaluation, "We don't like their sound. Groups of guitars are on their way out."

The same occurs in science. Not uncommonly, works that attain the status of scientific classics initially experienced rejection—which often came with hostile embellishments if novel ideas were discordant with concepts in vogue at the time. Consider the work of John Garcia, who eventually won well-deserved recognition for his fundamental discoveries in the study of conditioned taste aversion. His initial manuscripts were rejected, with one reviewer saying that one is no more likely to find the phenomenon he discovered than bird droppings in a cuckoo clock. Persistent scientific pursuit after verbal droppings of this type demands tenacious self-belief. When scientists reject theories and technologies that are ahead of their time, they delay the time between discovery and technical realization of basic scientific advance.

It is widely believed that misjudgment produces dysfunction. Certainly, gross miscalculation can create problems. But optimistic self-appraisals of capability that are not unduly disparate from what is possible can be advantageous, whereas veridical judgments can be self-limiting. When people err in their self-appraisal, they tend to overestimate their capabilities. This is a benefit rather than a cognitive failing to be eradicated. If self-efficacy beliefs always reflected only what people can do routinely, they would rarely fail but they would not mount the extra effort needed to surpass their ordinary performances.

Evidence suggests that it is often the so-called normals who are distorters of reality [e.g., Alloy & Abramson, 1979; but also see Allan et al., 2007], exhibiting self-enhancing biases that distort appraisals in the positive direction. The successful, the innovative, the sociable, the nonanxious, the nondespondent, and the social reformers take an optimistic view of their personal efficacy to exercise influence over events that affect their lives (Bandura, 1986; Taylor & Brown, 1988). If not unrealistically exaggerated, such self-beliefs foster the perseverant effort needed for personal and social accomplishments. The findings of laboratory studies are in accord with the records of human triumphs regarding the centrality of the motivational effects of self-beliefs of efficacy in human attainments. It takes a resilient sense of efficacy to override the numerous dissuading impediments to significant accomplishments.

Motivational processes not only are important to success on activities one faces in the present. The experience of success based on effort builds self-efficacy for future activities. Development of resilient self-efficacy requires some experience in mastering difficulties through perseverant effort. If people experience only easy successes they come to expect quick results and their sense of efficacy is easily undermined by failure. Some setbacks and difficulties in human pursuits serve a useful purpose in teaching that success usually requires sustained effort. After people become convinced they have what it takes to succeed, they persevere in the face of adversity and quickly rebound from setbacks. By sticking it out through tough times, they emerge from adversity with a stronger sense of efficacy.

Affective Processes

People's beliefs in their capabilities affect not only levels of motivation, but also how much stress and despondency people experience in threatening or taxing situations. Such emotional reactions can affect action both directly and indirectly by altering the nature and course of thinking. Threat is not a fixed property of situational events. Nor does appraisal of the likelihood of aversive happenings rely solely on reading external signs of danger or safety. Rather, threat is a relational property concerning the match between perceived coping capabilities and potentially aversive aspects of the environment.

People who believe they can exercise control over potential threats do not conjure up apprehensive cognitions and, therefore, are not perturbed by them. But those who believe they cannot manage potential threats experience high levels of stress and anxiety arousal. They tend to dwell on their coping deficiencies and view many aspects of their environment as fraught with danger. Through such inefficacious thought they distress themselves and constrain and impair their level of functioning (Bandura, 1988b, 1988c; Lazarus & Folkman, 1984; Meichenbaum, 1977; Sarason, 1975).

That perceived coping efficacy operates as a cognitive mediator of anxiety has been tested by creating different levels of perceived coping efficacy and relating them at a microlevel to different manifestations of anxiety. Perceived coping inefficacy is accompanied by high levels of subjective distress, autonomic arousal and plasma catecholamine secretion (Bandura, Reese, & Adams, 1982; Bandura, Taylor, Williams, Mefford, & Barchas, 1985). The combined results from the different psychobiological manifestations of emotional arousal are consistent in showing that anxiety and stress reactions are low when people cope with tasks in their perceived self-efficacy range. Self-doubts in coping efficacy produce substantial increases in subjective distress and physiological arousal. After perceived coping efficacy is strengthened to the maximal level, coping with the previously intimidating tasks no longer elicits differential psychobiological reactions.

Anxiety arousal in situations involving some risks is affected not only by perceived coping efficacy, but also by perceived self-efficacy to control intrusive perturbing cognitions. The exercise of control over one's own consciousness is summed up well in the proverb: "You cannot prevent the birds of worry and care from flying over your head. But you can stop them from building a nest in your hair." Perceived self-efficacy in thought control is a key factor in the regulation of cognitively-generated arousal. It is not the sheer frequency of aversive cognitions but the perceived inefficacy to turn them off that is the major source of distress (Kent, 1987; Salkovskis & Harrison, 1984). Thus, the incidence of aversive cognitions is unrelated to anxiety level when variations in perceived thought control efficacy are controlled for, whereas perceived thought control efficacy is strongly related to anxiety level when extent of frightful cognitions is controlled (Kent & Gibbons, 1987).

The role of perceived self-efficacy and anxiety arousal in the causal structure of avoidant behavior has also been examined extensively. The results show that people base their actions on self-percepts of coping efficacy in situations they regard as risky. The stronger the perceived coping efficacy, the more venturesome the behavior, regardless of whether self-percepts of efficacy are enhanced through mastery experiences, modeling influences or cognitive simulations (Bandura, 1988b).

Perceived self-efficacy accounts for a substantial amount of variance in phobic behavior when anticipated anxiety is partialed out, whereas the relationship between anticipated anxiety and phobic behavior essentially disappears when perceived self-efficacy is partialed out (Williams, Dooseman, & Kleifield, 1984; Williams, Kinney, & Falbo, 1989; Williams, Turner, & Peer, 1985). In short, people avoid potentially threatening situations and activities not because they are beset with anxiety, but because they believe they will be unable to cope with situations they regard as risky. They take self-protective action regardless of whether or not they happen to be anxious at the moment. The dual control of anxiety arousal and avoidant behavior by perceived coping efficacy and thought control efficacy is revealed in analyses of the mechanisms governing personal empowerment over pervasive social threats (Ozer & Bandura, 1989). One path of influence is mediated through the effects of perceived coping self-efficacy on perceived vulnerability and risk discernment, and the other through the impact of perceived cognitive control self-efficacy on intrusive aversive thoughts.

Perceived self-inefficacy to fulfill desired goals that affect evaluation of self-worth and to secure things that bring satisfaction to one's life can give rise to bouts of depression (Bandura, 1988a; Cutrona & Troutman, 1986; Holahan & Holahan, 1987a, b; Kanfer & Zeiss, 1983). When the perceived self-inefficacy involves social relationships, it can induce depression both directly and indirectly by curtailing the cultivation of interpersonal relationships that can provide satisfactions and buffer the effects of chronic daily stressors (Holahan & Holahan, 1987a). Depressive rumination not only impairs ability to initiate and sustain adaptive activities, but further diminishes perceptions of personal efficacy (Kavanagh & Bower, 1985). Much human depression is also cognitively generated by dejecting ruminative thoughts (Nolen-Hoeksema, 1987). Therefore, perceived self-inefficacy to exercise control over ruminative thought figures prominently in the occurrence, duration and recurrence of depressive episodes (Kavanagh & Wilson, 1988).

Other efficacy activated processes in the affective domain concern its impact on basic biological systems that mediate health functioning (Bandura, 1989a). Stress has been implicated as an important contributing factor to many physical dysfunctions. Controllability appears to be a key organizing principle regarding the nature of these stress effects. Exposure to physical stressors with ability to control them has no adverse physiological effects. But exposure to the same stressors without ability to control them impairs cellular components of the immune system (Coe & Levine, 1989; Maier, Laudenslager, & Ryan, 1985). Biological systems are highly interdependent. The types of biochemical reactions that have been shown to accompany perceived coping inefficacy are involved in the regulation of immune systems. For example, perceived self-inefficacy in exercising control over cognitive stressors activates endogenous opioid systems (Bandura, Cioffi, Taylor, & Brouillard, 1988). There is evidence that some of the immunosuppressive effects of inefficacy in controlling stressors are mediated by release of endogenous opioids. When opioid mechanisms are blocked by opiate antagonists, the stress of coping inefficacy loses its immunosuppressive power (Shavit & Martin, 1987).

In the laboratory research demonstrating immunosuppression through stress mediation, controllability is studied as a fixed dichotomous property in which animals either exercise complete control over physical stressors, or they have no control, whatsoever. In contrast, most human stress is activated in the course of learning how to exercise control over recurring cognitive and social stressors. It would not be evolutionarily advantageous if acute stressors invariably impaired immune function, because of their prevalence in everyday life. Indeed, in a recently completed project, we find that stress aroused in the process of gaining coping efficacy over stressors enhances immune function. The rate of efficacy acquisition is a good predictor of whether exposure to acute stressors enhances or suppresses immune function.

Additional lines of research provide converging evidence for the influential impact of perceived ability to exercise control over anxiety and stress reactions (Bandura, 1997; Averill, 1973; Levine & Ursin, 1980; Miller,1980). People who are led arbitrarily to believe they can control aversive events display lower autonomic arousal and less performance impairment than do those who believe they lack personal control, even though they are subjected equally to the painful events (Geer, Davison, & Gatchel, 1970; Glass, Singer, Leonard, Krantz, & Cummings, 1973). The same is true for stress reactions to clinical pain. Bogus physiological feedback that patients were effective relaxers raised beliefs in their efficacy to cope with their oral surgery (Litt, Nye, & Shafer, 1993). Self-efficacy enhancement surpassed relaxation and sedation drugs in reducing self-rated anxiety as well as anxiety reactions and behavioral agitation during surgery, as rated by the oral surgeon and dental assistant. Regardless of type of ameliorative treatment the patients received, the more their efficacy beliefs were raised by the preparatory ministrations, the lower the anxious agitation.

The power of control beliefs to transform frightening environments into benign ones is graphically demonstrated by Sanderson, Rapee, and Barlow (1989). Inhaling a CO_2 mixture induces panic attacks in agoraphobics. One group inhaled the mixture without control over it. Another group inhaled it under illusory control. They were told they could regulate how much CO_2 they got by turning a valve. But unbeknownst to them the valve was disconnected so they inhaled the same amount of the CO_2 mixture. Agoraphobics who had no control experienced mounting anxiety over time. They were plagued with catastrophic thoughts that they were going to disintegrate, go crazy or die. And 80% experienced panic attacks. Those who were led to believe they were exercising control remained unperturbed, and free of catastrophic thinking and relatively few of them experienced a panic attack.

Figure 3.1 summarizes the processes through which judgments of self-efficacy shape human achievement and well-being.

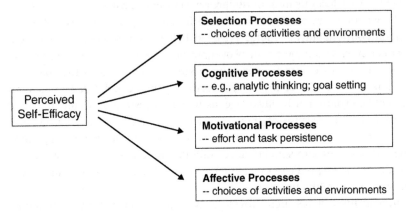

Figure 3.1 In Social Cognitive Theory, self-efficacy judgments are one proximal determinant of each of four classes of psychological processes—Selection Processes, Cognitive Processes, Motivational Processes, and Affective Processes—that, in turn, are highly consequential to achievement and well-being in a wide range of activities and social contexts.

Self-Efficacy Causality

A central question in any theory of the cognitive regulation of motivation and action is the issue of causality. Do beliefs of personal efficacy causally contribute to human functioning? This question is not one for idle speculation. It can be, and has been, extensively investigated empirically in the self-efficacy literature.

Meta-Analytic Results

One empirical strategy relates variations in self-efficacy beliefs to future psychological functioning. Multiple large-scale meta-analyses have assessed the resulting self-efficacy effects. They include analyses of work-related performances in both laboratory and field studies (Sadri & Robertson, 1993; Stajkovic & Luthans, 1998); psychosocial functioning in children and adolescents (Holden, Moncher, Schinke, & Barker, 1990); academic achievement and persistence (Multon, Brown, & Lent, 1991); health functioning (Holden, 1991); athletic performance (Moritz, Feltz, Fahrbach, & Mack, 2000); perceived collective efficacy in group functioning (Gully, Incalcaterra, Joshi, & Beaubien, 2002; Stajkovic & Lee, 2001). They encompass controlled investigations in which efficacy beliefs are altered experimentally (Boyer, et al., 2000). Reviewed studies include interindividual designs comparing groups raised to differential levels of perceived efficacy as well as intraindividual designs in which a given individual experiences increasing self-efficacy beliefs over time. They include multiple controls for other potential contributors to performance; diverse methods of instilling greater beliefs in self-efficacy; diverse populations in varying cultural milieus; and dependent measures encompassing cognitive, affective, and behavioral expressions. Moreover, efficacy beliefs are measured by different formats and domain-related scales, so that obtained relations are not peculiar to a particular instrument.

Evidence from these meta-analyses consistently shows that efficacy beliefs contribute significantly to motivation and performance. The conclusion holds for both intra-individual and inter-individual analyses of individuals at different levels of perceived self-efficacy, over changes in functioning in individuals at different levels of efficacy over time; and even variation within the same individual in the tasks performed and those shunned or attempted but failed. Evidence that divergent procedures produce convergent results adds to the explanatory and predictive generality of the self-efficacy determinant.

Altering Self-Efficacy Beliefs Directly, Without Enactive Experience

Meta-analyses do not portray the variety of creative experimental strategies that have been used to verify the functional properties of people's beliefs in their capabilities. Because of the centrality of this issue this section reviews, in some detail, the nature of these strategies, the multiple controls they institute, and evidence of the functional impact of self-efficacy beliefs. In the most stringent tests, perceived self-efficacy is raised directly to differential levels rather than by enactive[2] experiences. Such modes of influence provide no personal performance information for judging one's personal capabilities.

One direct way of altering perceived self-efficacy is to introduce a trivial factor devoid of any relevant information whatsoever, but that can bias perceived self-efficacy. Studies of anchoring influences show that arbitrary reference points from which judgments are made bias judgmental processes because the adjustments from the arbitrary starting points are usually insufficient (Tversky & Kahneman, 1974). For example, people will judge a larger crowd at a major sports event from an arbitrary starting number of 1,000 than from an arbitrary number of 40,000, even though these anchoring numbers are completely irrelevant to

---

2 The term "enactive" designates experiences in which an individual takes overt action in a given performance context rather than merely, for example, talking about the context and its challenges or observing someone else coping with the situation. The terminology is significant in that different forms of experience (enactive or not) differentially influence cognition and action. For example, in a classic study conducted with snake phobics, Bandura, Blanchard, & Ritter (1969) demonstrated that a condition in which a therapist and participant collaboratively engage with the phobic stimulus—i.e., an enactive therapy—more effectively improved behavior, affect, and cognition than systematic desensitization or a treatment condition in which participants merely observed a filmed model.

judging the size of the crowd. Cervone and Peake (1986) raised perceived self-efficacy by having individuals rate their efficacy from a supposedly randomly selected high number and lowered their self-efficacy from a low arbitrary starting number. The higher the instated perceived self-efficacy the longer individuals persevered on difficult and unsolvable problems before they quit. Mediational analyses showed that the biasing anchoring influence had no effect on performance motivation when perceived self-efficacy was controlled. Thus, the effect of the external anchoring influence on performance motivation was completely mediated by the degree to which it changed efficacy beliefs.

In a related study (Peake & Cervone, 1989), efficacy judgment was biased simply by having people judge their self-efficacy in relation to ascending or descending levels of possible attainments. The initial levels in these sequences served as anchoring influences that lowered or raised self-efficacy beliefs, respectively. Elevated self-beliefs of efficacy heightened effort, whereas lowered self-beliefs lessened effort on troublesome problems. In a further study, Cervone (1989) biased self-efficacy judgment through differential cognitive focus on things about the task that might make it troublesome or tractable. Dwelling on formidable aspects weakened people's belief in their efficacy, but focusing on doable aspects raised self-judgment of capabilities. The higher the altered self-efficacy beliefs, the longer people persevered in the face of repeated failure. In these various experiments, perceived self-efficacy predicts variance in motivation within treatment conditions, as well as across treatments. Mediational analyses reveal that neither anchoring influences nor cognitive focus has any impact on motivation when variations in self-efficacy beliefs are controlled. These external influences thus exerted their effect on motivation entirely through the mediation of changes in self-efficacy beliefs.[3]

---

3 Related findings are reported in Berry et al. (1989), Cervone and Palmer (1990), and Oh (2021). Note that this body of findings eliminates an "epiphenomenalist" alternative explanation of the self-efficacy literature. In this theoretical alternative, self-efficacy—performance relations could be driven by participants' skills, with greater motoric skills or procedural knowledge on a task causing higher levels of performance and also causing people to report higher self-efficacy beliefs when they reflect on their competencies. In studies of motivation and effort, in principle, a third variable such as participants' mood could cause people to spend more time on tasks and to make more positive self-reports of efficacy. In either case, the relation between self-efficacy beliefs and behavior would be epiphenomenal rather than causal. This epiphenomenalist counter-argument is ruled out *by* findings such as Cervone and Peake (1986) and Peake and Cervone (1989). It is implausible that a brief, subtle manipulation such as an anchoring cue could build participants' skills or systematically alter their mood states; this is particularly true in Peake and Cervone (1989; also see Berry et al., 1989) where, as Bandura notes, different experimental conditions present *identical* stimulus material, but merely in different orders, varying their order of presentation to produce anchoring effects. These results thus confirm the Social Cognitive Theory prediction that self-efficacy judgments causally impact behavior. Bandura reflects on the epiphenomenalist position later in this chapter.

Another direct mode of influence that involves no performance alters efficacy beliefs solely by observational means. In one such experiment, perceived self-efficacy was raised in snake phobics by modeling alone either to differential levels in different individuals, or to successively higher levels in the same individuals by modeling the same information repeatedly (Bandura, Reese, & Adams, 1982). The higher the induced level of perceived self-efficacy the more snake handling tasks they performed regardless of whether the functional relation of self-efficacy belief to coping performance was assessed intraindividually or interindividually. Microanalysis of efficacy-action congruences revealed a very close 85% fit between efficacy beliefs and snake-handling performance on individual tasks they had never done before. They successfully executed coping tasks with a snake that fell within their enhanced range of perceived self-efficacy, but they shunned or failed those that exceeded their perceived coping capabilities.

Efficacy enhancement merely through visualization is still another direct means of altering efficacy beliefs without the mediation of enactive experiences. Severe phobics visualized progressively more threatening snake scenes while deeply relaxed in symbolic desensitization until anxiety reactions to all the scenes were completely eliminated in everyone (Bandura & Adams, 1977). Their perceived self-efficacy and snake coping behavior were then measured. Even though completely desensitized, the participants varied in belief in their coping efficacy. The more their efficacy beliefs were raised the higher their coping performance.

In modes of influence that alter efficacy beliefs by observing models or visualizing threatening activities, people do not execute any behavior. Consequently, they have no personal performance data for reappraising their capabilities. In the pretest assessment forty percent of the phobics in the study receiving symbolic desensitization could not even perform a single task, such as enter the test room containing a caged snake (Bandura & Adams, 1977). None had ever touched a snake in their lives or had a physical encounter with one. The only thing that their performance history and pretest performance could tell them was that they could do nothing. Although they were all completely desensitized to the visualized threats, their perceived self-efficacy at the end of treatment differed markedly, ranging from 6% to 67% increase from their zero performance baseline. Their posttreatment coping behavior was similarly varied, ranging from a 6% to 58% increase in performance attainment. The microlevel congruence between self-efficacy belief at the end of treatment and subsequent coping behavior was a high 83%.

One might argue that anxiety extinction is a possible alternative mechanism. Williams (1992) analyzed numerous data sets from studies of efficacy-based treatment for agoraphobia in which perceived self-efficacy, anticipatory anxiety, and coping behavior were all measured. The findings are consistent in showing that perceived self-efficacy is a strong predictor of coping behavior when anticipatory anxiety is partialed out, whereas the relationship between anticipatory anxiety and coping behavior essentially disappears when the influence of perceived self-efficacy is partialed out. The predictive superiority of perceived self-efficacy is replicated in other domains of functioning. People's beliefs in their efficacy have an independent effect on their performance attainments, whereas their level of anxiety bears little or no relationship to their performances on stressful academic tasks (Meece, Wigfield, & Eccles, 1990; Pajares & Miller, 1994) and athletic activities (McAuley, 1985) after the influence of perceived self-efficacy is removed. Beliefs of personal efficacy similarly predict willingness to perform threatening activities, but anticipatory anxiety makes no independent contribution (Arch, 1992).

Many experiments have been conducted in which people receive veridical feedback concerning their performance, but their efficacy beliefs are altered by bogus normative comparison. Erroneous feedback serves as a form of persuasory influence. Litt (1988) used an intraindividual design for this purpose. After being tested for pain tolerance on a cold-pressor test, individuals were led to believe that they were either at a high (90th) or low (37th) percentile rank in pain tolerance compared to an ostensibly normative group, regardless of their actual performance. The bogus normative information produced differential levels of perceived self-efficacy which, in turn, were accompanied by corresponding changes in pain tolerance. The greater the changes in perceived self-efficacy, the larger the changes in pain tolerance.

In the second phase of the intraindividual design, the bogus normative feedback was opposite to that provided originally. Those who were led to believe that they had lost their comparative superiority lowered their perceived self-efficacy, whereas those led to believe they had allegedly gained comparative superiority raised their belief in their capability to tolerate pain. Their subsequent level of pain tolerance changed in the direction of their efficacy beliefs. The condition involving alleged change from high to low normative standing is especially interesting because perceived self-efficacy overrode past performance as a predictor of subsequent performance.

The regulatory role of perceived self-efficacy instated by fictitious normative comparison has been replicated in markedly different domains of functioning. Bouffard-Bouchard (1990) instilled high or low efficacy beliefs in students by suggesting that they were of higher or lower standing compared to bogus peer norms irrespective of their actual performance. Students whose perceived efficacy was illusorily raised set higher goals for themselves, used more efficient problem-solving strategies, and achieved higher intellectual performances than students of equal cognitive ability who were led to believe they lacked such capabilities. The research corroborated not only the functional relation of perceived self-efficacy to behavior but also the well known impact of efficacy belief on aspiration and strategic thinking (Wood & Bandura, 1989).

Jacobs and his colleagues similarly demonstrated that efficacy beliefs raised by fictitious normative comparison heightened perseverant motivation in difficult problem solving (Jacobs, Prentice-Dunn, & Rogers, 1984). In research in which efficacy beliefs were altered by bogus information about a competitor's strength, the higher the illusory beliefs of physical strength, the more physical stamina the individuals displayed during competition (Weinberg, Gould, Yukelson, & Jackson, 1981). Failure in a subsequent competition spurred those whose perceived self-efficacy was arbitrarily raised to even greater physical effort, whereas failure further impaired the performance of those whose efficacy beliefs had been undermined. Beliefs of physical efficacy illusorily heightened in females and illusorily weakened in males obliterated large preexisting sex differences in physical stamina.

Efficacy beliefs, instilled illusorily, operate determinatively at the collective level as well at the individual level. Erroneous information given to group members that they performed better or worse than a fictitious norm altered belief in their collective capabilities (Prussia & Kinicki, 1996). The effect of this bogus information on groups' aspirations and performance attainments was mediated entirely through the changes it produced in perceived collective efficacy.

Epiphenomenonalists might argue that the bogus comparative information in the preceding studies constitutes the "performance" that generates the self-efficacy epiphenomenon. Let us examine the logic of such an argument. According to epiphenomenalism, self-referent thoughts are the concomitant by-products of performances, but they do not enter into the determination of behavior. The cybernetic system operates automatically. Hence, to argue that delayed phony information about other people's performances constitutes one's performance would be a most peculiar form of epiphenomenalism. The individuals do not know that they will receive comparative information later. Hence, the by-products of their performance would have to be mysteriously suspended or somehow obliterated by later phony information that is completely irrelevant to, or even contradicts, their actual performances. In point of fact, in experiments using bogus feedback self-efficacy beliefs are a product of social persuasion, not of their actual performances. Sociocognitive theory provides a great deal of particularized knowledge on how best to structure persuasory influences to increase their efficacy-enhancing impact (Bandura, 1997).

Relating Self-Efficacy Beliefs to Future Performance While Controlling for Past Performance

In early reactions to self-efficacy theory, epiphenomalists and behavior analysts would single out studies in which perceived self-efficacy is altered by enactive modes of influence, because there is a behavior to latch onto. They then contend that perceived self-efficacy is just a reflection of prior performance. This claim has long lost its credibility by evidence from countless studies demonstrating that perceived self-efficacy contributes independently to subsequent performance after controlling for prior performance and indices of ability. The following sections present a sample of experimental and prospective studies applying not only controls for past performance and ability, but often multiple controls for other factors that can influence performance.

The unique contribution of self-efficacy is verified in numerous experiments by Schunk in which perceived efficacy is developed in children who are markedly deficient in mathematical ability by self-directed instruction (Schunk, 1982), and those with severe reading deficiencies by training in verbal self-guidance (Schunk & Rice, 1993). Children's beliefs in their efficacy account for variance in performance after controlling for level of skill development and performance attainment in the self-instruction. In path analyses in other studies, children's perceived efficacy to regulate their learning activities and to master academic subjects raises academic aspirations and final grades independently of their prior grades in the subject matter and the academic aspirations the parent holds for their children (Zimmerman, Bandura, & Martinez-Pons, 1992).

Locke and his colleagues conducted an experimental test of the role of perceived self-efficacy and goals in the development of creative proficiency (Locke, Frederick, Lee, & Bobko, 1984). In path analysis, perceived group efficacy predicted creative performance both directly and mediationally through its impact on goal setting after applying multiple controls. These controls included training in creativity and use of brainstorming strategies, preexisting creative ability, and post-training creative performance in the prediction of subsequent level of creative performance.

Prussia and Kinicki (1996) examined experimentally how perceived collective efficacy operates in concert with other social cognitive determinants of the quality of group problem solving. Groups received videotaped instruction in brainstorming strategies either in a lecture format or by observing a group modeling the same strategies behaviorally and cognitively. Participants received accurate feedback about their own performance attainments, but prearranged comparative feedback leading them to believe that their group performed either above or below the normative productivity standard. The groups' subsequent success in adopting the strategic processes and generating novel solutions was measured. The impact of performance feedback on group performance operated entirely through its effects on affective reactions and perceived collective efficacy. Group dissatisfaction with substandard performance combined with a strong sense of collective efficacy spurred group productivity. Perceived collective efficacy also completely mediated the effects of the positive and negative bogus feedback on the goals the groups set for themselves, and partially mediated the benefits of instructive modeling on group effectiveness. The unique contribution of collective efficacy to group productivity remains after controlling for prior group performance.

The crucial role of perceived self-efficacy under challenging conditions is revealed in path analyses of determinants of athletic performance in different phases of tournament matches (Kane, Marks, Zoccaro, & Blair, 1996). In preliminary wrestling matches, contestants with less secure self-efficacy can triumph over weaker contestants because of differential ability. Wrestling ability, as measured by athletic level and prior performance record in contests, predicts competitive performance directly but also through the mediated effect of self-efficacy belief and personal goals. However, in pressure packed overtime matches, where contestants are more evenly matched, perceived self-efficacy is the sole determinant of overtime performance and prior competitive performance has no predictive value.

In experimental tests of the extent to which self-regulatory influences determine response to varying degrees of goal discrepancy, participants performed on an ergometer and their effortful performance was measured in kilopond meter units (Bandura & Cervone, 1983, 1986). To equate for individual differences in physical performance, participants rated their self-efficacy for 14 levels of performance attainment ranging from a 50% decline to and 80% increase in effortful performance compared to their baseline performance level. Their subsequent percent change in effortful performance was also measured relative to their baseline performance level. The higher the participants perceived self-efficacy and the greater their discontent with just matching their past performance the higher their performance output.

Social cognitive theory of career choice and development has sponsored wide-ranging programs of research with special focus on the role played by beliefs of personal efficacy in occupational choice and preparation (Lent, Brown, & Hackett, 1994: Betz & Hackett, 1997). These lines of research help to clarify the impact of self-efficacy beliefs on decisional behavior. The findings of this substantial body of research show that the higher the perceived self-efficacy to fulfill educational requirements and occupational roles the wider the career options people seriously consider pursuing, the greater the interest they have in them, the better they prepare themselves educationally for different occupational careers, and the greater their staying power in challenging career pursuits. Efficacy beliefs predict occupational choices and level of mastery of educational requirements for those careers, and persistence in technical/scientific pursuits when variations in actual ability, prior level of academic achievement, scholastic aptitude and vocational interests are controlled (Lent, Brown, & Larkin, 1989; Lent, Brown, & Larkin, 1984, 1986, 1987; Lent, Lopez, & Bieschke, 1993).

Self-development during formative years forecloses some types of occupational options and makes others realizable. A multifaceted longitudinal project examined by the path analytic method shows how sociostructural determinants operating in concert with different facets of perceived self-efficacy at the beginning of junior high school predict the types of occupational pursuits students are seriously considering toward the end of junior high (Bandura, Barbaranelli, Caprara,

Pastorelli, 2001). The impact of familial socioeconomic status and parental self-efficacy and aspirations on their children's occupational preferences are entirely mediated through the children's perceived occupational self-efficacy and academic aspirations. Perceived occupational self-efficacy rather than their actual academic achievement is the key determinant of the kinds of career pursuits children seriously consider for their lifework and those they disfavor.

Multivariate investigations using panel designs with path analytic and structural equation modeling also can be used to estimate the unique contribution of efficacy belief to subsequent performance after controlling for past performance, as well as multiple other possible determinants. Results show that perceived self-efficacy is a significant contributor to subsequent performance over and above the influence of other factors including past performance (reviewed in Bandura, 1997).

The issue of past performance and the determinative function of perceived self-efficacy can, of course, be addressed experimentally rather than by partialling out variances statistically. This experimental strategy was used in an intraindividual experimental design with sequential microanalytic comparison of the relative predictiveness of prior performance and perceived efficacy (Bandura & Adams, 1977).[4] Coping tasks for severe snake phobics were hierarchically ordered in terms of severity of threat, i.e., touching a snake, holding it, letting it loose and retrieving it as it slithered around, tolerating the snake crawling in their laps. The phobics received guided mastery treatment until they could perform the uppermost coping task they failed in pretest assessment, whereupon they rated their perceived self-efficacy for all the succeeding coping tasks they had never performed. Their coping behavior was then assessed. Contrary to the view that perceived self-efficacy simply reflects past performances, the same performance attainment gives rise to widely different levels of perceived self-efficacy. For example, having achieved the same performance level at the midpoint of the hierarchical coping tasks, some phobics judged themselves capable of performing only 10% of the higher level tasks, others 20%, still other 35%, and some felt supremely efficacious to perform 100% of the tasks. Efficacy beliefs predicted at an 84% level of accuracy performance on the highly threatening tasks that the phobics had never done before. All that past performance

---

4 The term "microanalytic" refers to a research strategy in which self-efficacy—behavior relations are analyzed at the level of individual acts. The prediction is that, for any given person confronting an array of challenging activities, the individual will (will not) be capable of performing those actions for which they possess high (low) self-efficacy beliefs. In the language of personality psychology (Caprara & Cervone, 2000), this is a "within-person" strategy, in that thoughts and actions are explored across multiple contexts for an individual person. It can also be characterized as an "idiographic" strategy, given its sensitivity to potentially idiosyncratic patterns of high/level self-efficacy beliefs and action patterns. Statistical methods designed to analyze the microanalytic congruence indices Bandura cites reveals that the observed positive relations between self-efficacy appraisal and behavior are highly statistically significant (Cervone, 1985).

could tell phobics regarding coping tasks they had never attempted is that they can do what they had just done, which has no predictive value.

Studies that apply performance controls provide a conservative estimate of the regulatory function of perceived self-efficacy because of statistical overcontrol. Behavior is not a cause of behavior. Correlations between prior and subsequent behavior simply reflect the degree of commonality of their determinants. If the determinants are similar across time, the performances will be highly correlated. Performance is not an unadulterated measure of ability (Bandura, 1990; Sternberg & Kolligian, 1990). It is heavily infused with many motivational and self-regulatory determinants. Past performance is thus a conglomerate index encompassing the set of unmeasured sociocognitive factors operating at the time. Perceived self-efficacy is an important part of that constellation of unmeasured determinants of performance. Thus, past performance is itself affected by beliefs of personal efficacy. Efficacy beliefs are autocorrelated and affect both prior and later performance. Using unadjusted past performance scores thus also removes some of the effects of efficacy beliefs on future performance. Therefore, control for past performance ideally should use the residual after partialling out the prior self-efficacy contribution to variance in performance (Wood & Bandura, 1989).

The field has moved beyond the simple-minded view that efficacy beliefs are just reflectors of performance to analyses of the unique contribution of efficacy beliefs in multifaceted causal structures. In these structural analyses the relation of past performance to subsequent performance is heavily, if not fully, mediated through efficacy beliefs, goals and aspirations, outcome expectations, and other sociocognitive determinants (Bandura, 1997).

On Self-Efficacy Scales

Development of useful tools of measurement often accelerates scientific progress. Progress in psychology, however, has often been impeded by measurement tools that are far from optimal. In the assessment of personal determinants of sociocognitive functioning, investigators commonly have chosen to employ omnibus tests. Such measures include a fixed set of items that—in an effort to serve varied predictive purposes across diverse domains of functioning and age groups—may each be cast in a very general form.

This omnibus assessment strategy has substantial drawbacks. When all-purpose tests are employed in specific applications, many of the test items may have little relevance to the domain of functioning being analyzed. When items are cast in a more general form [e.g., "I can usually handle whatever comes my way," a test item in Schwarzer & Jerusalem, 1995], the greater is the burden on respondents to define what is being asked of them. One cannot expect omnibus tests to predict with high accuracy how people will function in different domains under diverse circumstances. Personality researchers are, therefore, increasingly adopting multidimensional, domain-linked measures of personal determinants of sociocognitive functioning [for overviews of this trend, see Caprara & Cervone, 2000; Cervone & Shoda, 1999; Shoda, Cervone, & Downey, 2007].

Domain-linked assessment strategies are crucial to the assessment of self-efficacy beliefs. Well-formulated self-efficacy scales focus on a psychological domain selected for study, and ideally measure people's beliefs in their capabilities to fulfill different levels of task demands within that domain. By measuring perceptions of self-efficacy across a wide range of task demands, one can identify the upper limits of people's perceptions of their capabilities as well as gradations of perceived efficacy below that point. By contrast, a circumscribed measure that asks people to report their perceived efficacy for attaining a singular performance level would not distinguish between individuals who judge themselves inefficacious to perform the most arduous memory task but differ in their perceived efficacy for less taxing ones. The curtailed distributions that such a measure yields would lower the magnitude of correlations, artificially underestimating the strength of self-efficacy—behavior relations. Expanded self-efficacy assessments in which individuals judge the strength of their efficacy to fulfill gradations of task demands are more sensitive to variations in perceived self-efficacy in any given sample.

An exemplary case of self-efficacy assessment can be found in the study of memory performance. Berry, West, and Dennehey (1989) devised a psychometrically sound set of self-efficacy scales that accord well with guidelines from self-efficacy theory and methodology. They include several valuable features. Separate self-efficacy scales are devised for different types of memory. The intercorrelations corroborate that the set of scales represents a common domain but taps different dimensions of memory. They measure gradations of self-efficacy strength rather than just categorical judgments of whether one can execute a given level of memory performance. The scales are highly reliable and they account for a good share of the variance in memory performance. The scale format can be easily extended to other types of memory.

Berry and colleagues also tested whether the format in which the scale items are presented has an effect on self-efficacy judgment. The initial reference points in a sequence of items can have an anchoring influence on self-efficacy judgments (Peake & Cervone, 1989). The authors found that a descending format, ordering the items from most to least difficult task demands, tended to produce slightly higher self-efficacy appraisals than did an ascending or random order (the latter two did not differ from each other). Because the ascending order of presentation does not bias self-efficacy judgment, it should be the preferred format.

In comparative studies, domain-linked measures of personal efficacy typically predict changes in functioning better than do general measures. Examples are found in health research. Domain-linked efficacy scales have been shown to be more predictive of changes in health behavior than perceived locus of health control (Alagna & Reddy, 1984; Beck & Lund, 1981; Brod & Hall, 1984; Kaplan, Atkins,

& Reinsch, 1984; Walker & Franzini, 1983). General items linked to particular activity domains are an improvement over omnibus measures that are disembodied from clearly defined activities and contextual factors. But ill-defined items still sacrifice explanatory and predictive power even though they may be tied to a designated domain. Relations obtained with suboptimal measures may underestimate or misrepresent the causal contribution of given factors. Lachman and Leff (1989) note this problem in reviewing evidence from studies showing that generalized scales fail to reveal any age differences where more sensitive domain-linked scales do.

Use of domain-linked scales does not mean that there is no generality to perceived self-efficacy. If different classes of activities require similar functions and subskills, one would expect some generality in judgments of self-efficacy. Even if different activity domains are not subserved by common subskills, some generality of perceived self-efficacy can occur if development of competencies is socially structured so that the cultivation of skills in dissimilar domains covaries. Commonality of subskills and covariation of development will yield generality. Multidomain measures reveal the patterning and degree of generality of people's sense of personal efficacy. One can derive a degree of generality from multidomain scales, but one cannot extract the patterning of perceived personal efficacy from conglomerate omnibus tests.[5]

---

5 The Editor notes two developments that occurred subsequent to Bandura's authoring of these passages. Both are fully consistent with the overall Social Cognitive Theory position Bandura outlined. One is that generality of perceived self-efficacy is observed not only if objective competencies covary across domains. Generality also is observed when people *subjectively believe that* a skill they possess (or lack) is pertinent to multiple domains. People are found to display high and low patterns of self-efficacy appraisal across domains if they believe that a personal quality they possess advances or impedes success across the different contexts (Cervone, 2004, 2021). These contexts can vary widely and idiosyncratically from person to person. For example, one individual reported the belief that diverse challenges involving weight loss, classroom performance, and both warm-hearted and assertive interpersonal challenges benefitted from a common competency that they possessed: being a "determined" person (Cervone, 1997). The second development involves the concept of validity of psychological measures. Borsboom, Mellenbergh, & van Heerden (2004) explain that validity claims inherently rest on ontological claims; to claim that one is validly measuring an attribute, one must believe that the attribute exists. "I am measuring X, but I do not think X exists" is not a viable position. The omnibus, generalized self-efficacy measures that Bandura critiques on predictive validity grounds also struggle to pass the ontological test. What evidence is there, one may ask, that individuals, at the level of individual cases, possess a "generalized self-efficacy belief" (that, in turn, can be measured; cf. Schwarzer & Jerusalem, 1995)? In practice, almost all individuals display diverse patterns of *high and low* self-efficacy appraisal across situations— even situations that each occur within a given domain of functioning, such as academic performance (Cervone, Mercurio, & Lilley, 2020). When, as Bandura notes, personality researchers adopt domain-linked measures, they do so in part because mean scores on omnibus tests are a mathematical construction that may not correspond to any psychological quality that individuals actually possess (also see Mischel & Shoda, 1995). Detailed critiques of traditional personality trait theory and measurement processes can be found in Bandura (1986, 1999).

Boosting Self-Efficacy Beliefs and Sources of Self-Efficacy Information

Self-efficacy is not a static trait. Self-efficacy judgments are elements of a dynamic system of self-beliefs. A wide variety of interventions, conducted in diverse psychosocial settings, have been shown to affect people's beliefs in their efficacy to handle the challenges of everyday life (reviewed in Bandura, 1997).

Although interventions are diverse in practice, their key ingredients can be understood in a simple manner, namely, by analyzing the different types of information they provide. Efficacy-inducing interventions rely on four principal sources of efficacy information; any given intervention may, of course, combine one or more of the four:

a) *performance accomplishments*, that is, first-hand experiences of mastery
b) *vicarious experiences*, especially the observation of successful efforts by persons similar to oneself
c) *verbal persuasion*, in which individuals in one's social world try to convince people of their capacity to succeed
d) *emotional arousal*; people may evaluate their emotional arousal and overall bodily state when judging their efficacy for future performance

Following is a brief review of each of these four sources of self-efficacy information.

Performance Accomplishments

Performance accomplishments, including guided mastery experiences in which individuals collaborate with an aidful instructor, generally provide the most effective way of enhancing self-efficacy beliefs. Accomplishments, especially those gained through perseverant effort and ability to learn from setbacks and mistakes, build a sense of self-efficacy that is resilient. In any domain, individuals benefit from experiences that combine three components (Bandura, 1986): the modeling of skills that convey the basic strategies and rules in a domain; opportunities for the learner personally to practice these skills in conditions that simulate those of the naturally-occurring environment; and transfer effort, so that learners see how the new competencies (acquired with the aid of an instructor, or therapist, or other such guide to the mastery experience) will translate to independent success in the future, and thus will gain in self-efficacy beliefs for personally handling the upcoming challenges.

Vicarious Experiences

Modeling is a key first step in conveying strategies and building in others a sense of efficacy for performance. Regarding strategies, it is valuable to break down complex skills into sub-skills that observers can master in achievable steps. Regarding self-efficacy beliefs, the impact of modeling on beliefs about one's capabilities is greatly increased by perceived similarity to the models. A model's success more readily builds personal beliefs among observers if those observers judge that the model is similar to themselves. Learners adopt modeled ways more readily if they see similar others solve problems successfully with modeled strategies than if they regard the models as very different from themselves.

Verbal Persuasion

A third form of information that may impact self-efficacy beliefs is verbal persuasion. People commonly try to instill confidence in others by convincing them, through exhortation, of their capacity for success.

A number of factors determine the success—or not—of such efforts. Verbal persuasion is more likely to succeed when communicators are credible and possess expertise in the domain in which they are trying to persuade. When there is more than one communicator, consensus raises the likelihood that communications will be convincing.

But even in cases of credible verbal communication, verbal persuasion is a less reliable means of producing resilient efficacy beliefs. Words lose impact if they are contradicted by evidence. Verbal inputs do sometimes produce self-efficacy increases with behavioral consequences (e.g., Weinberg et al., 1979, 1980). But if verbal persuasion increases self-beliefs to an unrealistic degree, contradictory failure feedback will erode confidence both in oneself and in the credibility of the communicator. In therapeutic efforts, social persuasion alone is not a powerful means of effecting change (see Bandura, 1977).

Emotional Arousal and Somatic State

People often become aware of their level of emotional arousal and their overall bodily state. When this happens, physiological states become a fourth source of information that bears on appraisals of personal efficacy.

The influence of this fourth information source depends on multiple factors beyond the initial question of whether people attend to their physiological state. Physiological arousal is subject to personal interpretation. The interpretations may include questions on the course of the arousal and the circumstances in which they occur; high heart rate at halftime of a sporting event has different meaning than the same arousal just prior to taking an exam or giving a public speech.

These distinctions among sources of self-efficacy information are significant theoretically. But, as noted, in practice interventions commonly combine multiple sources. To illustrate the power of such practical applications, we close this chapter by considering applications in two domains, organizational effectiveness and cognitive performance among older adults. Chapter 6 reviews further applications, including ones that use media technologies to foster beneficial change on a global level.

Organizational Effectiveness

Work life is increasingly structured on a team-based model in which management and operational functions are assigned to the workers themselves. A self-management work structure changes the model of supervisory managership from hierarchical control to facilitative guidance that provides the necessary resources, instructive guidance, and support that teams need to do their work effectively (Stewart & Manz, 1995). This change heightens the importance of personal agency executed by employees at lower levels of a corporate hierarchy. Enabling organizational structures builds managers' efficacy to operate as facilitators of productive team work (Laschruger & Shamian, 1994). The perceived collective efficacy of self-managed teams predicts the members' satisfaction and productivity (Lindsley, Mathieu, Heffner, & Brass, 1994; Little & Madigan, 1994).

Personal agency also is key to entrepreneurship. The development of new business ventures and the renewal of established ones depends heavily on innovativeness. With many resourceful competitors around, viability requires continual ingenuity. Entrepreneurs have to be willing to take risks under uncertainty. Those of high efficacy focus on the opportunities worth pursuing, whereas the less self-efficacious dwell on the risks to be avoided (Krueger & Dickson, 1993, 1994). Hence, perceived self-efficacy predicts entrepreneurship and which patent inventors are likely to start new business ventures (Chen, Greene, & Crick, 1998; Markman & Baron, 1999). Venturers who achieve high growth in companies they have founded, or transform those they bought, have a vision of what they wish to achieve and a firm belief in their efficacy to achieve it (Baum, 1994 [for a meta-analysis of entrepreneurial self-efficacy and firm performance, see Miao et al., 2017]).

Effective organizational leadership requires receptivity to innovators that can improve organizational quality and productivity. Managers' perceived technical efficacy influences their readiness to adopt electronic technologies (Jorde-Bloom & Ford, 1988). Efficacy beliefs affect not only managers' receptivity to technological innovations, but also the readiness with which employees adopt them (Hill, Smith, & Mann, 1987; McDonald & Siegall, 1992). Efficacy-fostered adoption of new technologies, in turn, alters the organizational network structure and confers influence on early adopters within an organization over time (Burkardt & Brass, 1990).

Perceived self-efficacy to fulfill occupational demands affects the level of stress and physical health of employees. Those of low efficacy are stressed both emotionally and physiologically by perceived overload in which task demands exceed their perceived coping capabilities, whereas those who hold a high belief in their efficacy and that of their group are unfazed by heavy workloads (Jex & Bliese, 1999). Perceived self-efficacy must be added to the demands-control model of occupational stress to improve its predictability. High job demands with opportunity to exercise control over various facets of the work environment is unperturbing to job-holders of high perceived efficacy, but cardiovascularly stressful to those of low perceived efficacy (Schaubroeck & Merritt, 1997). Efforts to reduce occupational stressfulness by increasing job control without raising efficacy to manage the increased responsibilities will do more harm than good.

For the self-efficacious, job underload can be a stressor. Indeed, employees of high efficacy are stressed by perceived underload in which they feel thwarted and frustrated by organizational constraints in developing and using their potentialities (Matsui & Onglatco, 1992). Exposure to chronic occupational stressors combined with low perceived self-efficacy for managing job demands and enlisting social support at times of difficulty increases vulnerability to burnout (Brouwers & Tomic, 2000; Leiter, 1992 [for a meta-analysis of empirical findings relating perceived self-efficacy to job burnout, see Shoji et al., 2016]). This syndrome is characterized by physical and emotional exhaustion, depersonalization of clients, lack of any sense of personal accomplishment, and occupational disengagement through cynicism about one's work.

A resilient sense of efficacy provides the necessary staying power in the tortuous pursuit of innovation and excellence. Yet the very undaunted self-efficacy that breeds success in tough ventures may perpetuate adherence to courses of action that hold little prospect of eventual success. Thus, for example, managers of high perceived efficacy are more prone than those of low efficacy to escalate commitment to unproductive ventures (Whyte & Saks, 1999; Whyte, Saks, & Hook, 1997) and to remain wedded to previously successful practices despite altered realities that place them at competitive disadvantage (Audia, Locke, & Smith, 2000). The corrective for the perils of success is not enfeeblement of personal efficacy. Such a disenabling remedy would undermine aspiration, innovation, and human accomplishments in endeavors presenting tough odds. Individuals who are highly assured in their capabilities and the effectiveness of their strategies are disinclined to seek discordant information that would suggest the need for corrective adjustments. The challenge is to preserve the considerable functional value of resilient self-efficacy, but to institute information monitoring and social feedback systems that can help to identify practices that are beyond the point of utility.

Self-Efficacy Beliefs and Cognitive Performance Among Older Adults

The later years of life bring changes: retirement, relocation, physical infirmities, and loss of friends or spouses. Change, in turn, creates demands; skills and effort are required to cultivate new social relationships and activities that may foster personal well-being. The presence of uncertainty and challenge raises the significance of self-reflections on personal efficacy.

Perceived social inefficacy is costly. It increases the vulnerability of older people to stress and depression, both directly and indirectly, by impeding development of social supports that serve as a buffer against life stressors (Holahan & Holahan, 1987a, 1987b). Growing physical infirmities and perceived inability to fulfill valued performance standards that were achievable at an earlier time can also be highly depressing.

Yet, many sustain well-being into older adulthood. Longitudinal studies with multiple cohorts similarly reveal that older adults manage to preserve a favorable sense of personal efficacy well into the later years (Lachman, 1986). This is an interesting finding provided it does not reflect insensitivity of the global measurement of personal efficacy. There are several processes by which older adults can preserve a high sense of self-efficacy, even when they are outperformed by younger cohorts. Longitudinal studies reveal no universal or general decline in intellectual abilities until the very advanced years, but, in cross-sectional comparisons of different age groups, the young surpass the old (Baltes & Labouvie, 1973; Schaie, 1974). The major share of age differences in intelligence seems to be due to differences in educational experiences across generations rather than to biological aging. It is not so much that the old have declined in intelligence but that the young have had the benefit of richer intellectual experiences enabling them to function at a higher level. If older adults do not experience a decline in actual capability and avoid social comparison with younger cohorts, they can achieve an enduring sense of personal efficacy through favorable self-comparison over time. Even if they experience a decline in ability, they can sustain their sense of efficacy by ignoring younger cohorts and appraising their capabilities through social comparison with their age-mates. By maintaining or improving their relative standing among agemates, they can preserve their sense of self-efficacy in the face of changing capabilities (Frey & Ruble, 1990).

People also have some leeway in self-appraisal in how heavily they weight different domains or facets of functioning. If they remain good problem solvers and bring a broadened perspective to bear on judgments regarding important matters, they will not necessarily downgrade their sense of personal efficacy because they process information a bit slower or have experienced some decline in physical stamina [Artistico et al., 2011, review such self-efficacy processes in older adulthood, including the role of self-efficacy processes in everyday problem solving]. A balanced self-appraisal can help sustain a favorable sense of personal efficacy.

A challenging domain in which research documents the benefits of robust self-efficacy beliefs to older adults is memory. Human memory is an active constructive process in which information is semantically elaborated, transformed, and reorganized into meaning memory codes that aid recall. People who view memory as a cognitive skill that they can improve are likely to exert the effort needed to convert experiences into recallable symbolic forms. Consistent with this expectation, the more strongly older adults believed in their memory capabilities, the more time they devoted to processing memory tasks cognitively (Berry, 1987). Higher processing effort, in turn, produced better memory performance. In the analysis of the causal structure, perceived self-efficacy affects actual memory performance both directly and indirectly through level of cognitive effort. Those who regard memory as an inherent capacity that declines with biological aging have little reason to try to exercise control over their memory functioning. They are quick to read instances of normal forgetting as indicants of declining cognitive capacity. The more they disbelieve their memory capabilities, the poorer use they make of their cognitive capabilities. The negative cultural stereotyping of the elderly can foster a sense of declining cognitive capability [also see Berry, 1999].

Perceived self-efficacy may operate on memory functioning through an affective modality. West, Berry, and Powlishta (1989) report findings in which depression was accompanied by perceived memory inefficacy, which, in turn, was associated with deficient memory performances.

Modeling interventions may boost both skills and self-efficacy beliefs at any point in the lifespan. The diverse sources of self-efficacy information outlined above can be enlisted to the benefit of the cognitive performance of older adults. For example, in an intervention to boost memory efficacy, individuals could be given efficacy demonstration trials in which they perform memory tasks both with and without mnemonic aids; evidence that the aids enhance memory performance would be a persuasive demonstration that one can exercise some agentic control over one's own memory by enlisting readily available cognitive strategies. Modeling influences can be used to demonstrate how others have been able to improve their memory by habitual use of mnemonic aids. Persuasory influences also can contribute, especially when they instill self-beliefs that encourage people optimally to utilize the many skills they possess despite experiencing some cognitive declines. Combining information sources—for example, combining verbal persuasion with a structuring of cognitive tasks that ensures experiences of mastery—would best put the theoretical principles outlined in this chapter into practice.

4
Shaping One's Future through Self-Regulation

The conceptions of motivation that psychologists have proposed over the decades are diverse. Yet, despite the diversity, there is a curious common theme: the claim that people's actions are not under their control.

Consider psychodynamic theory (Freud, 1917, 1933). Behavior was said to driven by a dynamic interplay of forces that functioned substantially outside of consciousness. Since they were outside of awareness, these forces could not be agentically controlled. The psychodynamic formulation thus greatly discounted the human capacity for agency. Psychodynamic theory gained widespread acceptance despite possessing substantial drawbacks (Bandura, 1986). The inner drives it proposed were inferred from behavior, but generally could not be assessed independently in order to *predict* behavior. This made the theory substantially untestable. When empirical tests could be derived, psychodynamic theory sometimes blatantly failed them – as we saw in Chapter 2, which reviewed evidence that children do not display the cathartic releases of aggressive energy that psychodynamic theory predicted. In general, theories which contend, as did psychoanalysis, that a small set of drives, impulses, or motives account for human action struggle to predict and explain the marked strategic shifts in behavior that individuals often display as their situational circumstances vary across time and place.

In radical behavioristic theory, behavior was said to be under external control. Environmental stimuli purportedly trigger emotional responses and shape frequencies of one or another class of behavior. In this view, agency resides in environmental forces. People are like weathervanes, twisting and turning in the winds of momentary stimulus control. Even the most casual observations of human behavior contradict this perspective. People commonly commit themselves to extended, arduous courses of action and pursue them in the absence of tangible rewards. It is certainly true that the external influences on which behaviorists

Social Cognitive Theory: An Agentic Perspective on Human Nature, First Edition. Albert Bandura.
© 2023 John Wiley & Sons, Inc. Published 2023 by John Wiley & Sons, Inc.

focused are significant to human behavior. But they do not independently control that behavior. External rewards and punishments serve as sources of information that people use to predict events, and as sources of influence on the self-processes that are discussed later in this chapter.

Echoes of these old views are still heard today. For example, some postulate models of personality and motivation that focus exclusively on limbic system structures that are shared widely across mammalian species and that are triggered by select environmental stimuli. No one denies the existence of limbic structures that subserve various forms of reward-seeking or punishment-avoiding response. But no such theoretical model could possibly provide a comprehensive account of human motivation and its cognitive and emotional accompaniments. People do not merely respond automatically to environmental triggers. They also select environments, construct environments, and reconstruct the environments they encounter. People are not motivated merely by external stimuli. They are motivated also to meet socially acquired personal standards that indicate forms of behavior that are appropriate and desirable. Failures to meet these socially acquired standards bring not only simple emotions of fear and anxiety, but complex emotions of shame and guilt that are distinctive to our species. Achievements bring not only the arousal states that accompany impending tangible rewards, but also uniquely human experiences of pride. A theory of human motivation must account for the distinctive actions, thoughts, and experiences of humans.

Three Broad Classes of Motivation

Motivation is a general construct. Progress in understanding human motivated action is advanced by recognizing discriminably different aspects of the overall phenomenon. Social cognitive theory distinguishes among three broad classes of motivation (Bandura, 1986).

One class of motivators is biologically based. Biological conditions arising from cellular deficits create physically discomforting effects that foster consummatory and protective behaviors. The early psychological theorists conceptualized motivation largely in terms of such physiological activators. However, the activating potential of physiological states is substantially under anticipatory and generative cognitive control. Infants become active not solely based on how hungry they are, but on when they expect to be fed (Marquis, 1941). Humans can be sexually stirred more by erotic fantasies than by hormonal injections (Beach, 1969). People's construal of aversive events alters the degree to which objective events produce subjective experiences (Bandura, 1990a; Cioffi, 1989; McCaul & Malott, 1984). Thus, even in the so-called biological motivators, human behavior is extensively activated and regulated by anticipatory and generative cognitive mechanisms rather than simply impelled by biological urges.[1]

The second class of motivators operates through social incentives. In the course of development, physically positive experiences often occur in conjunction with expressions of interest and approval of others, whereas unpleasant experiences are associated with disapproval or censure. Through such correlative experiences, social reactions, themselves, become predictors of primarily rewarding and punishing consequences and, thereby, become incentives. People will do things for approval and refrain from activities that arouse others' displeasure or wrath. The effectiveness of social reactions as incentives thus derives from their predictive value rather than inhering in the reactions themselves. For this reason, identical reactions from different people have differential effects. The approval or disapproval of those who exercise rewarding and punishing power operate as stronger incentives than similar expressions by individuals who cannot affect one's life. Indiscriminate praise that never carries any tangible effects becomes an empty reward, and disapproval that is never backed up with any tangible consequences becomes an empty threat devoid of motivating power.

Several factors contribute to the durability of social incentives. The same expressions can predict an array of possible rewarding or punishing experiences. Disapproval, for example, may result in such unpleasant effects as physical punishment, deprivation of privileges, monetary penalties, dismissal from a job, or ostracism. An event that signifies diverse possible consequences will have greater potency than if it portends only a single effect. Moreover, social reactions are not invariably accompanied by primary experiences: Praise does not always bring material benefits, and reprimands do not always result in physical suffering. Unpredictability protects social and symbolic incentives from losing their effectiveness (Mowrer, 1960). Because of intermittency and diversity of correlates, social reactions retain their incentive function even with minimal primary support.

The third major class of motivators – and the one that is the focus of the present chapter –is cognitively based. In cognitively-generated motivation, people motivate themselves and guide their behavior by the aspirations and challenges they set. Such self-motivation is especially robust. Once people commit themselves to a goal, they seek self-satisfaction from seeing their aspiration fulfilled and intensify their efforts as a result of discontent if they see that efforts are falling short.

---

1 An interesting illustration of Bandura's point about the cognitive control of responses that one might expect to be controlled exclusively by physiological deficits comes from Rozin et al. (1998), who found that amnesic patients will, if it is offered, consume a second lunch because they have no memory of having consumed the first one.

Prolonged self-directed efforts have fueled many of the humankind's great, and hard-earned, achievements.

Goal-Directed Action, Goal Effects, and Goal Theory

Goal-directed motivation has been the subject of extensive research. Evidence from numerous laboratory and field studies supports the claim that the assignment of specific and challenging goals enhances motivation.[2] This research is particularly compelling in that basic goal effects have been across heterogeneous activity domains, settings, populations, social levels and time spans (Locke & Latham, 1990; Mento, Steel, & Karren, 1987 [Latham & Locke, 2018]).

Goal effects are related systematically to properties of goals, as was postulated in Locke's goal theory (1968). Three aspects of goals that determine their motivational impact are goal *specificity*, level of goal *challenge*, and goal *proximity*.

Goal Specificity

The extent to which goals create guides for action is partly determined by their specificity. Specific goals are ones that designate explicitly the type and amount of effort required to attain them. Explicit standards regulate performance by designating the type and amount of effort required to attain them, and they generate self-satisfaction and build self-efficacy by furnishing unambiguous signs of personal accomplishments. General intentions, which are indefinite about the level of attainment to be reached, provide little basis for regulating one's efforts or for evaluating how one is doing.

Studies that compare the effects of goals differing in specificity demonstrate that specific attainable goals produce higher levels of performance than do vague intentions to "do your best," which usually have little or no effect (Locke &

---

2 The scientific literature is this area features a linguistic ambiguity that, if not noted, may be confusing to the reader. The natural language term "goal" is used in diverse ways in the literature. In research on the effects of goal *assignment*, the term refers to a performance aim established by an authority figure (e.g., a work manager). In research on individuals' personal aspirations, the term may refer to an aim that is unrelated to any directive from an authority. A second ambiguity involves the distinction between enduring psychological structures and dynamically shifting psychological processes (see, e.g. Cervone, 2004, 2005; Cervone & Pervin, 2023). The term "goal" sometimes refers to enduring mental representations of aims to which a person may aspire across an extended period of time (e.g., the goal of saving $X for retirement). Yet, in other discussions (including Bandura's analysis of the adjustment of personal goals in the course of acting and receiving feedback on one's efforts), the term refers to near-term aims that are established and re-established across brief time frames.

Latham, 1990; Bandura & Cervone, 1983 [for a meta-analysis of such results, see Kleingeld et al., 2011]). Specific performance goals serve to motivate the unmotivated and to foster positive attitudes toward the activities (Bryan & Locke, 1967).

Goal Challenge

A second consequential property of goals is level of goal challenge. The amount of effort and satisfaction that accompany variations in goals depends on the level at which they are set. Locke postulates a positive linear relationship between goal level and performance motivation. A large body of evidence does show that the higher the goals the harder people work to attain them and the better is their performance (Locke & Latham, 1990). However, the linear relationship is assumed to hold only if performers accept the goals and remain strongly committed to them. Most people, of course, eventually reject performance goals they consider unrealistically demanding or well beyond their reach. However, people often remain surprisingly steadfast to goals they have little chance of fulfilling, even when given normative information that others reject them as unrealistic (Erez & Zidon, 1984). When assigned goals are beyond their reach and failure to attain them carries no cost, people try to approximate high standards as closely as they can rather than abandon them altogether (Garland, 1983; Locke, Zubritzky, Cousins, & Bobko, 1984). As a result, they achieve notable progress even though the accomplishment of distal goal aspirations eludes them.

The generality of evidence of unshaken pursuit of unreachable goals must be qualified, however, by the fact that laboratory simulations may differ from actual conditions on several important dimensions: the endeavor usually involves only a brief effort, failure carries no costs, and no opportunities exist for alternative pursuits. Unattainable goals are more likely to be abandoned when the activities require extensive investment of effort and resources, failure to meet the goals brings aversive consequences, and other activities are available in which one's efforts might be more fruitfully invested. When goals are set unrealistically high, strong effort produces repeated failure that can eventually weaken motivation by undermining perceived self-efficacy.

Much of the experimentation on level of goal challenges involves a single effort to achieve an individual goal. Social cognitive theory distinguishes between complementary regulative functions of distal goals and a graduated system of proximal subgoals in ongoing endeavors (Bandura, 1986). Superordinate distal goals give purpose to a domain of activity and serve a general directive function, but subgoals are better suited to serve as the proximal determinants of specific choice of activities and how much effort is devoted to them. Self-motivation is best sustained through a series of proximal subgoals that are hierarchically organized to ensure successive advances to superordinate goals. The relationship between probability of goal attainment and effort expenditure will differ for subgoals and for end goals. Pursuit of a formidable distal goal can sustain a high level of motivation if it is subdivided into subgoals that are challenging but clearly attainable through extra effort (Bandura & Schunk, 1981). To strive for unreachable subgoals is to drive oneself to unrelenting failure. By making complex tasks easier through their subdivision into more manageable units, one can perhaps retain the power of goals that otherwise tend to have lesser impact on complex tasks than on simpler activities (Wood, Mento, & Locke, 1987). It is not that challenging goals are necessarily ineffective or debilitating for complex pursuits, but instead that complex activities must be structured in such a way that goals enhance and helpfully channel efforts rather than misdirecting them. When complex tasks are aidfully structured, challenging goals are transformed from debilitators to enhancers of performance (Earley, Connolly, & Ekegren, 1989; Earley, Connolly, & Lee, 1989).

Distal and Proximal Goals

Goal effects depend, in part, on how far into the future the goals are projected. A third important quality of goals thus is their proximity. A proximate standard serves to mobilize self-influences and direct what one does in the here and now. By contrast, distal goals alone are too far removed in time to provide effective incentives and guides for present action. In the face of many competing attractions, focus on the distant future makes it easy to put off matters in the present on the belief that there is always ample time to mount the effort later.

In any given domain of activity, people may contemplate both a long-term distal aim and any number of shorter-term achievements that are steps toward the distal aspiration. The superordinate distal goal gives purpose to a domain of activity while also serving a general directive function. But self-motivation is best sustained by combining the distal goal with a series of proximal subgoals. Ideally, the subgoals are organized hierarchically, to ensure successive advances toward the superordinate aim. Concrete, near-term subgoals are better suited to serve as proximal determinants of choices among activities and how much effort is devoted to them than are long-term aspirations alone.

The complementary regulation of motivation by hierarchically-related goals of differential achievability characterizes most everyday strivings. Even when long-range aspirations are not yet fulfilled, here-and-now achievements can sustain the long-term goal pursuit. As people achieve (or fail to achieve) lower-level goals, the perceived difficulty of a superordinate goal of course does not remain constant. When people see themselves progressing toward a superordinate goal that lies in the distant future, their observations of progress alter their subjective estimates of eventual success; with progress, the distal attainment appears less formidable.

Self-Referent Processes in Goal Motivation

Goals operate largely through self-referent processes rather than motivating action directly. That is, the motivational effects do not stem from the goals themselves, but rather from the fact that people respond evaluatively to their own behavior.

Social Cognitive Theory distinguishes among three types of self-influences in cognitive based motivation. They include 1) affective self-evaluation, 2) perceived self-efficacy for goal attainment, and 3) ongoing adjustment of personal aims, or self-set goals. The three constitute a self-regulatory system in that they functionally interact with one another and with the social contexts in which individuals regulate their actions.

Affective Self-Evaluative Reactions

Goals motivate by enlisting self-evaluative reactions; when people commit themselves to specific goals, they become involved in the activity. Some self-evaluative processes are anticipatory. People seek the self-satisfaction that occurs when standards are fulfilled. Some are concurrent. People are prompted to intensify their efforts by their own discontent with substandard performances. Without the prospect of self-satisfaction from personal accomplishments, unremitting discontent would eventually take a toll on self-motivation.

Studies have experimentally varied the direction and the level of discrepancy between attainments and goals, and have determined the impact of affective self-reaction in the various discrepancy conditions (Bandura & Cervone, 1983, 1986). The higher the discontent with performances that are moderately or highly substandard, the higher the subsequent effortful performance; affective self-reactions serve as significant predictors of subsequent performance within each of these discrepancy levels. Other studies have similarly shown that affective self-reactions to one's performances contribute to variance in subsequent individual and group performance (Cervone, Jiwani, & Wood, 1991; Prussia & Kinicki, 1996).

Perceived Self-Efficacy

Perceived self-efficacy is the second self-referent process that contributes to cognitive-based motivation. As reviewed in the previous chapter, it is partly on the basis of self-beliefs of efficacy that people choose what challenges to undertake, how much effort to expend in the endeavor, and how long to persevere in the face of difficulties.

Furthermore, levels of stress and despondency also are partly shaped by appraisals of personal efficacy for coping with difficulties and failures. When people are falling short of their aspirations, the negative discrepancies between aims and attainments can be either motivating or discouraging, and people's beliefs in their efficacy for goal attainment substantially determine which of the two responses predominates. Those who harbor self-doubts about their capabilities are easily dissuaded by failure, whereas those who remain assured of their capabilities tend to intensify their efforts when falling short and to persist until they succeed. That strong belief in one's efficacy heightens level of effort and perseverance in difficult pursuits is corroborated by evidence across diverse domains of functioning for both children and adults (Bandura & Cervone, 1986; Brown & Inouye, 1978; Cervone & Peake, 1986; Jacobs, Prentice-Dunn, & Rogers, 1984; Schunk, 1984; Weinberg, Gould, & Jackson, 1979).

Self-Set Goals

The exact goals people set for themselves during an endeavor are likely to change. People evaluate their level of success and general pattern of progress they are making and readjust their aspirations accordingly (Campion & Lord, 1982). They may maintain their original goal, lower their sights, or adopt an even more challenging goal. Thus, the third constituent self-influence in the ongoing regulation of motivation concerns the readjustment of personal goals in light of one's attainments.

The social-cognitive analysis of personal goal setting differs substantially from a theoretical perspective known as "control theory." Consider the control theory of human functioning proposed by Powers (1973). It developed as an outgrowth of cybernetic models in engineering which show how mechanical devices are regulated through feedback based on the results of their previous motions. The core idea is a proposed negative feedback loop in which a deviation from the desired programmed state or reference value is detected by a sensor, and automatically triggers movements that will drive the system toward the preprogrammed state. This model takes discrepancies between the programmed state and the perceived input from the output of the system as the fundamental driving force behind motion within the system: "Action is driven by the difference, or error" (Powers, 1991, p. 152). If there is no disturbance, there is no adjustment. The system either maintains its present movements or remains at rest. According to this conceptual scheme, the nervous system embodies a hierarchy of interconnected feedback loops with upper-level loops providing the reference signals that serve as goal settings for subordinate loops.

Despite claims to the contrary, Powers's (1978) control theory is founded on austere materialistic reductionism. In this view, the human organism is "nothing more than a connection between one set of physical quantities in the environment (input quantities) and another set of physical quantities in the environment (output quantities)" (Powers, 1978, p. 421). Experiments in which subjects are instructed to control a cursor by manipulating a stick are used to verify the theory. In the posited "behavioral law," action is "determined strictly and quantitatively by the inverse of the feedback function and is, therefore, a property of the environment and not of the subject" (Powers, 1978, p. 432). Powers (1978) also noted, "We are not modeling the interior of the subject, so we need not worry about how this effect is created" (p. 430). Such a view is hardly conducive to understanding human motivation and action, which are extensively cognitively regulated.

In Social Cognitive Theory, humans are proactive and are more apt to look forward than to look backward, locked in a negative feedback loop (Bandura, 2001). They extend their aspirations distally well beyond their proximal performance level and override a lot of negative feedback along the way in pursuit. It is through this proactive self-management that people turn aspirations into reality. In conditions of rapid change, human success requires a forward-looking perspective.[3]

Documenting the Engagement of Self-Influences in Goal Motivation

The role of this full range of self-influences can be examined through a research strategy introduced in the previous chapter's coverage of self-efficacy processes. People commonly reflect on themselves when coping with challenges. Therefore, in research, one can directly assess these self-reflections. In self-report measures, participants can be asked to report not only their perceived self-efficacy for future achievement, but also their evaluative reactions (their levels of self-satisfaction or dissatisfaction with current achievements and prospective future efforts) and

---

3 Bandura's emphasis on forward-looking cognition is consistent with the view that the brain functions substantially to predict events. Rather than merely responding to stimuli, as control theory discusses, the brain function "to create simulations that predict incoming sensory events before their consequences arrive to the brain. . . to anticipate future events that must be dealt with" (Feldman-Barrett, 2017, p. 7).

their aspirations for upcoming performance to their current level of success (in order to determine whether people have adjusted their personal goal levels).[4]

Such assessments of self-regulatory influences have been employed in studies with the following structure. Participants are asked to engage in challenging activities. Experimental conditions vary the nature of the task goals toward which participants work and of the feedback that they receive on their task progress. The activities selected are novel tasks that allow researchers to provide feedback in which discrepancy levels (i.e., degrees of discrepancy between an assigned goal and feedback indicating one's current level of goal progress) are pre-arranged; in other words, the feedback participants receive is manipulated systematically across experimental conditions. The self-reactive influences that, in Social Cognitive Theory, are posited to regulate goal-directed motivation are assessed at a number of time points during task performance. Conducting assessments in this manner enables one to determine whether self-processes at any given point in time predict levels of effort and performance at a subsequent time point. Through this strategy, one can identify the manner in which self-reactive influences operate in concert in the regulation of motivation through goal systems.

One such experiment examined how self-evaluative and efficacy mediators contribute to motivation under a moderate negative goal discrepancy (Bandura & Cervone, 1983). Experimental conditions varied the presence/absence of performance goals and numerical feedback on goal progress as participants engaged in a physically effortful task. In the condition combining goals and feedback, the experimentally-controlled feedback indicated that efforts were moderately short of the goal. Key results are displayed in Figure 4.1. As shown, affective self-evaluation and perceived self-efficacy were good predictors of the degree of change in motivation in this condition, in which attainments fell short of the goal being pursued. Discontent over substandard performance combined with high perceived self-efficacy for goal attainment produces a marked heightening of effort.

---

4 A colloquial language that complements Bandura's analysis employs the everyday concept of "talking to oneself." When engaged in an activity, people not uncommonly talk to themselves about how they are doing. This self-talk naturally takes on different linguistic forms. Sometimes people talk to themselves about their personal capabilities (e.g., "I wonder if I can do any better than this?"); sometimes they subjectively evaluate the goodness or worth of their current efforts (e.g., "that stinks, what I just did; I don't want to keep performing at this level"); and sometimes their thoughts turn to aims for future action (e.g., "next time, I'll just try to make some small progress"). These three classes of self-talk illustrate the 1) self-efficacy judgments, 2) self-evaluative reactions, and 3) self-set personal goal adjustments that Bandura presents. This self-talk rephrasing also underscores the logic of using direct self-reports as measurement tools. If people are already talking to themselves about their ongoing efforts, it is a simple matter to tap into their thinking via self-report. As Ericsson and Simon (1980) explained years ago when discussing cases in which verbal reports provide valid data, in such cases the pertinent material (the self-reflections) is in short-term memory in a linguistic form, and thus can be directly reported.

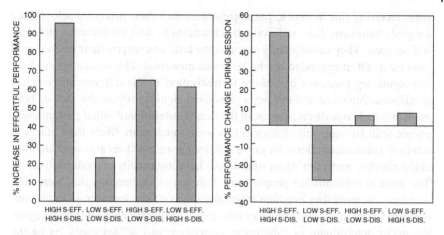

Figure 4.1 Mean percentage changes in motivational level under conditions combining goals and performance feedback as a function of different combinations of levels of self-dissatisfaction (S-DIS) and perceived self-efficacy for goal attainment (S-EFF). The left-hand panel shows the mean change in motivation for the entire session; the right-hand panel shows the mean motivational change between the initial and the final segment of the session. From Bandura & Cervone, 1983, p. 1024. Copyright 1983 by the American Psychological Association. Adapted by permission of the publisher.

A low sense of self-efficacy with low discontent over a substandard performance mobilizes little effort. Either high discontent or high perceived self-efficacy alone results in a moderate increase in motivation. The joint operation of the self-reactive influences even predicts whether motivation is enhanced, sustained, or debilitated over the course of a given attempt. The discontented self-efficacious ones intensified their effort as time went on, whereas those who judged themselves inefficacious to reach the goal and were satisfied with a substandard performance slackened their efforts and displayed a substantial decline in motivation as they continued the activity.

The three self-regulatory influences exert differential impact on motivation in different contexts. Specifically, their impact varies when current attainments diverge, to varying degrees, from one's goal on a task (Bandura & Cervone, 1986). In research, the degree of discrepancy between aspirations and current attainments has been varied systematically over a wide range of discrepancy levels. As in the prior work (Bandura & Cervone, 1983), this experimental paradigm featured a physically strenuous task: exertion on a novel type of exercise bicycle. Participants periodically received feedback on their performance. The feedback was prearranged such that, in different experimental conditions, participants learned that their efforts were falling either markedly, moderately, or minimally short of an assigned goal – or, in a fourth condition, that it had exceeded the standard.

After receiving this feedback, participants recorded their perceived self-efficacy for goal attainment, their self-evaluative reactions to their attainments, and their self-set goals. They subsequently resumed the task, whereupon their motivational level (their effort expended on the task) was measured. This design reveals how self-regulatory processes contribute to motivation in the different discrepancy conditions. Perceived self-efficacy contributed significantly in the face of both moderate and large discrepancies; in the face of substandard initial performance, people with stronger self-efficacy beliefs were much more likely than others to intensify subsequent efforts. Negative self-evaluative reactions also were an influential affective motivator when attainments fall substantially or moderately short. The more self-dissatisfied people were with initial attainments that were substandard, the more they heighten their subsequent efforts. By contrast, in the condition in which initial performances fell short of the goal to only a minimal degree, the major determinant of subsequent motivation was self-set goals. As people approached or surpass the initial standard, the new goals they set for themselves serve as an additional motivator. The higher the self-set goals, the more effort invested in the endeavor.

Taken together this set of self-reactive influences accounted for the *major share of* variation in motivation. Self-reactive influences predict the impact of success, as well as of failure, on motivation. When attainments surpass challenging goals, people's beliefs in their efficacy and their self-set goals determine their level of motivation (Figure 4.2). Those who hold a strong belief in their efficacy motivate themselves by setting even higher goal challenges that create new discrepancies to be mastered. Thus, notable attainments bring temporary satisfaction, but people enlist new challenges as personal motivators for further accomplishment. Those who doubt they could muster the same level of effort again lower their goals. Their motivation declines.

In the flow of behavior and self-reflection, the relation between attainments, on the one hand, and self-referent thought, on the other, can vary. For example, a given performance attainment can give rise to diverse self-set goals depending on level of perceived self-efficacy (Bandura & Cervone, 1986). When people fail to fulfill a challenging standard, some become less sure of their efficacy and lower their goals, whereas others remain confident, persist in the face of failure, and even raise their goals. Surpassing a taxing standard through sustained strenuous effort does not necessarily raise efficacy beliefs. Although for most people, high accomplishment strengthens beliefs of personal efficacy, many who drive themselves to hard-won success are left with self-doubts that they can duplicate the feat and so adopt more modest goals for future pursuits. Strength of perceived efficacy and goal commitment predict whether people redouble their efforts, react apathetically, or become despondent when they fail to fulfill a valued standard (Bandura, 1991).

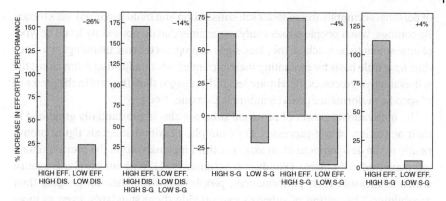

Figure 4.2 Mean percentage changes in motivational level by people who are high or low in the self-reactive influences identified by hierarchical regression analyses as the critical motivators at each of four levels of preset discrepancy between a challenging standard and level of performance attainment. EFF signifies strength of perceived self-efficacy to attain a 50% increase in effort; DIS, the level of self-dissatisfaction with the same level of attainment as in the prior attempt; and S-G, the goals people set for themselves for the next attempt. The second set of graphs at the −4% discrepancy level summarize the results of the regression analysis performed with perceived self-efficacy averaged over the 30%–70% goal attainment range. From Bandura & Cervone, 1986, p. 108. Reprinted by permission of Academic Press, Inc.

Goal Properties and the Differential Engagement of Self-Processes

It earlier was noted that, in Social Cognitive Theory, goals operate largely through self-referent processes rather than by motivating action directly. Here we emphasize a second point: These self-reactive influences are not always active. In other words, people are not continuously, in all life circumstances, engaged in each of the three aspects of self-referent thinking outlined above: 1) affective self-evaluation, 2) perceived self-efficacy for goal attainment, and 3) ongoing adjustment of personal aims – outlined above. Instead, the self-influences are *differentially* engaged in goal-directed motivation (Bandura & Cervone, 1986). Certain properties of goal structures, and the feedback structures that can provide indication of goal progress, determine how strongly the self-system will become enlisted in any given endeavor.

Consider again a goal property noted above: specificity. As reviewed, specific goals generally produces higher levels of motivation and performance than do vague aims such as doing "your best." Why do these motivational effects occur reliably? Specific goals gain motivational power by enlisting self-influences. As people observe themselves making progress toward specific aims, the unambiguous signs of personal accomplishment foster self-satisfaction and build perceived self-efficacy. By contrast, when people possess only vague aims that do not specify levels or types of attainment to be reached, they lack signs of progress that are unambiguous. They thus have little basis for evaluating their current efforts or adjusting future aims; the self-evaluative processes thereby are less fully engaged than they are in the presence of specific performance goals (Bandura & Cervone, 1983).

The motivational power of proximal subgoals also is substantially grounded in their activation of self-processes. For example, proximal subgoals figure prominently in the development of an aspect of thinking analyzed in the previous chapter: perceived self-efficacy (Bandura & Schunk, 1981). Without standards against which to measure their performances, people have little basis for gauging their capabilities. The setting of subgoals can provide these standards, even as more distal aims are reached. Subgoal attainments provide rising indicants of mastery for enhancing self-percepts of efficacy. By contrast, distal goals by themselves are too far removed in time to serve as favorable markers of progress along the way to ensure a growing sense of personal efficacy.

The standards against which attainments are compared also contribute, in several ways, to the development of intrinsic interest in the things being pursued. People develop enduring interest in activities at which they feel self-efficacious and from which they derive self-satisfaction. Challenging standards enlist sustained involvement in tasks needed to build competencies that foster interest. Moreover, when people aim for and master valued levels of performance, they experience a sense of satisfaction (Bandura & Cervone, 1983; Bandura & Jourden, 1989; Locke, Cartledge, & Knerr, 1970). The satisfactions derived from goal attainments build intrinsic interest. However, when distal goals are used as the comparative standard, current attainments may prove disappointing because of wide disparities with lofty future standards. As a result, interest fails to develop even though skills are being acquired in the process. To the extent that proximal subgoals promote and authenticate a sense of efficacious agency, they heighten interest through enhancement of perceived personal causation (Bandura & Schunk, 1981). Perceived self-efficacy is thus a better predictor of intrinsic interest than is actual ability (Collins, 1982).

These diverse effects of proximal self-motivation were revealed in a study in which children who were grossly deficient and uninterested in mathematics pursued a program of self-directed learning under conditions involving either proximal subgoals leading to a distal goal, only the distal goal, or without any reference to goals (Bandura & Schunk, 1981). Within each of the goal conditions, children could observe how many units of work they had completed in each session and their cumulative attainment. Under proximal subgoals children progressed rapidly in self-directed learning, achieved substantial mastery of mathematical operations, and developed an increased sense of efficacy (Figure 4.3). Distal goals had

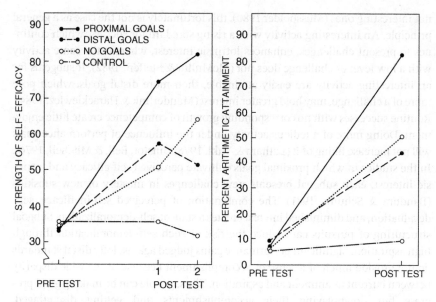

Figure 4.3 The left panel shows the strength of children's perceived arithmetic efficacy at the beginning of the study (pretest), after they completed the self-directed learning (Post 1), and after they took the arithmetic posttest (Post 2). Children in the control group were assessed without the intervening self-directed learning. The right panel displays the children's level of arithmetic achievement before and after the self-directed learning. From Bandura & Schunk, 1981, p. 592. Copyright 1981 by the American Psychological Association. Reprinted by permission of the publisher.

no demonstrable effects. Subgoal attainments also created intrinsic interest in arithmetic, which initially held little attraction for the children.

The value of proximal subgoals in cultivating intrinsic interest and promoting academic attainment is further corroborated by Morgan (1985) in an extended field experiment designed to improve the academic competence of college students. People not only perform better under goal proximity; they also prefer a proximal to a distal focus (Jobe, 1984).

Like any other form of influence, goals can be applied in ways that breed dislikes rather than nurturing interests. Goals have their strongest positive psychological effects when they serve as mastery devices rather than as onerous dictums. As already noted, personal standards that subserve valued aspirations promote interest. But if goals assigned by others impose severe constraints and burdensome performance requirements the pursuit can become oppressive. Because the effects of goals depend on their properties, propositions about the impact of goals on interest must be qualified by the nature and structure of the goals and the purposes they serve. Although some findings suggest that goals enhance interest in dull tasks but not interesting ones (Mossholder,1980), this fortunately is not the case as a general principle. An interesting activity with a rising standard for success, which continues to present challenges, enhances intrinsic interest, whereas the same activity with a low level of challenge does not (McMullin & Steffen, 1982). If subgoals for an interesting activity are easily attainable, then more distal goals, which pose more of a challenge, may hold greater interest (Manderlink & Harackiewicz, 1984). Routine successes with no corresponding growth of competence create little enjoyment. Doing more of a tedious activity under the influence of performance goals will not increase liking of it (Latham & Yukl, 1976; Umstot, Bell, & Mitchell, 1976). In the studies in which proximal goals cultivate perceived self-efficacy and intrinsic interest, each subgoal presents new challenges in mastery of new subskills (Bandura & Schunk, 1981). The combination of perceived self-inefficacy, self-devaluation, and diminished interest creates a state of self-demoralization. Subgoal structuring of pursuits can reduce the risk of such self-demoralization through high aspiration. Significant performance gains judged against lofty distal standards do not provide much of a sense of accomplishment because of the wide disparity between current attainment and aspiration. Thus, people can be making good progress but downplaying their accomplishments and getting discouraged. Hierarchical subgoals minimize dispiriting mismatches. We shall return shortly to the self-debilitating affective consequences of unfulfilled striving.

Csikszentmihalyi (1979) examined what it is about activities that fosters continuing deep engrossment in life pursuits. The common factors found to be conducive to enduring motivation include adopting personal challenges in accordance with one's perceived capabilities and having informative feedback of progress.

Goal proximity should be distinguished from specificity of planning. Planning specificity includes not only temporal variation in goals but a host of additional factors. For example, consider studies that compare self-control programs featuring specific daily plans to self-control programs with more general monthly plans. The detailed proximal systems prescribe higher levels of onerous busywork involving, for example, the creation of daily flow charts indicating when and where activities will be performed, and an associated monitoring and recording of one's performances (Kirschenbaum, Humphrey, & Mallet, 1981; Kirschenbaum, Tomarken, & Ordman, 1982). Self-influence strategies that require excessive busywork usually are applied less faithfully, yielding less beneficial results. The optimal way to reveal the motivating potential of goal proximity is to vary only whether attainments are compared to close or distant standards, without confounding these goal variations with bothersome, time-consuming oversight routines.

Efforts to clarify how goal proximity operates in self-regulatory mechanisms often encounter another methodological obstacle: People spontaneously transform suggested goals during the course of their pursuits. When encouraged to set distal goals for themselves, many individuals quickly improvise their own

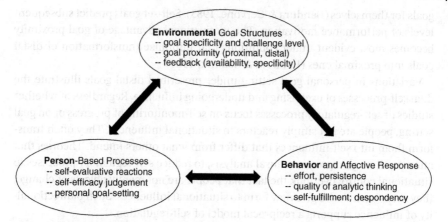

Figure 4.4 The figures summarizes Bandura's analysis of self-processes in goal-directed motivation by relating it to his conception of reciprocal causality, presented in Chapter 1. The earlier model is an overarching framework within which more specific theoretical analyses can be formulated in specific domains. As this chapter explains, in the domain of goal-directed motivation, the key social-cognitive person-based processes are self-evaluative reactions, self-efficacy judgments, and the setting and adjustment of personal goals. The key environmental factors involve the structure of goal systems: the nature of the goals one sets and the feedback one receives on progress. These person and environmental factors interact dynamically in a number of ways. A relatively obvious point is that environmental factors influence the level of self-referent variables; for example, successes tend to raise self-satisfaction and self-efficacy judgment. A second point, which is distinctive to Social Cognitive Theory, is that the environmental factors influence whether people *engage in* the various forms of self-referent thinking. Compared to conditions in which clear task goals and specific performance feedback are absent, the presence of specific goals and feedback prompts people to engage in self-referent thinking processes that, in turn, affect subsequent motivation and performance (Bandura & Cervone, 1983, 1986; Cervone, Jiwani, & Wood, 1991; Cervone & Wood, 1995). Finally, behavior and the environment inherently interact. For example, in many circumstances, substandard behavior at one point in time (e.g., a poor answer early in a job interview; a blown play early in a sporting event) inherently creates, at subsequent time points, a more challenging environment (e.g., the interviewer becomes skeptical and asks harder questions; your team falls behind and must execute riskier plays to catch up). [Figure created by Editor, following the principles of Bandura's analyses.]

proximal goals by partitioning desired future attainments into more easily realizable, near-term subparts (Bandura & Simon, 1977; Dubbert & Wilson, 1984; Weinberg, Bruya & Jackson, 1985). Performances become the product of self-created goals rather than of externally assigned ones. The effects of proximal goals are untestable if uncontrolled personal goal setting largely eliminates experimentally assigned temporal variation in goals. Similarly, even when people simply monitor their performances, without any reference to goals, many begin to create goals for themselves (Bandura & Cervone, 1983). Self-set goals predict subsequent levels of performance motivation. The motivational advantage of goal proximity becomes most evident under conditions that minimize transformation of distal goals into proximal ones (Bandura & Schunk, 1981).

Variations in personal goal setting under prescribed distal goals illustrate the dual self-processes of exercising and undergoing influence. Regardless of whether studies of self-regulatory processes focus on self-monitoring of progress or on goal setting, people are not simply reactors to situational influences. They often transform them into self-influences that differ from what others intend. Theories that attempt, through regressive causal analysis, to reduce self-regulatory processes to situational control overlook the fact that people are not merely objects of change; they act as agents who give new form to situational influences. Such bidirectionality of influence supports a reciprocal model of self-regulation.

In research that has examined intraindividual change, goals enhanced performance at the outset before any feedback was provided to create a discrepancy (Bandura, 1991). Framing feedback of the same performance discrepancy as progress toward a desired goal (e.g., 75%) versus shortfall from the same goal (e.g., 25%) had markedly different effects (Jourden, 1991). Feedback framed as gains toward goal attainment is found to sustain high perceived self-efficacy, raise self-set goals, and support self-satisfaction and group productivity in the management of a simulated organization. By contrast, when factually equivalent discrepancy feedback is framed in term of goal shortfalls, perceived self-efficacy plummets, self-set goals decrease, self-satisfaction declines, and organizational performance progressively deteriorates. So much for the driving power of negative feedback. The removal of a negative is not the same as the attainment of a positive.

Affective Consequences of Goal Discrepancies

Self-regulatory processes produce emotional effects that can alter level of performance motivation. Negative discrepancies between attainments and standards selected as indices of personal merit can give rise to self-devaluation and despondent mood. Given stringent standards, even notable achievements appear trivial and undeserving of self-satisfaction. A growing body of evidence reveals that negative cognitive biases in the constituent processes of self-regulation increase vulnerability to depression (Kanfer & Hagerman, 1981; Rehm, 1982).

Of special interest is evidence that faulty goal setting may be conducive to despondency and performance debilitation. Compared to nondepressed persons, the depressed tend to set higher standards for themselves relative to their attainments and to react less positively to similar successes and more self-critically to similar failures (Golin & Terrill, 1977; Loeb, Beck, Diggory, & Tuthill, 1967;

Schwartz, 1974; Simon, 1979). Goal stringency is a relational characteristic reflecting the match between personal capabilities and goals, not a matter of absolute level. Depression is most likely to arise when personal standards of merit are set well above one's perceived self-efficacy to attain them (Kanfer & Zeiss, 1983). Negative discrepancies in self-appraisal of capabilities by social comparison can also breed despondency. Perceived self-inefficacy to accomplish valued performances that others find readily attainable creates a depressive mood and impairs cognitive functioning (Davies & Yates, 1982). Much attention has been given to the adverse effects of unfavorable social comparison. In studies that vary the social performance standard for comparative appraisal, the higher the accomplishments of similar others, the less self-satisfied people are with their own performance attainments (Simon, 1979).

The self-belittling effect of adverse social comparison is especially evident in persons who are prone to depression. When exposed to high attainments of others, the depressed judge their own accomplishments as less praiseworthy than do the nondepressed (Ciminero & Steingarten, 1978). Self-devaluative reactions to adverse social comparative appraisal is even more pronounced in depressed women (Garber, Hollon, & Silverman, 1979). To mitigate the deleterious effects of social comparison, it is often recommended that human endeavors be structured so that people judge themselves in reference to their own standards and progress, rather than by comparing themselves against others. Self-comparative standards provide the benefits of personal challenge and success experiences for self-development without the cost of invidious social comparison. However, striving to meet one's own standards of excellence can be a source of self- devaluation if they are too stringent. In competitive, individualistic systems, social comparison inevitably intrudes on self-appraisal. Social arrangements in which one person's success is another person's loss or hindrance force social comparison unless one cedes competitive pursuits. However, some leeway exists in how much weight individuals give to self-comparison and to social comparison in their self-appraisals (Bandura, 1990c; Frey & Ruble, 1990). Continued progress in a valued activity does not necessarily ensure perpetual self-fulfillment. The strides at which activities are mastered can drastically alter self-evaluative reactions (Simon, 1979). Performers received prearranged feedback of a decelerating pattern of improvement (improve fast initially but then taper off), or an accelerating pattern of improvement (improve slowly at first but then make large gains). Different rates of improvement produced strikingly different patterns of self-evaluation. Accomplishments that surpass earlier ones bring a continued sense of self-satisfaction. But people derive little satisfaction from smaller accomplishments, or even devalue such accomplishments, after having made larger strides. People who are prone to depression display even greater affective reactivity to their rate of progress. They are more self-satisfied with accelerating strides, but they find even less satisfaction in modest improvements after achieving large performance attainments. Early spectacular accomplishments reflecting notable proficiency can thus be conductive to later self-dissatisfaction even in the face of continuing personal attainments.

With success comes the tribulation of fulfilling not only rising personal standards but social expectations. As the great songwriter Irving Berlin, who achieved early fame and then sustained a career of more than a half century, once noted. "The toughest thing about success is that you've got to keep on being a success." Those who experience spectacular early successes often find themselves wrestling with self-doubts and despondency if their later work falls short of their earlier triumphs. The two-time Nobel Laureate Linus Pauling prescribed the absolute remedy for the woes of belittling self-comparison; when asked what one does after winning a Nobel Prize, he replied, "Change fields, of course!"

Self-regulatory theories of motivation and of depression make seemingly contradictory predictions regarding the effects of negative discrepancies between attainments and standards. Standards that exceed attainments are said to enhance motivation through goal challenges, but negative discrepancies are also invoked as activators of despondent mood. Moreover, when negative discrepancies do have adverse effects, they may foster apathy rather than despondency. A conceptual scheme is needed that differentiates the conditions under which negative discrepancies will motivate, depress, or induce apathy.

Whether negative discrepancies are motivating or depressing will depend on people's self-efficacy beliefs for matching them. Social cognitive theory posits that the directional effects of negative goal discrepancies are predictable from the relationship between perceived self-efficacy for goal attainment and level of self-set goals (Bandura, 1986). Negative disparities are likely to foster high motivation and little despondency among people who believe they have the efficacy to fulfill a difficult goal. The same objective disparities are likely to diminish motivation and foster despondent mood among those who judge themselves inefficacious for goal attain while simultaneously continuing to demand it of themselves. Finally, it is people who judge themselves inefficacious and abandon difficult goals as personally unrealistic who are likely to experience apathy, as reflected in lowered motivation without despondent mood.

Thus far the discussion has been concerned with depression arising from perceived self-inefficacy to fulfill valued standards of achievement. Perceived self-inefficacy to exercise control over other things people long for can also be depressing. The desired outcomes can be diverse, involving, for example, perceived inefficacy to cultivate social relationships (Holahan & Holahan, 1987a, b; Stanley & Maddux, 1986), manage child rearing demands (Cutrona & Troutman, 1986), or other aspects of life that mean a great deal (Devins, et al., 1982;

Rosenbaum & Hadari, 1985). The greater the perceived self-inefficacy, the higher the depression.

Two biasing processes have been postulated to explain how mood states can affect self-efficacy judgment. According to an affective priming theory proposed by Bower (1983), when past successes and failures are stored in memory, they are stored in association with representations of their accompanying affective states (Bower, 1983). The set of memories provides the data base on which judgmental processes operate. Mood activates, through an associative mood network, the subset of memories congruent with it. Thus, negative mood activates the failure subset, whereas a positive mood activates the success subset. The spread of activation from the emotion node makes mood-congruent memories salient. Self-appraisal of efficacy is enhanced by selective recall of past successes but diminished by recall of failures. By contrast, in a cognitive priming view, specific successes or failures that induce the affect also produce cognitions that cue thoughts of other past successes and failures. This view places greater emphasis on the thought content of the inducing event than on the aroused affect as the primer of other positive or negative thoughts. Cognitive availability biases self-efficacy judgment.

Kavanagh and Bower (1985) have shown that, indeed, induced positive mood enhances perceived self-efficacy, whereas despondent mood diminishes it. The impact of induced mood on self-efficacy judgment was widely generalized across diverse domains of functioning.

Self-Regulatory Processes, Education, and Occupational Opportunities

The choices one makes in adolescence and young adulthood have lasting consequences for professional life. Self-development during these formative years opens the door to some occupations while foreclosing other occupational options. Self-regulatory processes in this time of life thus shape one's future.

Self-Efficacy Beliefs, Aspirations, and Career Trajectories

An understanding of these processes and their impact requires longitudinal methods. One such effort was a multifaceted longitudinal project examined conducted with children, as well as their mothers and teachers, in a residential community located near Rome (Bandura, Barbaranelli, Caprara, & Pastorelli, 2001). In this setting, after completing middle school, children experience a major life transition. They must choose one an educational system from among seventeen options classical, scientific, or artistic lyceums; professional schools in the fields of engineering, commerce, or education; or technical schools that prepare students for various technical, social service, or agricultural and horticultural vocations.

To explore the potential role of self-efficacy judgment in career choice, perceived career self-efficacy and occupational choices were measured before an educational system was chosen. In keeping with the principles of self-efficacy assessment discussed in Chapter 3, perceived self-efficacy was measured in a contextualized manner; children judged their efficacy to execute designed activities in each of seven domains of functioning. For example, some items measured perceived self-efficacy for regulating one's own learning activities (Zimmerman et al., 1992). The challenging activities for which children judged their efficacy for perfomance included structuring environments conducive to learning, planning and organizing academic activities, and getting teachers and peers to help them with academic problems when needed. As an example of a second item domain, some items assessed children's self-regulatory efficacy, including their beliefs in their abilities to resist peer pressure to engage in high-risk activities involving alcohol, drugs, and transgressive behavior.

The study's longitudinal methods enabled the research to address the question of whether the different facets of perceived self-efficacy as measured at the beginning of junior high school would predict the types of occupational pursuits students considered seriously toward the end of junior high (Bandura et al., 2001). Path analytic methods were employed to explore relations among sociostructural determinants, the various facets of perceived self-efficacy, and educational aspirations. The findings revealed the role of self-efficacy beliefs in mediating the relation between sociostructural factors and career preferences. Specifically, the impact of familial socioeconomic status and parents' self-efficacy and aspirations on their children's occupational preferences was entirely mediated through the children's perceived occupational self-efficacy and academic aspirations. Perceived occupational self-efficacy rather than actual academic achievement was found to be the key determinant of the kinds of career pursuits children seriously considered for their lifework and those they disfavor.

Aspirational Standards, Achievement Motives, and External Incentives

Social Cognitive Theory of course is not the only framework that researchers have adopted in efforts to understand motivational processes and their role in life trajectories. In a prominent alternative, personality theories often have portrayed human strivings and accomplishments as products of achievement needs or motives.

In such efforts, the achievement motive is usually inferred from responses to items containing cues relevant to achievement. Theories in which motives are inferred from the types of behavior they supposedly cause create problems of circularity. The motive is inferred from a given class of behavior and is then used to explain the activation of that class of behavior.[5]

The processes of self-motivation through self-reactive influence described above are significant ingredients in the variety of motivational phenomena that come under different names in other theoretical conceptions. Achievement motivation is one such instance. High achievers tend to invest their self-satisfaction in attainment of challenging goals; low achievers adopt easy goals as sufficing. The higher the aspirational standards people set for themselves, the harder they strive to fulfill them and the more likely they are to excel in their attainments. The functional properties ascribed to the achievement motive are much the same as those that characterize aspirational standards. Both are said to direct and activate courses of action that lead to desired accomplishments. However, there is a major conceptual difference between a motive force and self-generated incentives arising from internal standards and self- reactive influence. Motives impel behavior, whereas self-incentives motivate and direct behavior through anticipatory cognitive mechanisms. Research in which achievement motive and aspirational standards are measured sheds some light on these alternative motivational mechanisms. High need for achievement is associated with high goal setting. However, need for achievement has no influence on performance independently of personal goals. The relationship between need for achievement and performance disappears when level of self-set goals is controlled (Dossett, Latham, & Mitchell, 1979; Latham & Marshall, 1982; Matsui, Okada, & Kakuyama, 1982). The goals people set for themselves predict their performance level and self-satisfaction better than do the traditional personality measures of need for achievement (Arvey & Dewhirst, 1976; Ostrow, 1976; Yukl & Latham, 1978).

The inclination of high need achievers to select high goals does not necessarily mean that performance standards are the products of an underlying motive, as is

---

5 For a more extended critique of explanatory strategies in personality psychology, see Bandura (1999). Additional discussion can be found in Boag (2011, 2018) and Cervone (1999, 2008). Boag (2018) explains that "part of the problem" in trying to identify basic motives or needs is that investigators tend "to determine whether a need is basic or not, simply based on what the need is said to do rather than the actual source of the need itself" (p. 31). This creates the "circularity" on which Bandura remarks. A related issue concerns a general principle of scientific explanation. "A fundamental explanation of the property" under consideration -- the philosopher Nozick (1981, p. 632) explains -- "will not refer to things with that very same property" (Nozick, 1981, p. 632). If the property is the blueness of the sky, the explanation would *not* refer to something that is blue (e.g., "blue molecules" or a "dispositional tendency of the sky to be blue"). Similarly, if the property is a person's tendency to engage in achievement-related behaviors, one would – in order to adhere to this principle – avoid explanations that refer to a need, motive, or tendency "to achieve." Bandura's Social Cognitive Theory *does* adhere to this explanatory principle in that explanation is grounded systems of determinants, no one of which corresponds to the class of overt behavior that is being explained.

commonly assumed. Personal standards of excellence may lead people to endorse achievement statements or to produce achievement imagery on personality tests, rather than such endorsements verifying an achievement motive fueling aspiring standards. Evidence that standard setting is a better predictor of ongoing level of performance than are indices of achievement motives lends causal priority to standard setting. Moreover, goal theory can explain rapid shifts in motivational level through changes in mediating self- processes, whereas quick changes pose explanatory difficulties for a dispositional motive determinant. Self-influence through internal standards also contributes to the motivational effects of extrinsic feedback and incentives. Extrinsic incentives can motivate partly by activating personal goals for progressive improvement. Indeed, a series of studies conducted by Locke and his associates shows that incentives increase performance to the extent that they encourage people to set motivating goals for themselves (Locke, Bryan, & Kendall, 1968). In research reporting mixed results on whether incentives influence performance partly by their effect on self-set goals, performers were given no information about their level of performance (Pritchard & Curtis, 1973). Self-evaluative motivators are not effectively activated in the absence of knowledge of how one is doing (Bandura & Cervone, 1983). People are certainly motivated by the prospect of valued extrinsic outcomes. But by applying evaluative standards to their ongoing performances, they create motivating challenges and fulfill them to please themselves as well. Even simple feedback of progress or trivial extrinsic incentives can enhance performance motivation once self-satisfaction becomes invested in the activity. Satisfaction in personal accomplishment becomes the reward.

Concluding Comment

The converging lines of evidence reviewed in this chapter testify to the paramount role played by self-regulatory mechanisms in human motivation across diverse realms of functioning. Self-regulation is a multifaceted phenomenon operating through a number of subsidiary cognitive processes including self-monitoring, standard setting, evaluative judgment, self-appraisal and affective self-reaction. Cognitive regulation of motivation relies extensively on an anticipatory proactive system rather than simply on a reactive negative feedback system. The human capacity for forethought, reflective self-appraisal and self-reaction gives prominence to cognitively-based motivators in the exercise of personal agency.

The process of evaluating one's actions in relation to standards of excellent is significant not only to motivated action in achievement-oriented settings. It also is central to the moral domain, as we will see in the chapter ahead.

5
Morality and the Disengagement of Moral Standards

A shared morality is vital to the humane functioning of any society. Many forms of behavior are advantageous to oneself but detrimental to others. Without some consensual moral codes, people would disregard each other's rights and welfare whenever their desires came into conflict.

Human morality is of considerable import not only collectively but also individually. Internalization of a set of standards is integral to the achievement of self-directedness and a sense of continuity and purpose in one's everyday life.

Moral rules and the social sanctions to which they give rise not only articulate moral principles. They also are meant to govern social conduct. External sanctions alone, however, are relatively weak deterrents to immoral action because, in practice, most transgressive acts can go undetected. Yet a great many people, in a great many contexts, do act in a moral manner. Their moral conduct is maintained substantially thanks to *self*-sanctions. People continuously preside over their own conduct; they adhere to moral principles in countless situations that present little or no threat of external sanctions if those principles were violated. Self-sanctions thus play a central role in the social cognitive theory of moral agency, presented in this chapter.

The analysis of moral conduct presented here in Chapter 5 follows directly from material presented in Chapter 4. The earlier analysis of self-regulation and motivation revealed that personal standards and self-evaluative reactions contribute substantially to motivation and performance. Findings also showed that these self-regulatory mechanisms are not always engaged; different external goal structures were found to engage, or to disengage, the psychological process of evaluating actions in relation to personal standards (Bandura & Cervone, 1983, 1986).

This concept—the engagement and disengagement of standards—figures prominently in Social Cognitive Theory's account of moral behavior, as is detailed later in the present chapter. Many transgressions of everyday life are committed

Social Cognitive Theory: An Agentic Perspective on Human Nature, First Edition. Albert Bandura.
© 2023 John Wiley & Sons, Inc. Published 2023 by John Wiley & Sons, Inc.

by people who adhere to virtuous personal standards in many domains of life, but in select circumstances disengage those standards and commit harmful acts.[1]

The social cognitive theory of morality contrasts with theoretical alternatives that, historically, have garnered considerable attention. In these alternatives, theorists have focused primarily on moral reasoning. But questions of major basic and applied interest involve moral *conduct*. The conspicuous neglect of moral conduct reflected both the rationalistic bias of major theories of morality and the convenience of investigatory method; it is considerably easier to examine people's reasoning about hypothetical moral dilemmas than their conduct in morally-charged settings. But it is conduct that counts. The psychological mechanisms that govern moral conduct involve far more than abstract reasoning about the domain. When perpetrators engage in inhumane actions, people suffer—no matter how the perpetrators might reason about and justify their actions.

Even moral thought is not solely an intrapsychic affair. The way people apply moral principles to everyday dilemmas varies depending on situational imperatives, activity domains, and constellations of social influence. It is not uncommon to observe otherwise good people engaging, in select contexts, in sophisticated justifications that subserve immoral endeavors. A comprehensive theory of morality must aim to explain how moral reasoning, in conjunction with other psychosocial factors, governs moral conduct.

To meet this aim, Social Cognitive Theory adopts the interactionist perspective reviewed in previous chapters. Applied to the moral domain, the principle of triadic reciprocal causation highlights ways that personal factors (in the form of moral thought and affective self-reactions), moral conduct, and environmental influences function as reciprocally interacting determinants. But, before presenting this Social Cognitive Theory of morality, we will analyze stage-theoretic cognitive structural analyses of moral reasoning.

Stage Theories of Moral Reasoning

Stage theorists assume that different types of moral thinking develop in an invariant sequence. Each stage is said to feature a distinctive, uniform way of thinking. Piagetian theory (1948) favors a developmental sequence progressing from moral realism, in which rules are seen as unchangeable and conduct is judged in terms of damage done, to relativistic morality in which conduct is judged primarily by the performer's intentions. In the latter stage, well-intentioned acts that produce

---

1 The definitive Social Cognitive Theory account of moral behavior and the disengagement of moral standards is Bandura (2016).

much harm are viewed as less reprehensible than ill-intentioned acts that cause little harm. Moral absolutism stems from unquestioning acceptance of adult prescripts and the egocentric outlook of young children; moral relativism develops from increasing personal experiences and reciprocal relationships with peers.

Following Piaget's lead, Kohlberg developed an expanded cognitive structural theory of morality that revitalized and altered the direction of the field. Kohlberg (1969, 1976) postulated a six-stage sequential typology of moral rules, beginning with punishment-based obedience, evolving through opportunistic self-interest, approval-seeking conformity, respect for authority, contractual legalistic observance, and culminating in principled morality based on standards of justice. Changes in the standards of moral reasoning are produced by cognitive conflict arising from exposure to higher levels of moral reasoning. [Specifically, in Kohlbergian theory, conflicts induce a "cognitive disequilibrium" that promotes movement toward a higher level of moral thought (see, e.g., Haan, 1985).]

Because the six Kohlbergian stages are said to be a fixed developmental sequence, individuals cannot acquire a given form of moral reasoning without first acquiring the preceding modes in order. Regarding social influences, it is presumed that exposures to forms of moral reasoning that are too discrepant from one's dominant stage have little impact because they are insufficiently understood to activate any changes. Judgmental standards of lesser complexity are similarly rejected because they have already been displaced in attaining more advanced forms of thinking. Views that diverge moderately above one's stage presumably create the necessary cognitive perturbations, which are reduced by adopting the higher stage of moral reasoning.

Hierarchical Moral Superiority

Theorists who endorse the stage-theoretic account must explain why people do not preserve their cognitive equilibrium simply by adhering to their own opinions and rejecting conflicting ones. They explain this by positing a universal, though not inborn, latent preference for higher modes of moral thinking (Rest, Turiel, & Kohlberg, 1969). What makes the "higher-stage" reasoning morally superior is not entirely clear. In thoughtful reviews of the stage theory of morality, Locke (1979, 1980) identified and refuted alternative bases of hierarchical superiority. It is not that higher stages of reasoning are cognitively superior because, in most of their judgments, people do not use the highest mode of thinking they understand. Findings suggest that, in many instances, tests of maturity in moral reasoning may be measuring personal preferences more than level of competence in moral reasoning (Mischel & Mischel, 1976). On the matter of stage progression, if people are actuated by an inherent drive for higher ways of moral thinking, it is puzzling why they rarely adopt the uppermost level as their dominant mode even though they comprehend it (Rest, 1973). It is similarly arguable that higher stage reasons are morally superior. By what logical reasoning is a morality rooted in law and order (stage 4) morally superior to one relying on social regard and concern for others (stage 3)? Minorities oppressed by a social order that benefits the majority and those subjected to the rule of apartheid would not think so. Nor would writers who argue that social responsibility and concern for others should be the guiding rule of morality (Gilligan, 1982).

Higher-stage reasoning cannot be functionally superior because stages provide the rationale for supporting either side of a moral issue but they do not prescribe particular solutions. Developmental stages determine the reasons given for actions, not what actions should be taken. Different types of moral thinking can justify stealing, cheating on income taxes, and military bombing of foes. Immorality can thus be served as well, or better, by sophisticated reasoning as by simpler reasoning. Indeed, the destructive social policies advocated by enlightened graduates of renowned academies is better explained by the social dynamics of group thinking than by the collective level of moral maturity (Janis, 1972). When people reason about moral conflicts they commonly face in their environment, Kohlberg and his associates find that moral reasoning is more a function of the social influences operating in the situation than of persons' stages of moral competence (Higgins, Power, & Kohlberg, 1984).

Kohlberg (1971a) underscores the point that his hierarchical stages of reasoning are behaviorally nonprescriptive because they are concerned with the "form" of reasoning not its "content." However, the end point of moral reasoning, which construes morality as justice, carries a fixed behavioral mandate. Unlike the preceding stages, where it is acknowledged that a given type of moral thinking can support either the transgressive or the conforming side of a moral issue, at the end-point stage, thought is said to prescribe what courses of action are morally right. Because movement through the stages is said to be achieved naturally by the force of reasoning, empirical "is" thus becomes philosophical "ought." Rationality dictates morality. The ordering of moral priorities is presumably revealed by switching perspectives in impartial cognitive role-taking of the position of each party in a moral conflict. However, as Bloom (1986) notes, simple perspective shifting in no way guarantees consensus on what aspects of a situation are morally relevant, the moral principles considered inherent in those aspects, and which principle should be granted priority unless there is already prior agreement on which principle should take precedence. It should also be noted that impartial role reversibility is imaginable in the abstract, but social experiences create too many human biases for impartiality of view and universalization of interests to be achievable in reality. For example, no amount of perspective shifting is likely to produce consensus among those who hold pro- and antiabortion views. The principle of freedom—for women and personalized fetuses—provides justification for both moral stances. The consensus most likely to be achieved is agreeing to disagree.

The evidence for the cultural universality of the "is" has not gone uncontested (Locke, 1979; Simpson, 1974) [Jia & Kreetenauer, 2017]. Other theorists argue that the moral idealization in Kohlberg's theory reflects preference for Western views of moral adequacy rather than objective standards or the dictates of reason (Bloom, 1986; Shweder, 1982). Societies that are less inclined toward ethical abstractions and idealization of autonomy come out looking morally underdeveloped even though in their moral conduct they may exhibit fewer inhumanities than Western societies that are ranked as morally superior.

Kohlberg's (1971b) prescriptive stance that moral education in the classroom should consist of moving children through the stages of moral reasoning, regardless of parental wishes, understandably draws heavy fire (Aron, 1977; Wonderly & Kupfersmid, 1980). It belies the egalitarian characterization of the theory. The view of moral superiority as an autonomous self operating above communal norms and concerns does not sit well with many moral theorists.

Some moral philosophers, who hardly lack competence for principled reasoning, regard the principle of justice as only one among other moral principles that either compete for the role of chief yardstick of morality or share in a pluralistic system of judgment (Carter, 1980; Codd, 1977). If, however, principled reasoning is defined as using justice as the supreme judgmental rule it becomes a conceptual truth incapable of empirical disproof (Peters, 1971). The common finding is that adults comprehend different moral principles but use them selectively or in a complementary way, depending on the interplay of circumstances and the domain of functioning. Moral development produces multiform moral thinking rather than following a single developmental track.

Another limitation of the Kohlbergian approach involves assessment. Empirical analyses of Kohlberg's theory generally rely on a test that includes only a few moral dilemmas that are sampled from a narrow range of moral conflicts. The dilemmas are stripped of factors that, in naturally-occurring circumstances, can greatly complicate efforts to find moral solutions. To contend that a few sketchy items verify moral truths is to invest a simple assessment tool with extraordinary revelatory power. A test that surveys only a limited range of predicaments while not systematically representing ecologically-relevant features of everyday life may provide a shaky empirical foundation for a theory of morality and the classification of people into moral types. In practice, a person's propensity for principled moral reasoning will vary depending on the information included in the depicted moral conflicts. For example, the moral dilemmas Kohlberg devised are ambiguous about the likely consequences of transgressive behavior. In the transactional realities of everyday life, people not only have to weigh considerations in moral reasoning; they also must live with the short- and long-term consequences of their moral choices. Anticipation of consequences may weigh heavily in naturally-occurring moral reasoning—especially in cases in which the consequences of moral decisions may alter the course of one's life. Consider research that has added to the commonly studied moral dilemmas varying information about consequences to be experienced by the hypothetical individuals that the dilemmas describe. As the severity of personal consequences increases, people favor self-interest over principled reasoning (Sobesky, 1983). How often people offer principled solutions for moral conflicts may partly reflect the gravity of the consequences they happen to imagine for the sketchy portrayals rather than their competence for principled reasoning.

The exact structuring of hypothetical moral dilemmas can markedly influence the priority people give to alternative moral principles and the amount of agreement obtained in moral judgment. To pit petty theft against human life, as in the oft quoted conflict of the husband faced with stealing an overpriced drug to cure his wife's cancer, will draw consensual judgments from principled thinkers. But adding more substance to the dilemmas, in the form of complicating elements, will elicit disagreement over which moral claims should take precedence (Bloom, 1986; Reed, 1987). The everyday moral dilemmas over which people agonize and feud often involve abhorrent alternatives that do not lend themselves easily to moral solutions.

Evaluating the Claims of Stage Theories

Stage theories assume that, over the course of development, moral judgments change into a series of uniform types representing discontinuous stages. A major problem with typologies is that people hardly ever fit them. Because differing circumstances call for different judgments and actions, unvarying human judgment is a rarity. A person's moral judgments typically rely on reasoning from several different moral standards rather than being based on only one type of standard. Stage theorists thus have to create transitional categories and substages. Stage theories classify people into types according to their modal form of reasoning, although any given individual usually displays coexisting mixtures of reasoning that span several "stages." Most people get categorized as being in varying degrees of transition between stages.

People not only display substantial variability in moral reasoning at any given period. Also, many years may elapse from when they first adopt a new standard of morality to when it becomes the preferred one (Colby, Kohlberg, Gibbs, & Lieberman, 1983). Fischer (1983) notes that such evidence contradicts stage theory, which depicts changes in thinking as pervasive transformations of preceding modes of thought. Clearly, moral thought is not hamstrung by a single cognitive structure that undergoes disjunctive developmental change. Rather than exhibiting wholistic reorganization of their moral thinking, people adopt new moral standards gradually, eventually discarding simpler ones. Adoption of one standard does not preempt all others. People may draw from among a co-existing set of standards in judging different moral predicaments. The mature mode of thinking is characterized by the consideration of diverse factors that may be morally relevant in any given situation, and the choice of a judgmental standard that is most germane in that setting.

One might question the practice of treating reasoning that draws on more than one moral standard as evidence of moral immaturity evolving toward justness as the ultimate standard of morality. Different moral standards are not necessarily contradictory. Hence, adoption of a certain standard need not require jettisoning another. To judge the morality of conduct by a system of complementary standards, such as justness and compassion, reflects a high level of moral reasoning rather than transitional immaturity in thinking. Indeed, Peters (1966) argues that justice is necessary but not sufficient for a moral system. He points out that people can be brutal, but entirely impartial or just in their brutality. A society that subscribes to a morality that integrates standards of justness and compassion will be more humane than a society concerned solely with justness.

The nature of moral judgment unquestionably changes across adulthood. The major question to ask when evaluating stage theories is not whether there exist some universalities in developmental order; it is whether the process of development validly can be described as changes in discrete lock-step stages. There surely are some culturally universal features to the developmental changes of standards of conduct and the locus of moral agency that arise from basic uniformities in the types of biopsychosocial changes that occur with increasing age in all cultures. Growth of personal competencies and increasing autonomy alter the types of morally relevant situations with which the growing child must contend, and the social structures within which these transactions take place. A broadening social reality changes the nature of the moral concerns as well as the social sanctions for transgressive conduct. Expanding moral choices require more generalized and complex moral standards.

Developmental change from concrete to more abstract forms of reasoning is also a natural order of development that all theories acknowledge. No one would contend that young children begin as sophisticated reasoners and become progressively simple-minded as they mature. Nor do young children recognize the prescripts of the social system before they recognize the prescripts of their immediate caretakers or companions. Another obvious natural order of development involves a broadening of perspective from individual to institutional prescripts for promoting human well-being. Change from external regulation to increasing autonomy and self-regulation is still another natural order of development.

Preparation for adult social roles requires adoption of standards appropriate to them. The standards must serve as guides for conduct over an expanding range of moral domains, across various settings involving multiple sources of influence.

Therefore, developmental change in moral standards is not simply a cumulative process. With increasing age, new standards are adopted rather than merely being appended to earlier ones. People vary in the standards they teach, model, and sanction with children of differing ages.

Social Foundations of Moral Standards

Social Cognitive Theory recognizes that the development and exercise of moral self-sanctions are rooted in human relations and the way in which those relations are structured by the larger society. This structuring changes across the course of development.

At first, guidance of behavior is necessarily external and physically oriented. To discourage hazardous conduct in children who do not understand speech, parents must rely on physical guidance. They structure situations physically to reduce the likelihood of problem behavior, such as injurious aggression and, should it arise, they try to check it by introducing competing activities or by disciplinary action. Sometimes they pair simple verbal prohibitions with physical intervention, so that eventually a "no" alone will suffice as a restrainer. At this earliest period of development, there is little that is asked of young children and there is little they can do that is transgressive. Their behavior is regulated and channeled mainly by physical sanctions and verbal proxies for them.

As children mature, some of the activities they pursue inevitably come into conflict with other people's aims and with social norms. Such occasions elicit social reactions designed to promote culturally valued behavior. Social sanctions increasingly replace physical ones as influential guides for how to behave in different situations. Parents and other adults explain standards of conduct and the reasons for them. Social sanctions that disapprove transgressive acts and commend valued conduct add substance to the standards. It is not long before children learn to discriminate between approved and disapproved forms of conduct and to regulate their actions on the basis of anticipated social consequences (Bandura & Walters, 1959; Sears, Maccoby, & Levin, 1957; Walters & Grusec, 1977).

Studies of socialization practices show that social sanctions combined with reasoning foster self-restraints better than do sanctions alone (Parke, 1974; Sears, Maccoby, & Levin, 1957). The reasoning that is especially conducive to development of self-regulatory capabilities appeals to behavioral standards and to empathetic concern for the adverse effects that detrimental conduct inflicts on others (Bandura & Walters, 1959; Hoffman, 1977; Perry & Bussey, 1984).

To instill a generalized self-regulatory moral capability, simply punishing an act is not optimal; it is more effective to use discipline as an occasion for explaining rules of conduct (LaVoie, 1974). Coercive threat may cause compliance in the given situation. But cognitive guides provide a basis for regulating future conduct under changing circumstances.

Qualitative differences in the use of reasoning are evident when comparing families of aggressively antisocial and prosocial adolescents (Bandura & Walters, 1959). The former emphasize that misconduct can bring punishment, whereas the latter stress the injury and suffering that misconduct inflicts on others.

Parents cannot always be present to guide their children's behavior. Successful socialization requires gradual substitution of internal controls for external sanctions. As moral standards are gradually internalized, they begin to serve as guides and deterrents to conduct by the self-approving and self-reprimanding consequences children produce for themselves. Not only do the sanctions change from a social to a personal locus, but with advancing age the range of moral considerations expands. As the nature and seriousness of possible transgressions change with age, parents and other significant adults in the child's life add new aspects to the moral persuasion. For example, they do not appeal to legal arguments when handling preschoolers' misconduct, but they do explain legal codes and penalties to preadolescents to influence future behavior that can have serious legal consequences. It is hardly surprising that adolescents are more likely than young children to consider legalities in their reasoning about transgressive acts.

People develop moral standards from a variety of influences. They form standards for judging their own behavior partly on the basis of how significant persons in their lives react to it.

Parents and others are generally pleased when children meet or exceed valued standards and disappointed when their performances fall short of them. Children notice this, and eventually come to respond to their own behavior in self-approving and self-critical ways, depending on how it compares with the evaluative standards set by others.

Standards also can be acquired through direct instruction in the precepts of conduct (Liebert & Ora, 1968; Rosenhan, Frederick, & Burrowes, 1968). In direct instruction, moral standards may be drawn from the tutelage of people in one's own environment or from the writings and examples of influential figures in society. The moral standards to which adults subscribe guide the type of morality they teach to children (Olejnik, 1980). As in other forms of influence, direct tuition is most effective in fostering development of standards when it is based on shared values and is supported by social feedback to conduct.

People not only prescribe self-evaluative standards for others, they also exemplify them in responding to their own behavior. The power of modeling in influencing standards of conduct is well documented (Bandura, 1986). Modeling is a dynamic constructive process, as Chapter 2 explained. People do not passively absorb standards of conduct from whatever influences happen to impinge upon them. Rather, they construct generic standards from the numerous evaluative rules that are prescribed, modeled, and taught. This process is complicated because those who serve as socialization influencers, whether designedly or unintentionally, often display inconsistencies between what they practice and what they preach. When these two sources of social influence conflict, example often outweighs the power of precept (Hildebrandt, Feldman, & Ditrichs, 1973; McMains & Liebert, 1968; Rosenhan, Frederick, & Burrowes, 1968). Moreover, people usually differ in the standards they model, and even the same person may model different standards in different social settings and domains of conduct (Allen & Liebert, 1969). Such discrepancies reduce the impact of modeling on the development of personal standards. Exemplified standards also carry more force when models possess social power and status (Akamatsu & Farudi, 1978; Grusec, 1971; Mischel & Liebert, 1967).

Televised modeling, which dramatizes a vast range of moral conflicts that transcend viewers' immediate social realities, constitutes another integral part of social learning. Values modeled in print can similarly impart moral standards for judging conduct (Walker & Richards, 1976). Symbolic modeling influences the development of moral judgments by what it portrays as acceptable or reprehensible conduct, and by the sanctions and justifications applied to it. In sum, a varied array of interacting societal influences contribute to the development of moral perspectives.

Multifaceted Nature of Moral Judgment and Action

When people adopt an internal standard, it does not necessarily encompass every domain of activity or completely supplant other forms of control. The degree to which a given individual's actions adhere to socially prescribed norms thus may vary from one setting they encounter to another. Even the most principled individuals may, in some domains and under some circumstances, regulate their behavior mostly by anticipated social or legal consequences rather by than self-guides. Indeed, even children, during the course of development, learn how to get around moral consequences of culpable behavior when that behavior can gain them personal benefits. They discover that they can reduce the likelihood of reprimands by invoking extenuating circumstances for their misdeeds (Bandura & Walters, 1959). As a result, different types of vindications become salient factors in moral judgments. Even very young children are quite skilled in using mitigating factors to excuse wrongdoing (Darley, Klosson, & Zanna, 1978). Later they learn to weaken, if not completely avoid, self-censure for reprehensible conduct by invoking self-exonerating justifications. A theory of moral reasoning must, therefore, address how exonerative moral reasoning can make the immoral inconsequential or even moral. We shall return later to the forms that these mechanisms of moral disengagement take.

Cognitive Conflict as the Automotivator for Change

A theory of morality must explain both the motivators for cognitive change in moral principles and the motivators for acting morally. Stage theorists address the motivation for cognitive change but largely ignore the motivation for pursuing moral courses of action, some of which are self-denying whereas others may bring adverse reactions from certain quarters. Cognitive conflict is posited as the major motivator of cognitive change in stage theories.

According to this equilibration mechanism (Piaget, 1960), discrepancies between the cognitive schemas that children already possess and the events they perceive create internal conflict. This motivates exploration of the source of discrepancy until the internal schemas are altered to accommodate the contradictory experiences. Events that differ markedly from what one knows or expects are too bewildering, and those that differ minimally are too familiar, to arouse interest and exploration. It is moderately discrepant experiences that presumably arouse cognitive conflict that prompts cognitive reorganization. Piagetian theory thus proposes cognitive perturbations by moderately discrepant experiences as the basic automotivator for cognitive change.

Empirical tests of this type of automotivator reveal that discrepancy of experience alone does not guarantee cognitive change (Kupfersmid & Wonderly, 1982; Wachs, 1977). Indeed, if disparities between perceived events and mental structure were, in fact, automatically motivating, everyone should be highly knowledgeable about the world around them and continually progressing toward ever higher levels of reasoning. The evidence does not seem to bear this out. Although motivation presumably springs from cognitive conflict between beliefs held and the information conveyed by situations encountered, surprisingly little effort has been made to verify the causal links between discrepant influences, indicants of internal conflict, and the quest for new understanding. What little evidence there is on this point shows that discrepant influences foster cognitive changes but they seem unrelated to level of cognitive conflict (Zimmerman & Blom, 1983). This finding receives support from a study by Haan (1985) comparing the power of induced social and cognitive disequilibrium to change moral reasoning. Cognitive disequilibrium had little effect on moral reasoning. However, the experiences of coping with social discord around issues of morality produced changes in moral reasoning. The impact of divergent views seems to stem more from how persuasive they are than from how cognitively conflictful they are. Role-playing higher levels of moral reasoning is no more effective in altering moral judgments than simply observing the same moral arguments being modeled (Matefy & Acksen, 1976).

Simply demonstrating that children are unmoved by what they already know or what they do not comprehend because it exceeds their cognitive capabilities is a mundane result that can be explained without reference to an elaborate automotivating mismatch mechanism. Until objective criteria are specified for what level of disparity constitutes moderate discrepancy, the equilibration model of self-motivation does not lend itself readily to empirical test. Langer (1969) maintains that it is the cognitive perturbations children spontaneously produce by themselves rather than those externally activated by discrepant events that are the effective instigators of cognitive change. Moreover, the cognitive conflict is said to be often unconscious, which makes it even less accessible to study. Unless independent measures of unconscious self-perturbation are provided, the posited incongruity motivator is incapable of verification.

As a rule, people do not pursue most activities that differ moderately from what they know or can do. Indeed, if they were driven by every moderately discrepant event encountered in their daily lives they would be rapidly overwhelmed by innumerable imperatives for cognitive change. Effective functioning requires selective deployment of attention and inquiry. Self-motivation through cognitive comparison requires distinguishing between standards of what one knows and standards of what one desires to know. It is the latter standards that exert selective influence over which of many activities that create discrepant experiences will be actively pursued.

A moderately discrepant experience, even in areas of high personal involvement, does not guarantee cognitive change. When people confront views that are discordant from their own, they often resolve the conflict by discounting or reinterpreting the discordant information rather than by changing their way of thinking. It has been shown in other domains of cognitive functioning that the degree of cognitive change generated by exposure to discrepant information is better predicted from the credibility of those voicing discrepant views than from the degree of disparity *per se*. When high credibility sources express views that are more discrepant with those of a listener, greater cognitive change results, but when low credibility sources express such views, their positions are more likely to be rejected (Bergin, 1962; McGuire, 1985). Social factors thus powerfully influence the cognitive processing of discrepant conceptions.

Some efforts have been made to test the equilibration mechanism of developmental change within Kohlberg's framework. Researchers have exposed children to moral arguments that increasingly diverge from views the children already hold. In the initial investigations of stage constraints on moral change, children were presented with a few hypothetical moral dilemmas and then were given conflicting moral advice by persons using reasons from different stages (Rest, Turiel, & Kohlberg, 1969; Turiel, 1966). The investigators report that children reject modeled opinions below their dominant mode of thinking, were unaffected by those that were too advanced, but were likely to adopt modeled views one stage above their own.

Subsequent research indicated that the restricted changeability of moral reasoning may lie more in how the modeling influence was used than in constraints of children's stages. It is unreasonable to expect entrenched moral perspectives to be markedly altered by a transitory influence, especially if presented in a weak form. Theories predicting null results should apply social influences in their most powerful form because one can easily fail to produce cognitive changes by using weak influences. Children do not remember the essential details of moral situations presented to them briefly, but they show good recall with greater exposure (Austen, Ruble, & Trabasso, 1977). Fleeting information that goes by unrecognized or unrecalled cannot affect moral thinking. In the studies conducted by Rest and Kohlberg, not only is the modeling influence unusually brief, but the models disagree in their views by advocating opposing solutions. Although results are not entirely uniform (Walker, 1983), models who are consistent in how they judge different moral predicaments generally have greater impact on children's moral reasoning than do models who disagree with each other (Brody & Henderson, 1977; Keasey, 1973). When the modeled views are consistent, children's moral perspectives are changed more by exposure to moral reasoning two stages above their own than by reasoning one stage more advanced (Arbuthnot, 1975; Matefy & Acksen, 1976). These findings accord with substantial evidence in social psychology cited earlier that the more discrepant persuasive reasoning is from one's own views, the more one's attitudes change. Immaturity, of course, places some limits on the power of discrepant influences. Young children cannot be influenced by reasoning so advanced that it is completely incomprehensible to them.

Children also adopt modeled modes of reasoning labeled as more primitive in the stage hierarchy, but the findings are mixed on how well they adhere to them over time. Here, too, the variable adherence may reflect more how persuasively modeling is used than stage constraints. The views of a lone model, or one who disagrees, can be easily discounted as atypical. It is consensual multiple modeling that carries the strong persuasive impact necessary to override pre-existing orientations. Indeed, the propensity of children to pattern their preferences after models increases as the level of consensus among models increases (Perry & Bussey, 1979). Viewers are likely to conclude that if everyone firmly believes something, it must have merit.

It could be argued that judging by the intentionality of actions does not necessarily represent a higher level of reasoning than judging by the consequences that flow from the acts. In judging the morality of nuclear strategies, for example, the overriding consideration should be the awesome destructiveness of an attack, not the intentions of those who launch it. Prioritizing an attack's devastating consequences would hardly be considered "regressive" or "primitive" thinking. Dwelling on the degree to which it is morally well intended would reflect an excessive reverence for intention and personal principle.

One need not adopt stage-theory principles to explain why children display age trends in moral judgment, fail to adopt standards they do not fully comprehend, or are disinclined to maintain views considered immature for their age. Furthermore, evidence that modes of thinking that invert or skip stages can change moral reasoning is at variance with the stage theory contention that, to alter how one thinks about moral issues, one must pass through an invariant sequence of stages, each displacing lower ones along the way, from which there can be no return. Some stage theorists acknowledge the intra-individual diversity of moral reasoning (Rest, 1975) and thus redefine stage progression as a shifting distribution of mixed modes of thinking that are affected by many environmental factors. This does reduce the mismatch between theory and actuality. But it raises this question: Why adhere to a stage doctrine stripped of its major defining properties: change by structural displacement, steplike discontinuity, uniformity of cognitive structure, and judgment unarbitrated by either the situational factors or the domain of activity? If stage progression is recast as a multiform, gradualistic, contextualized process, the result differs little from developmental theories that do not invoke stages.[2]

Apparent deficiencies in moral reasoning, which often are attributed to cognitive limitations or insensitivity to certain moral issues, also have been shown to depend partly on how moral thought is assessed (Chandler, Greenspan, & Barenboim, 1973; Gutkin, 1972; Hatano, 1970; Leming, 1978b). The same individuals express different types of moral judgments depending on how morally

---

2 The Editor notes that the argument structure of Bandura's critique of developmental stage theories applies, in identical form, to personality trait theories, which Bandura critiques elsewhere (Bandura, 1986, 1991b, 1999, 2011, 2015). In the most popular trait conception of the 1990s, personality traits were said to be i) universal ii) mean-level tendencies that are iii) genetically determined, uninfluenced by the environment, and thus unchanging across the life course and, ontologically, are iv) intra-individual structures with causal force (McCrae & Costa, 1996). Today, a great many writers recognize that each of those four claims has been contradicted by substantial evidence—yet still cling to some form of the original trait theory (i.e. they still "adhere to a . . . doctrine stripped of its major defining properties"). This sociology-of-science phenomenon is the reverse of Mischel's (2008) "toothbrush problem." Mischel explained that writers avoid using other's theories (as if they are toothbrushes) and seek their own, even if the other's theory is empirically validated. Conversely, writers continue to use their own theory, and avoid others', even when the unique defining claims of their theory are empirically discredited. For reviews of evidence that significant inter-individual personality traits i) vary across cultures, ii) include variability in action, not merely mean-level tendencies, iii) are environmentally influenced and thus change, and iv) cannot credibly be construed as intra-individual causal forces, see Cervone and Pervin (2023).

relevant factors are presented (e.g., verbally or through portrayals); whether conflicts are common or outlandishly rare; whether people express moral orientations in abstract opinions or specific sections applied to transgressors; and whether they judge the transgressive acts of others or give moral reasons for how they themselves would act if facing a similar moral dilemma. The view that stages constrain people to think in a uniform way is difficult to reconcile with the notable variability of moral thinking observed with even small changes in how moral conflicts are presented and judgments rendered.

Moral Judgment As Application of Multidimensional Rules

In the social cognitive view, moral thinking is a process in which multidimensional rules or standards are used to judge conduct. Situations with moral implications may contain many decisional ingredients. They may vary in importance, and may be given lesser or greater weight depending on the particular constellation of events in a given social context. Among the factors that enter into judging the reprehensibility of conduct are the nature of the transgression; its baserate of occurrence and thus degree of norm variation; perceived situational and personal motivators for action; immediate and long-range consequences of the actions; whether it produces injury to persons or to property; whether it is directed at faceless agencies or identifiable individuals; the demographic characteristics of the wrongdoers; and the characteristics of victims and their perceived blameworthiness. In dealing with moral dilemmas, people may extract, weigh, and integrate this diverse range of morally relevant information.

We saw earlier that moral rules or standards of conduct are fashioned from varied social sources including precepts, evaluative social reactions, and models of moral commitments. From such diverse experiences, people learn which factors are morally relevant and how much weight to attach to them. With increasing experience and cognitive competence, moral judgments change from single-dimensional to multidimensional rules of conduct. The more complex rules involve configural or relativistic weighting of morally relevant information. Factors that are weighed heavily in some circumstances may be disregarded or de-weighted in others.

Research has explored rules through which children weigh and integrate information in making moral judgments (Kaplan, 1989; Lane & Anderson, 1976; Surber, 1985). When considering situations that vary in degree of maliciousness and harm, children do not reason dichotomously—using harm when young and intention when older—as Piagetian theory proposed. Rather, they apply varied integration rules in which the different factors are combined additively with the same absolute weight regardless of other information, or configurally in which the amount of weight given to a factor depends on the nature of another factor. However, additive rules seem to predominate (Leon, 1980, 1982). The form of the integration rule used varies more across individuals than ages.

Parental modeling accounts for a large part of the individual differences in complexity of moral decision making (Leon, 1984). Parents differ in how they integrate information into moral judgments, ranging from a simple multidimensional rule based solely on damage done, to a composite linear rule combining intent and damage, to a more complicated configural rule that weighs damage differentially depending on intent. In their own cognitive processing of information regarding the morality of conduct, children model their parents' rules in form and complexity.

Children at all ages evaluate both intention and harm in forming their judgments, with developmental changes in the weight given these factors being gradual rather than stage like (Grueneich, 1982; Surber, 1977). Analyses that separate what judgmental factors are selected from constellations of events, what weight is given to the factors that are singled out, and the decision rule by which they are combined are especially well suited to clarify developmental changes in moral reasoning. Multifaced analyses of judgments of factorial combinations of different types of information are more informative than coding verbal protocols or selecting global attributions of whether outcomes are attributed to personal causation or to external circumstances.

More work remains to be done on how people deal with large sets of morally relevant factors, how social influences alter the weight they give to different factors, what types of combinatorial rules they use, and how these different aspects of moral judgment change with development. Humans are not particularly adept at integrating diverse information (Kahneman, Slovic, & Tversky, 1982). As in other judgmental domains, when faced with complexities in moral judgment, most people probably fall back on judgmental heuristics that overly weight a few moral factors while ignoring others that are relevant. Consistent social feedback can produce lasting changes in the rules used to judge the morality of action (Schleifer & Douglas, 1973). However, in everyday life social consensus on morality is difficult to come by, thus creating ambiguity about the correctness of judgment. In the absence of consistent feedback, reliance on convenient heuristics may become routinized to the point where moral judgments are rendered without giving much thought to individuating features of moral situations. The susceptibility of moral judgment to change depends in part on the effects of the actions it fosters. Over time, people alter what they think by experiencing the social effects of their actions.

Relation Between Moral Reasoning and Conduct

An issue that has received surprisingly little attention is the relationship between moral reasoning and moral conduct. The relationship between thought and conduct is mediated through the exercise of moral agency (Bandura, 1986; Rottschaefer, 1986). The nature of moral agency will be examined shortly. The study of moral reasoning would be of limited interest if people's moral codes and thoughts had no effect on how they behaved. In the stage theory of moral maturity, the form of moral thought is not linked to particular conduct. This is because each level of moral reasoning can be used to support or to disavow transgressive conduct. People may act prosocially or transgressively out of mutual obligation, for social approval, for duty to the social order, or for reasons of principle. A person's level of moral development may indicate the types of reasons likely to be most persuasive to that person, but it does not ensure any particular kind of conduct. The implications of the stage theory of moral maturity for human conduct are difficult to test empirically because conflicting claims are made about how moral reasoning is linked to behavior. On the one hand, it is contended that the level of moral reasoning does not sponsor a particular kind of behavior (Kohlberg, 1971a). The theory is concerned with the form of the reasoning, not with the moralness of the conduct. Hence, in studies designed to alter moral perspectives through exposure to moral argument, the same level of reasoning is used, for example, for and against stealing (Rest, Turiel, & Kohlberg, 1969). On the other hand, a positive relationship is claimed between level of moral reasoning and moral conduct—the higher the moral reasoning, the more likely is moral conduct, and the greater is the consistency between moral judgment and conduct (Kohlberg & Candee, 1984).

Studies on whether stages of moral reasoning are linked to characteristic types of conduct are inconsistent in their findings (Blasi, 1980; Kurtines & Greif, 1974). Some researchers report that moral conduct is related to the level of moral reasoning, but others have failed to find strong evidence of such a relationship. Some of the studies routinely cited as corroborating such a link have not withstood replication. Others are seen under close scrutiny as contradicting it or as uninterpretable because of methodological deficiencies (Kupfersmid & Wonderly, 1980). Moreover, relationships may disappear when controls are applied for other differences between persons at varying levels of moral reasoning, such as general intelligence (Rushton, 1975).

Efforts to verify the link between moral thought and action have raised disputes about the designation of moral conduct. Kohlberg and Candee (1984) argue that performers' intentions define their actions as moral or immoral. If the morality of conduct is defined by the intentions voiced by transgressors, then most behavior that violates the moral codes of society will come out laundered as righteous. People can easily find moral reasons to redefine their misdeeds as well-intentioned acts. They become more adept at self-serving justifications as they gain cognitive facility. Presumed intent always enters in as one factor in the social labeling of behavior (Bandura, 1973), but intention is never used as the decisive definer of conduct. A robber who had good intent would not thereby transform robbery into nonrobbery. A theory of morality must explain the determinants and the mechanisms governing transgressive conduct, not only how perpetrators justify it. This requires a broader conception of morality than is provided by a rationalistic approach cast in terms of skill in abstract reasoning. Affective factors play a vital regulative role in moral conduct.

Self-Regulatory Mechanisms in Moral Agency

The regulation of moral conduct is not achieved by disembodied moral thought or by a simple feat of willpower. To explain the relation between moral reasoning and conduct, one must specify the psychological mechanisms by which moral standards get translated into action.

In Social Cognitive Theory, transgressive conduct is regulated by two major sources of sanctions: social sanctions and internalized self-sanctions. Both operate anticipatorily. People refrain from transgressing against social sanctions because they anticipate that such conduct will bring social censure and other adverse consequences, and fear those consequences. When action is governed by internalized self-processes, people behave prosocially because they anticipate that acting well will bring self-satisfaction and self-respect; they refrain from transgressing norms because they know that antisocial conduct—even if it is not detected by external social systems—will give rise to self-reproof. Moral conduct is motivated and regulated mainly by the ongoing exercise of self-reactive influence.

Psychological Subfunctions in the Self-Regulation of Moral Conduct

This overall self-regulatory process operates through three major subfunctions: the self-monitoring of conduct; judgment of conduct in relation to personal standards and environmental circumstances; and affective self-reaction.

Self-Monitoring. To exercise self-influence, people have to monitor their behavior and their situational circumstances. The self-monitoring process is not a simple mechanical audit of performances and social instigators. Pre-existing conceptions and affective states can bias how one's actions and the instigators for it are perceived and cognitively processed.

Self-monitoring is the first step toward exercising influence over one's conduct. By itself, however, such information provides little basis for self-directed reactions—which brings us to the next self-regulatory subfunction.

Personal Standards. Observed and anticipated actions give rise to self-reactions through a judgmental function in which conduct is evaluated against moral standards. The pertinent standards are understood in situational contexts. Situations with moral implications contain many judgmental ingredients that not only vary in importance but may be given lesser or greater weight depending upon the particular constellation of events in a given moral predicament.

In dealing with moral dilemmas, people must, therefore, extract, weigh, and integrate the morally relevant information in the situations confronting them. Factors that are weighed heavily under some combinations of circumstances may be disregarded or considered of lesser import under a different set of conditions. This process of moral reasoning is guided by multidimensional rules for judging conduct.

Affective Self-Reactions. The judgmental subfunction sets the occasion for self-reactive influence. Affective self-reactions provide the mechanism by which standards regulate conduct.

The anticipatory self-respect and self-censure for actions that correspond with, or violate, personal standards serve as the regulatory influences. People do things that give them self-satisfaction and a sense of self-worth. They ordinarily refrain from behaving in ways that violate their moral standards because it will bring self-condemnation. There is no greater punishment than self-contempt. Anticipatory self-sanctions thus keep conduct in line with internal standards.

Self-Efficacy Beliefs and Moral Conduct

There is a difference between possessing self-regulatory capabilities and being able to apply them effectively and consistently under the pressure of contravening influences. Effective self-regulation of conduct requires not only self-regulatory skills but also strong self-belief in one's capabilities to effect personal control. Therefore, people's belief in their efficacy to exercise control over their own motivation, thought patterns and actions (see Chapter 3) also plays an important role in the exercise of human agency.

The stronger the perceived self-regulatory efficacy, the more perseverant people are in their self-controlling efforts and the greater is their success in resisting social pressures to behave in ways that violate their standards. A low sense of self-regulatory efficacy heightens vulnerability to social pressures for transgressive conduct.

If people encounter essentially similar constellations of events repeatedly, they need not engage in a deliberate judgmental process of weighting and integrating moral factors each time before they act. Nor need they conjure up self-sanctions anticipatorily on each occasion. Judgment and action becomes routinized. People may execute actions with little accompanying thought. However, when morally relevant factors change significantly, the change reactivates self-evaluative and other self-regulatory processes.

In Social Cognitive Theory, the self is not disembodied from social reality. People make causal contribution to their actions and the nature of their environment by exercising self-influence. However, in accord with the model of reciprocal causation, social influences affect the operation of the self system in at least three major ways. They contribute importantly to the development of self-regulatory competence. Analyses of regulation of moral action through affective self-reaction distinguish between two sources of incentive motivation operating in the process. There are the conditional self-generated incentives that provide guides and proximal motivators for moral courses of action. Then there are the more distal social incentives for holding to a moral system. Thus, the second way in which social influences contribute to morality is by providing collective support for adherence to moral standards. The third way in which social realities affect moral functioning is by facilitating selective activation and disengagement of moral self-regulation. The various psychosocial mechanisms of moral disengagement are analyzed in sections that follow. It might be noted in passing that the wealth of particularized knowledge on how self-regulatory competence is acquired and exercised (Bandura, 1986) stands in stark contrast to the ill-defined internalization processes commonly invoked in theories of morality. A complete theory of morality, whatever its theoretical allegiance, must include these verified mechanisms of self-regulation.

Interplay Between Personal and Social Sanctions

The self-regulation of conduct is not entirely an intrapsychic affair, as the more radical forms of cognitivism might lead one to believe. Nor do people operate as autonomous moral agents impervious to the social realities in which they are enmeshed. As has been reviewed, Social Cognitive Theory favors a causal model involving triadic reciprocal causation. From this interactionist perspective, moral conduct is regulated by a reciprocity of influence between thought and self-sanctions, conduct, and a network of social influences.

After standards and self-reactive functions are developed, behavior usually produces two sets of consequences: self-evaluative reactions and social effects. These two sources of consequences may operate as complementary or opposing influences on behavior.

Conduct is most congruent with moral standards when transgressive behavior is not easily self-excusable and the evaluative reactions of significant others are compatible with personal standards. Under conditions of shared moral standards, socially approvable acts are a source of self-pride and socially punishable ones are self-censured. To enhance the compatibility between personal and social influences, people generally select associates who share their standards of conduct. This ensures social support for their own system of self-evaluation (Bandura & Walters, 1959; Elkin & Westley, 1955; Emmons & Diener, 1986). Diversity of standards in a society, therefore, does not necessarily create personal conflict. Selective association can forge consistency out of diversity.

Behavior is especially susceptible to external influences in the absence of strong countervailing internal standards. People who are not much committed to personal standards adopt a pragmatic orientation, tailoring their behavior to fit whatever the situation seems to call for (Snyder & Campbell, 1982). They become adept at reading social situations and guiding their actions by expediency.

One type of conflict between social and self-produced consequences arises when individuals are socially punished for behavior they value highly. Principled dissenters and nonconformists often find themselves in this predicament. Here, the relative strength of self-approval and social censure determine whether the behavior will be restrained or expressed.

Should the threatened social consequences be severe, people hold in check self-praiseworthy acts in risky situations but perform them readily in relatively safe settings. There are individuals, however, whose sense of self-worth is so strongly invested in certain convictions that they will submit to prolonged maltreatment rather than accede to rules they regard as unjust or immoral.

People commonly experience conflicts in which they are socially pressured to engage in behavior that violates their moral standards. When self-devaluative consequences outweigh the benefits for socially accommodating behavior, the social influences do not have much sway.

However, the self-regulation of conduct operates through conditional application of moral standards. Self-sanctions can be weakened or nullified by exonerative moral reasoning and social circumstances. People display different levels of detrimental behavior and offer different types of moral reasons for it, depending on whether they find themselves in social situations that are conducive to humane or to hurtful conduct (Bandura, Underwood, & Fromson, 1975).

Because almost any conduct can be morally justified, the same moral principles can support different actions, and the same actions can be championed on the basis of different moral principles. However, moral justification is only one of many mechanisms that affect the operation of moral standards in the regulation of conduct.

Selective Activation and Disengagement of Moral Standards

Development of self-regulatory capabilities does not create an invariant control mechanism within a person, as is implied by theories of internalization that incorporate entities such as conscience or superego as continuous internal oversers of conduct. Self-reactive influences only operate when they are activated (see Chapter 4). There are many processes by which self-sanctions can be disengaged from inhumane conduct. Due to the selective activation and disengagement of standards and self-reactions, the same person, who continually possesses the same moral standards, may engage in different types of conduct in different settings as those standards are variously engaged or disengaged.

Figure 5.1 shows the four major points in the self-regulatory process at which internal moral control can be disengaged from detrimental conduct. Self-sanctions can be disengaged by reconstruing conduct, obscuring causal agency, disregarding or misrepresenting injurious consequences, and blaming and devaluing the victims.

A set of psychological mechanisms is primarily responsible for this disengagement of moral control. This chapter concludes with a review of these mechanisms of moral disengagement.

Moral Justification

One set of disengagement practices operates on the construal of the behavior itself. People do not ordinarily engage in reprehensible conduct until they have

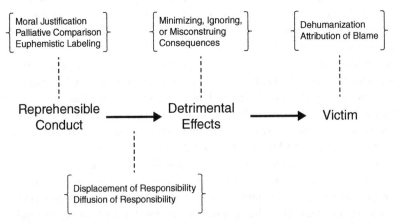

Figure 5.1 Mechanisms through which internal control is selectively activated or disengaged from reprehensible conduct at different points the regulatory process.

justified to themselves the morality of their actions. What is culpable can be made righteous through cognitive reconstrual. In this process, detrimental conduct is made personally and socially acceptable by portraying it in the service of moral purposes. People then act on a moral imperative.

Radical shifts in destructive behavior through moral justification is most strikingly revealed in military conduct. People who have been socialized to deplore killing as morally condemnable can be transformed rapidly into skilled combatants, who may feel little compunction and even a sense of pride in taking human life. The conversion of socialized people into dedicated combatants is achieved not by altering their personality structures, aggressive drives, or moral standards, but instead accomplished by cognitively restructuring the moral value of killing so that it can be done free from self-censuring restraints (Kelman, 1973; Sanford & Comstock, 1971). Through moral sanction of violent means, people view themselves as fighting ruthless oppressors who have an unquenchable appetite for conquest. They thereby see themselves as protecting cherished values and way of life, preserving world peace, saving humanity from subjugation to an evil ideology, and honoring their country's international commitments. The task of making violence morally defensible is facilitated when nonviolent options are judged to have been ineffective. Utilitarian justifications portray the suffering caused by violent counterattacks as outweighing the human suffering inflicted by the foe.

Over the years, much reprehensible and destructive conduct has been perpetrated by ordinary, decent people in the name of religious principles, righteous ideologies, and nationalistic imperatives. Individuals espousing high moral principles are inclined to resist arbitrary social demands to behave punitively, but they will aggress against people who violate their personal principles (Keniston, 1970a). Throughout history countless people have suffered at the hands of self-righteous crusaders bent on stamping out what they consider evil. Rapoport and Alexander (1982) document the lengthy blood-stained history of holy terror wrought by religious justifications. Acting on moral or ideological imperatives reflects a conscious offensive mechanism, not an unconscious defensive mechanism.

Although moral cognitive restructuring easily can be used to support self-serving and destructive purposes, it can also serve militant action aimed at changing inhumane social conditions. By appealing to morality, social reformers are able to use coercive, and even violent, tactics to force social change. Vigorous disputes arise over the morality of aggressive action directed against institutional practices. Powerholders often resist, by forcible means if necessary, making needed social changes that jeopardize their own self-interests. Resistance to warranted changes invites social activism. Challengers define their militant actions as morally justifiable means to eradicate harmful social practices. Powerholders, in turn, condemn the same acts as unwarranted violent solutions or as efforts to coerce changes that lack popular support.

Euphemistic Labeling

Language shapes the thought patterns on which people base many of their actions. Activities can take on different appearances depending on what they are called. Euphemistic language makes destructive conduct benign and thereby relieves actors of a sense of personal agency in the commission of unacceptable acts.

In an insightful analysis of the language of nonresponsibility, Gambino (1973) identifies different varieties of euphemisms. Palliative expressions are used to make the reprehensible respectable. Through hygienic words, even killing a human being may lose much of its repugnancy; soldiers "waste" people rather than kill them, intelligence operatives "terminate (them) with extreme prejudice" (Safire, 1979). When mercenaries speak of "fulfilling a contract," murder is transformed by admirable words into the honorable discharge of duty. Terrorists label themselves as "freedom fighters." Bombing attacks become "clean, surgical strikes" and the killed civilians are "collateral damage" (Hilgartner, Bell, & O'Connor, 1982). Sanitizing euphemisms, of course, perform heavy duty in less loathsome yet unpleasant activities. In some organizations, people are not fired, they are "selected out," as if receiving preferential treatment. A corporate memo speaks not of laying people off work, but of "resizing our operations." In teaching business students how to lie in competitive transactions, an instructor may speak euphemistically of "strategic misrepresentation" (Safire, 1979).

The agentless passive form serves as a linguistic device for creating the appearance that culpable acts are the work of nameless forces, rather than of people (Bolinger, 1982). This language portrays actors as not really being the agents of their acts. Instead, even inanimate objects may be invested with agency: "The telephone pole was approaching. I was attempting to swerve out of its way when it struck my front end" (San Francisco Chronicle, 1979b).

Laboratory studies reveal the disinhibitory power of euphemistic language (Diener et al., 1975). Adults behave more aggressively when assaults are given a sanitized label rather than being called aggression.

Advantageous Comparison

Whenever two events occur contiguously, the first may color how the second one is appraised. This principle can be exploited in the moral domain; judgments of a morally-relevant act can be influenced by expedient structuring of the act against which it is compared. Self-deplored acts, for example, can be made righteous by contrasting them with flagrant inhumanities. The more outrageous the comparison practices, the more likely it is that one's own destructive conduct will appear trifling or even benevolent.

In the 1960's, promoters of the Vietnamese war and their supporters, for example, minimized the slaying of countless people as a way of checking massive communist enslavement. Given the trifling comparison, perpetrators of warfare remained unperturbed by the fact that the intended beneficiaries were being killed at an alarming rate. Domestic protesters, on the other hand, characterized their own violence against educational and political institutions as trifling, or even laudable, by comparing it with the carnage perpetrated by their country's military forces in foreign lands. Analogously, terrorists minimize their slayings as the only defensive weapon they have to curb the widespread cruelties inflicted on their people.

In the eyes of their supporters, risky attacks directed at the apparatus of oppression are acts of selflessness and martyrdom. Those who are the objects of terrorist attacks, in turn, characterize their retaliatory violence as trifling, or even laudable, by comparing them with carnage and terror perpetrated by terrorists. In social conflicts, injurious behavior usually escalates with each side lauding its own behavior but morally condemning that of their adversaries as heinous.

Cognitive restructuring of behavior through moral justifications and palliative characterizations is a particularly effective means of disengaging moral self-sanctions. The restructuring not only eliminates self-deterrents. It also promotes self-approval of destructive exploits. Once destructive means become invested with high moral purpose, functionaries work hard to become proficient at them and take pride in their destructive accomplishments.

Displacement and Diffusion of Responsibility

Self-sanctions are activated most strongly when people realize, unambiguously, that they themselves are the agents responsible for detrimental effects. Such self-sanctions thus can be reduced by obscuring or distorting the relation between one's actions and harmful outcomes. People will behave in ways they normally repudiate if a legitimate authority accepts responsibility for the consequences of conduct (Diener et al., 1975; Milgram, 1974).

When displacing responsibility, people commonly view their actions as springing from the dictates of authorities rather than from their own motives and choices. Once people view themselves as not being the agents responsible for their actions, they are spared self-prohibiting reactions. Displacement of responsibility not only weakens self-restraints but also diminishes concern over the well-being of those mistreated by others (Tilker, 1970).

Exemption from self-devaluation for heinous deeds by displacement of responsibility has been most gruesomely revealed in socially sanctioned mass executions. Nazi prison commandants and their staffs divested themselves of personal responsibility for their unprecedented inhumanities (Andrus, 1969). They were simply carrying out orders. Impersonal obedience to horrific orders was similarly evident in military atrocities, such as the My Lai massacre (Kelman, 1973).

A related disengagement mechanism is diffusion of responsibility. The deterrent power of self-sanctions is weakened when the link between personal conduct and its consequences is obscured by diffusing responsibility for culpable behavior. This is achieved in several ways. Responsibility can be diffused, for example, by division of labor. Most enterprises require the services of many people, each performing fragmentary jobs that seem harmless in themselves. The fractional contribution is easily isolated from the eventual function, especially when participants exercise little personal judgment in carrying out a subfunction that is related by remote, complex links to the end result. After activities become routinized into programmed subfunctions, attention shifts from the import of what one is doing to the details of one's fractional job (Kelman, 1973).

Another practice that diffuses responsibility is group decision making. When policies are formulated collectively, no single individual feels responsible for the group's decision. As a result, otherwise considerate people may take part in inhumane group decisions that, individually, they would reject. Social organizations often go to great lengths to devise sophisticated mechanisms for obscuring responsibility for decisions that may adversely affect others.

Collective action is still another diffusion mechanism that weakens self-restraints. Any harm done by a group can always be ascribed, in large part, to the behavior of other members. People may act more harshly when individual responsibility is obscured by collective action (Bandura, Underwood, & Fromson, 1975; Diener, 1977; Zimbardo, 1969).

Disregard or Distortion of Consequences

Another form of moral disengagement involves construal of the consequences of actions. Individuals may weaken self-reactions by disregarding or misrepresenting consequences that are harmful to others. When reflecting on acts that were personally beneficial but harmful to others, people more readily recall information about the benefits than the harms (Brock & Buss, 1962, 1964). People are especially prone to minimize injurious effects when they act alone and, thus, cannot easily escape responsibility (Mynatt & Herman, 1975). In a related cognitive distortion, people may discredit the evidence of harm. Once the harmful consequences of personal conduct are ignored, minimized, distorted, or disbelieved, the self-censure that would otherwise restrain personal conduct may be disengaged.

It is relatively easy to hurt others when their suffering is not visible and one's causal actions are physically and temporally remote from their effects. Remotely-controlled weapons systems, for example, eliminate direct awareness of the weapons' consequences. By contrast, when people witness the suffering they cause, vicariously aroused distress and self-censure serve as self-restraining influences. In Milgram's (1974) studies of commanded aggression, heightened personal awareness of the victims' pain reduced obedience.

Dehumanization

A final set of disengagement practices involves the conceptualization of the recipients of harmful acts. Others may be viewed as more or less human. Perceiving others as human activates empathetic and vicarious emotional reactions to similar others. Dehumanization ("they're animals") reduces those feelings. It is difficult to mistreat humanized persons without risking personal distress and self-censure.

When given punitive power, people treat dehumanized individuals much more punitively than those invested with human qualities. Dehumanization fosters self-exonerative patterns of thought (Bandura, Underwood, & Fromson, 1975). Level of personal disapproval of punitive conduct is shaped by whether others retain, or have been deprived of, their humanness.

Assessing the Set of Moral Disengagement Mechanisms

Research on the self-regulation of moral conduct had, for many years, been hampered by a lack of measures of moral disengagement. A challenge is that disengagement mechanisms operate in concert. One must therefore devise measurement tools that assess a range of mechanisms that may impact morally-relevant conduct.

The mechanisms of moral disengagement have been measured in research by Bandura, Barbaranelli, Caprara, and Pastorelli (1996a). In a study conducted with a large number of elementary and junior high school students in a community near Rome, Italy, participants completed a self-report measure of their acceptance of statements that represented each of a wide variety of moral disengagement mechanisms. Items measured, for example, endorsement of moral justification ("It is alright to fight when your group's honour is threatened"), euphemistic language ("To hit obnoxious classmates is just giving them 'a lesson'"), distorting consequences ("Teasing someone does not really hurt them"), and dehumanization of victims ("Someone who is obnoxious does not deserve to be treated like a human being"). In addition, the researchers obtained data from the children, parents, peers, and teachers indicating the given child's levels of prosocial, aggressive, and transgressive behavior.

Path analyses revealed that moral disengagement influenced morally-relevant conduct not only directly but also indirectly. For example, when predicting levels of aggressive behavior, moral disengagement predicted higher levels of aggression proneness (a latent factor consisting of hostile rumination and irascibility) and lower levels of prosocial behavior (i.e., kind and cooperate actions). In turn, prosocial behavior was negatively related, and aggression proneness was strongly positively related, to aggressive behavior. Overall, the findings indicate that those who endorse moral disengagement mechanisms tend to engage in patterns of thought and to experience emotions that are conducive to conduct that is detrimental to others. High moral disengagers are more readily angered, more prone to ruminate about grievances, and ultimately more likely to engage in conduct that transgresses moral norms (Bandura et al., 1996).

Power of Humanization

Psychological research tends to focus on the ease with which one can bring out the worst in people through dehumanization and other self-exonerative means. Such findings draw the greatest attention. Milgram's obedience studies, for example, are widely cited as evidence that good people can be talked into performing cruel deeds. However, in that work, to get people to carry out punitive acts the overseer had to be physically present, repeatedly ordering them to act cruelly while overriding their concerns and objections. When orders were issued remotely, commands to escalate punishment to intense levels were largely ignored or subverted. As Helm and Morelli (1979) noted, this is hardly blind obedience to an authoritative mandate. Moreover, what is rarely noted, is the equally striking evidence that most people steadfastly refuse to behave punitively, even in response to strong authoritarian commands, if the situation was personalized by their seeing the victim or by inflicting pain directly rather than remotely.

The emphasis on obedient aggression is understandable. Harmful actions and inhumanities are prevalent throughout society. However, the power of humanization to counteract cruelty (e.g., Bandura et al., 1975) also is of major theoretical and social significance.

The moderating influence of humanization is sometimes revealed in situations involving great threat of violence. Abductors may find it difficult to harm hostages after they have gotten to know them personally. With growing acquaintance, it becomes increasingly difficult to take a human life cold-bloodedly. The affirmation of common humanity can bring out the best in others.

6

Applying Science for Human Betterment

The field of psychology sometimes does not profit from its theoretical advances. When this occurs, it mostly reflects the lack of creative translational and social diffusion models. These are the vital, but weakest, links in the field of social change. Historically, researchers have devoted much attention to developing theories and to testing their predictive validity, but less attention to exploiting their utility for social welfare. In the final analysis, the evaluation of a science of personal and social change will rest heavily on its social utility.

The present chapter explains how the basic principles of Social Cognitive Theory, presented in Chapters 1–5, have been and can continue to be applied to the solution of individual and macrosocial problems. Social Cognitive Theory, as you have seen, does not merely describe what people "are like." It provides tools that facilitate personal and social change. One thus can evaluate the theory not only by contrasting it with alternative perspectives on human nature, as previous chapters often have done, but also by assessing its success in promoting changes that significantly better the quality of peoples' lives. This translation of theory to beneficial application is the focus of this book's final chapter.

The chapter addresses an array of applications. They range across areas that include literacy, population growth, and the health of our planet. But we begin with the pressing concern of human health.

Social Cognitive Theory and Health Promotion

Health status is especially critical to individual welfare because it can affect one's entire lifestyle. Disease and chronic disability compromise the quality of life that people lead.

Social Cognitive Theory: An Agentic Perspective on Human Nature, First Edition. Albert Bandura.
© 2023 John Wiley & Sons, Inc. Published 2023 by John Wiley & Sons, Inc.

Society has developed means to promote health and reduce the risk of disease. But these contemporary biomedical technologies and services, which do benefit so many, remain inaccessible to vast segments of the world's population. The health applications described in this chapter are initial steps in the development of models that hold promise of providing universal access to health promotive services that can advance the health of populations worldwide.

Health Promotion Systems Founded on Self-Regulation Principles

The field of health is witness to divergent emphases. On the one hand, societies—especially in the industrialized world—have for many years poured massive resources into medicalizing diseases: diagnosing then when they occur and developing treatments that alleviate their symptoms and, ideally, bring cures. But the fact that so many diseases result substantially from detrimental health habits leads to a second emphasis: The conception of health is shifting from a disease model to a health model. Rather than waiting for the ravages of disease to occur and then treating them, the health model is proactive. It emphasizes health promotion rather than mainly disease management. It is just as meaningful to speak of levels of vitality and healthfulness as of degrees of impairment and debility.

Health promotion should begin with goals, not means (Norden, 1999). The goal plainly is health. Biomedical interventions are not the only means of promoting health. Health quality is heavily influenced by lifestyle habits—which is good news. It means that people can exercise some measure of control over the state of their health. To stay healthy, people should exercise, reduce dietary fat, refrain from smoking, keep blood pressure down, and develop effective ways of managing stressors. By managing these health habits, people can live longer and healthier, and can retard the process of aging. Self-management is good medicine. If the huge benefits of health habits were put into a pill, one would declare it a scientific milestone in medicine.[1]

Healthy habits, however, do not offer a quick fix to health problems. Health gatekeepers thus are more inclined to write drug prescriptions than behavioral prescriptions. Current health practices focus heavily on the medical supply side. But the days of an exclusively supply-side health system are limited. People are living longer, which creates more time for minor dysfunction to develop into chronic diseases.

---

1 Cellular mechanisms through which behavioral factors such as diet and stress influence the aging process are revealed in research documenting that these factors influence the internal environment of the body in ways that, in turn, can reduce telomere length (Epel, 2009; Lin & Epel, 2022). Telomeres protect cells' chromosomes; thus, their shortening accelerates the aging process.

The social cognitive approach which, as you have seen, is rooted in an agentic model of human nature, focuses on the demand side of health promotion. The agentic focus draws attention to the self-management of health habits. People have the capacity to take actions that can keep them healthy through their life span. Psychosocial factors in interaction with personal capabilities influence whether the extended life is lived efficaciously or with debility, pain, and dependence (Fries & Crapo, 1981; Fuchs, 1974). Aging populations will force societies to redirect their efforts from supply-side practices to demand-side remedies. Absent such focus, nations will be swamped with staggering health costs that consume valuable resources needed for national programs.

The self-regulation skills discussed earlier (see Chapter 4) underpin the maintenance of healthful habits. Whatever social factors may serve as guides and motivators, they are unlikely to produce lasting behavioral changes unless individuals develop the means to exercise personal control over health-promoting behaviors. To regulate their health practices, people have to engage in the self-regulatory skills discussed previously: monitoring their behavior to diagnose where changes need to be made; setting goals for health-promoting achievements; and adhering to self-standards that trigger self-evaluative reactions to performances. Long-term health goals set the course of personal change, but are too distant to override the many competing influences on current behavior. In the health domain, as in others, short-term goals provide the guides, strategies, and motivators for the changes needed in the here and now.

Health Promotion through Self-Management

Health promotion and risk reduction programs are often structured in ways that are costly, cumbersome, and minimally effective. The net result is minimal prevention and costly remediation. Contemporary interactive technologies, however, now enable one to deliver personalized programs to promote health to large numbers of people, efficiently and inexpensively. A single program implementor, assisted by a computerized system, can oversee the self-managed behavioral changes of hundreds of participants concurrently. Such systems are effective guides to, and motivators of, self-directed change when they prompt participants to set short-range attainable subgoals and provide people with detailed feedback on their goal progress. As we saw in Chapter 4, neither goals without knowing how one is doing, nor knowing how one is doing without specific goals, has any motivational impact.

Knowledge of the major subfunctions of self-regulation, as well as of the contribution of self-efficacy beliefs to health behavior, has informed the development of self-management models that promote habits conducive to health. Consider applications to cardiovascular health. Debusk and colleagues implemented a computer-assisted program designed to promote behaviors that contribute to cardiovascular well-being (DeBusk et al., 1994). Their self-regulatory system equipped participants with the skills and personal efficacy to exercise self-directed change in a variety of health-relevant areas: exercise, weight reduction, smoking cessation, and the maintenance of healthy nutrition. For each of these behavioral factors, participants received detailed guides to the maintenance of behaviors that promote health. At selected intervals, they also received individually-tailored guides to change that provided attainable subgoals for progressive change. Computerized feedback portrayed graphically the progress patients made toward each of their subgoals, while also suggesting strategies to surmount difficulties. A program implementor maintained telephone contact with participants to provide extra guidance if needed.

The preventive value of this self-management system was tested in a cholesterol reduction program. The participants, employees drawn from work sites, were individuals with elevated cholesterol levels. Among these individuals, the self-management program proved highly effective. With the aid of the program, these individuals reduced their consumption of saturated fat and lowered their serum cholesterol (DeBusk et al., 1994). They achieved an even larger risk reduction if their spouses took part in the dietary change program.

Further studies have attested to the efficacy of the self-management system in reducing plasma cholesterol (Clark, et al., 1997; DeBusk et al., 1999). This work has shown that, thanks to the self-management skills that patients acquire, a substantial proportion of patients are able to lower their cholesterol by dietary means alone. Their self-directed success spares them both the costs and the side effects of cholesterol-lowering medications.

Haskell also used a self-management system to promote lifestyle changes in patients suffering from coronary artery disease (Haskell et al., 1994). This program targeted risk factors such as smoking, exercise, weight, and nutrition. After four years, patients in the self-management programs achieved substantial gains that exceeded those receiving the usual medical care. The program also altered disease progression, with those receiving the self- management program having, for example, 47% less buildup of plaque on artery walls.[2]

People consume a lot of foods high in sodium, which is linked to hypertension that, if left unchecked, increases the risk of stroke, heart disease, and kidney failure. Sodium-reduction programs can lower blood pressure sufficiently to reduce the need for antihypertensive medication, or even to discontinue it altogether

---

2 Recent years have seen the widespread deployment of mobile phone technologies to deliver self-management interventions for hypertension and the management of coronary heart disease. Meta-analyses document the effectiveness of these self-management programs, but with some variations in findings that suggest a need for continued research on the difficult challenge of medical adherence (Li et al., 2020; Sua et al., 2020).

(Whelton, et al., 1998), especially if combined with other lifestyle changes (Reid, et al., 1994). West and collaborators demonstrated the effectiveness of a self-management system that was designed to help patients with heart disease to cut back on sodium intake (West, et al., 1999). Foods high in sodium content were targeted for dietary change. Training in self-management enhanced patients' perceived self-efficacy to adopt a low sodium diet. Thanks to the training, patients not only reduced sodium to the target level, but also maintained the desired dietary change over time. At each point in the self-change program, higher self-efficacy beliefs predicted greater reduction in sodium intake.

Even among patients requiring antihypertensive medication, there is a significant behavioral component: adherence, or not, to prescribed medical regimens (Rudd, 1997). The challenge of adherence is particularly difficult with nonsymptomatic disorders, where drug routines have no noticeable health benefits while causing unpleasant side effects. In randomized controlled studies, Rudd and his collaborators (2002) found that hypertensive patients who received drug therapy via the self-management system were more adherent and achieved greater blood pressure reduction than patients receiving the usual physician care.

The self-management model combines the individualization of clinical applications with the large-scale applicability of the public health approaches. This system generally is well received by patients because it is tailored to their needs, provides personalized guidance, and provides informative feedback that enables self-control over health-relevant change.

The interactive capabilities of electronic technologies also have been enlisted for health promotion in children. Interactive video games have been used to raise children's perceived efficacy and enable them to manage chronic health conditions (Lieberman & Brown, 1995). In a video role-playing game for diabetic children, children won points depending on how well they understood the diabetic condition and regulated the diet, insulin, and blood sugar levels of two wacky diabetic pachyderms (Brown et al., 1997). They set out to retrieve diabetic supplies snatched by pesky enemy critters in a diabetes summer camp. The better the children manage the meals, blood glucose, and insulin dosage to stay in the safe zone of the elephants, the more stolen insulin they recover. Children quickly become experts in how to manage diabetes, with higher self-efficacy beliefs and better dietary and insulin practices that are maintained over time. [Oh et al. (2022) review 74 studies that have used digital media to promote health globally among children and adolescents.]

Asthmatic children have learned self-management skills thanks to a helpful asthmatic dinosaur named Bronchiasaurus. In a gaming environment, children learn to manage their character's asthma by avoiding asthma triggers, keeping the air free of respiratory irritants, tracking peak flow, and taking medication (Lieberman, 2001). The role-playing simulation raised the children's own self-efficacy for asthma self-care in comparison to merely watching an instructive video on how to manage asthma.

Self-Management of Chronic Diseases

Another domain that illustrates how an agentic theory can be translated into effective applications is the management of chronic disease. Such diseases do not lend themselves well to biomedical approaches devised primarily for acute illness. The treatment of chronic disease must focus on self-management of physical conditions over time, to retard the potential progression from impairment to disability.

A prototypic model for the self-management of chronic diseases was devised by Holman and Lorig (1992). People were taught cognitive pain control techniques, self-relaxation, and proximal goal setting combined with self-incentives as motivators to increase level of activity. They also were taught problem solving and self-diagnostic skills for monitoring and interpreting changes in their health status, skills in locating community resources and managing medication programs. The effectiveness of this self-management approach was tested with patients suffering from arthritis. They received instruction from program implementors who themselves suffered similar physical impairments but overcame them in their daily life. These role models of success inspired participants while providing them with instructive guides and incentives for personal change. The program greatly increased patients' beliefs in self-efficacy for exerting control over their physical condition. People with higher perceived self-efficacy were less disabled by their arthritis, reported less pain experience, and experienced reduced joint inflammation (O'Leary, Shoor, Lorig, & Holman, 1988). A 4-year follow-up showed that the self-management program fostered prolonged health benefits (Lorig, Chastain, Ung, Shoor, & Holman, 1989; Lorig, Seleznick, et al., 1989). [Meta-analyses also have shown that digitally delivered arthritis self-management programs can reduce pain and improve physical functioning, Safari et al., 2020.]

Different types of chronic diseases present overlapping problems: pain management; overcoming physical impairments; maintaining self-sufficiency; accessing medical services. The self-management approach, therefore, is a generic model that is adaptable to diverse conditions (Lorig et al., 1999). Across multiple diseases, compared to nontreated controls, those who benefit from self-management programs tend to make greater use of cognitive symptom management, reported better health; less fatigue, disability, and distress over their physical condition; and fewer everyday limitations. They also tend to experience fewer hospitalizations and shorter hospital stays. Adding to the generic model mastery components that address disease-specific problems may further enhance health benefits.

Internet-Based Health Promotion Systems

Vast populations worldwide have no access to services that promote health by modifying behavioral habits with long-term health risk. Solving this problem of access requires the development of implementational models with global reach that are readily adaptable to diverse populations. Internet-based psychosocial health programs can enable people worldwide to exercise some control over their health, at a time of their own choosing and at little cost. People at risk for health problems may ignore preventive or remedial services that they must access in person, but may embrace online services that are convenient while also providing a higher feeling of anonymity.

A growing body of evidence based on randomized controlled trials attests to the potential of online self-management programs. Consider two examples. In research on anorexia and bulimia, which are serious health problems among adolescent girls and young women, Taylor and colleagues developed online programs for young women that reduced dissatisfaction with body weight and shape, altered dysfunctional attitudes, and prevented the onset of eating disorders in women at risk of developing such disorders (Taylor, et al., 2006; Taylor, Winzelberg, & Celio, 2001). In an internet-based program for smoking reduction, Muñoz and colleagues provided participants with instruction in how to quit smoking, how to cope with relapse, and how to refuse offered cigarettes (Muñoz, et al. 2006).

Medical service providers often are ill-equipped to promote health by psychosocial means; they lack both the expertise and the time needed to develop clients' self-management skills. To achieve results, physicians would have to assess their clients' social realities, have good strategies to offer for personal change, manage resistance, gauge progress and readjust strategies accordingly, and motivate patients to stick with their efforts through failures and setbacks. Not surprisingly, physicians report a low sense of efficacy to alter detrimental health habits (Hyman, Maibach, Flora, & Fortmann, 1992). Physicians give up trying when they doubt that they can affect behavioral change. Evidence-based self-management systems can provide physicians with the option of behavioral prescriptions to online health-promotion programs that are of demonstrated effectiveness. If online self-management programs are proven more effective in randomized controlled trials than the usual medical service or drug regimens, then behavioral prescriptions should be instituted as a regular part of health care systems.

Societal efforts to get people to adopt healthful practices rely heavily on public health campaigns. These population-based approaches promote changes mainly in people with high perceived self-regulatory efficacy for and positive expectations that the prescribed changes will improve their health. However, there is only so much that large-scale health campaigns can do on their own, regardless of whether they are tailored or generic. Public health campaigns provide a convenient way to link people to online systems that can provide the intensive, personalized guidance they need.

Macrosocial Applications Addressing Urgent Global Problems

The most ambitious applications of Social Cognitive Theory are those that aim to abate global problems. Consider some problems faced by our world. Soaring population growth has severe ecological consequences, including the destruction of ecosystems that sustain life. Population shifts from rural to urban areas create mega-cities with millions living under squalid conditions and lacking life's necessities. As Cleland and collaborators (2006) explain, a strategy for addressing this issue that is unique in its scope of benefits is the promotion of family planning. Family planning can reduce the cycle of poverty, decrease maternal and child mortality, liberate women for personal development by relieving the burden of excessive childbearing, contribute to achievement of universal primary education, and aid environmental sustainability by stabilizing the planet's population [which is projected to increase from 8 to more than 11 billion by the end of the century (United Nations, 2022)]. Efforts to reduce energy consumption at the individual level will be swamped by the large increase in the number of consumers worldwide.

The global ecosystem cannot sustain burgeoning population growth and high consumption of finite natural resources indefinitely. Humans, by wielding powerful technologies that amplify control over the environment, are producing hazardous global changes of huge magnitude—deforestation, desertification, global warming, glacial melting, flooding of low-lying coastal regions, topsoil erosion and sinking of water tables in the major food-producing regions, depletion of fisheries, and degradation of other aspects of the earth's life-support systems. Expanding economies that fuel consumptive growth by billions of people will continue to intensify competition for the earth's vital resources, overwhelming efforts to secure an environmentally and economically sustainable future. These practices are neither economically nor environmentally sustainable, because they destroy their own environmental basis. Through collective practices driven by a foreshortened perspective, humans may be well on the road to outsmarting themselves into irreversible ecological crises.

Another widespread problem is the pernicious gender inequality in familial, educational, health, and social life. In multiple societies, women continue to be subjugated and denied liberty, dignity and opportunities to develop their talents. This is ethically indefensible in any historical era. But, in the current one, it additionally is counterproductive economically. The demands of an information era favor intelligence over brawn. Societies that marginalize or subjugate women—who, of course, constitute approximately half of their population—undermine their own social, technological, and economic viability by neglecting this vast human resource. Fostering the talents and social rights of women provides nations with powerful leverage for national development and renewal. The same is true for ethnic minorities.

Epidemics are another mounting global problem. Whether it is the AIDS epidemic or the COVID-19 crisis,[3] biomedical problems can be countered with behavioral strategies through which people can reduce their disease risk.

Televised Modeling for Society-Wide Change

How can psychological interventions be delivered at a large-enough scale to make even a dent in problems of global scope? One valuable strategy came to my attention through a most fortuitous phone call.

One morning, I was contacted by Miguel Sabido, a creative producer at Televisia in Mexico City. He explained that he was developing long-running serial dramas founded on Social Cognitive Theory's principles of modeling (see Chapter 2). The dramas were designed to promote literacy and family planning in Mexico (Sabido, 1981).

Sabido's strategy for these productions was to dramatize people's everyday lives and the problems they have to manage. The enabling dramas help viewers to see a better life and provide them with strategies and incentives that enable them to take steps to achieve it. The long running serial dramas serve as the principal vehicle for promoting personal and social changes. Productions bring life to people's everyday struggles and the consequences of different social practices. The storylines speak ardently to people's fears, hopes, and aspirations for a better life. They inform, enable, motivate, and guide viewers for potentially life-altering personal and social change.

The dramatic productions are not just fanciful stories. They deal with the sometimes harsh realities of life and the impediments with which people struggle. Storylines model contemporary issues and life strategies: family planning, women's equality, degrading dowry systems, spouse abuse, environmental conservation, AIDS prevention, and a variety of life skills. The episodes engage viewers in the evolving lives of characters who model the challenges and strategies of life.

---

3 Riley et al. (2021) review efforts to combat the COVID-19 crisis that employ the strategy Bandura reviews in the immediately upcoming section of this text, broadcast education-entertainment.

There are three major components to this social cognitive approach to fostering society-wide changes (Bandura, 2001b). The first component is a theoretical model. It specifies the determinants of psychosocial change and the mechanisms through which they produce their effects. This knowledge provides the guiding principles. The second component is a translational and implementational model that converts theoretical principles into an operational model with specified content, change strategies, and a mode of implementation. The third component is a social diffusion model designed to promote adoption of psychosocial programs in diverse cultural milieus. Population Communications International (PCI) and the Population Media Center (PMC) serve as the global diffusion mechanisms (Poindexter, 2004; Ryerson, 1999). These two nonprofit organizations raise funds from various sources to cover production costs and provide the given nations' media personnel with instructive guidance and technical assistance to create engrossing serial dramas tailored to the particular cultural milieus. The creative process is a collaborative partnership with the host country's production teams.

Cultural and Value Analyses

These serial dramas are not foisted on nations by outsiders pursuing self-interest. The dramatic serials are created only on invitation by countries seeking help with intractable problems. The host production team, drawing on a wide variety of sources, including public health systems, religious organizations, women's groups and other constituencies identify unique cultural life conditions, social practices and prevailing values, and itemize the types of changes the dramatizations should address. These data provide the culturally relevant information for developing realistic characters and engrossing functional plotlines. Once a program is aired, producers monitor how viewers perceive the characters, with whom they are identifying, how they view the obstacles and the dramatized options, and the types of futures they envision.

Value disputes are often fueled by wrangling over stereotypes with emotive surplus meanings rather than deliberating about changes in real-life terms. But in the broadcast productions, value issues are cast in concrete terms that portray the tangible detriments and benefits of particular lifestyles. The tangible values embody respect for human dignity and equitable familial, social, health and educational opportunities that support common human aspirations; indeed, the dramatizations are grounded in internationally endorsed human values that are codified in United Nations' covenants and resolutions. The dramas enable viewers to see how alternative life options can affect the course of life. They thereby assist people to make informed lifestyle choices.

Elements of Enabling Serials

Four basic principles guide the construction of the dramatic serials. The first principle enlists the power of social modeling for personal and social change.

Social Modeling. Seeing people similar to themselves change their lives for the better not only conveys strategies for how to do it, but raises viewers' sense of efficacy that they too can succeed. Viewers come to admire and are inspired by characters in their likenesses who struggle with difficult obstacles and eventually overcome them.

Three types of contrasting models are used to highlight the personal and social effects of different styles of behavior. The episodes include positive models portraying beneficial lifestyles. Other characters personify negative models exhibiting detrimental views and lifestyles. Transitional models are shown transforming their lives by discarding detrimental styles of behavior in favor of beneficial ones. Viewers are especially prone to draw inspiration from, and identify with, transforming models by seeing them surmount similar adverse life circumstances.

Vicarious Motivators. The second feature of the dramatic productions enlists vicarious motivators as incentives for change. Unless people see the modeled lifestyle as improving their welfare they have little incentive to adopt it. The personal and social benefits of the favorable practices, and the costs of the detrimental ones are vividly portrayed. Depicted beneficial outcomes instill outcome expectations that serve as positive incentives for change, whereas depicted detrimental outcomes create negative outcome expectations that function as disincentives.

Efforts at social change typically challenge power relations and entrenched societal practices supported by individuals who have a vested interest in preserving the adverse practices. Successes do not come easily. To change their lives for the better, people have to challenge adverse traditions and inequitable constraints. They must be prepared for the obstacles they are likely to encounter. There are several ways of building resilience to impediments through social modeling. Prototypical problem situations and effective ways of overcoming them are modeled. People are taught how to manage setbacks by modeling how to recover from failed attempts. They are shown how to enlist guidance and social support for personal change from self-help groups and other agencies in their localities. Seeing others succeed through perseverant effort also boosts staying power in the face of obstacles.

Attentional and Emotional Engagement. To change deeply held beliefs and social practices requires strong emotional bonding to enabling models who exemplify a vision of a better future and realistic paths to it. Plotlines that dramatize viewers' everyday lives and functional solutions get them deeply involved. They form emotional ties to models who speak to their hopes and aspirations. Unlike brief exposures to media presentations that typically leave most viewers untouched, ongoing engagement in the evolving lives of the models provides numerous opportunities to learn from them and to be inspired by them.

In a radio serial drama in India, with a listenership of about 25 million, a mother challenges restrictive cultural norms for her daughter Taru, and promotes her education. Taru inspired formerly illiterate teenagers who had no access to education to become avid readers and pursue their schooling. Here is an example of Taru's powerful impact on teenage listeners: "*There are moments when I feel that Taru is directly talking to me, usually at night. She is telling me, 'Usha, you can follow your dreams.' I feel she is like my elder sister . . . and giving me encouragement.*" Modeling after the educational practices of Taru's mother, one of the viewers created a school for illiterate women. Several teenage girls started a school for poor children, who attend classes around the village water well. The teenagers fight for social justice, for gender equality, against class discrimination and forced teenage marriage. Their efforts alter community norms to fit the changing times.

In another serial drama in India, 400,000 viewers sent letters supporting, advising, or criticizing the various models in the drama. In a serial in Tanzania, women spotted a negative role model at a market and drove him out under a rain of tomatoes and mangos. In Brazil, 10,000 people showed up for a filming of a marriage of two of the characters in a serial drama.

Environmental Supports. Efforts to motivate change have little effect unless people also are provided with resources and environmental supports to realize the changes they desire. The serial dramas thus aim to enlist and create environmental supports, as an additional aid in the overall goal of developing and sustaining the changes promoted by the given media effort.

To achieve and sustain change, the dramatic productions are designed to operate through two pathways. In a direct pathway, the serials promote change by informing, enabling, motivating, and guiding individual viewers. In a socially-mediated pathway, program elements connect viewers to valuable social networks and community settings. These groups and places provide continued personalized guidance, as well as natural incentives and social supports for desired changes. The major share of behavioral and valuational changes are promoted within these social milieus. In addition, epilogues delivered by culturally admired figures provide contact information to relevant community services and support groups.

Global Applications

There have been many applications, worldwide, of the sociocognitive serial drama strategy. Efforts in Africa, Asia, and Latin America have promoted personal and society-wide changes that have bettered the lives of millions. Some of these applications are reviewed here; more extensive reviews are in Bandura (2002) and Singhal, Cody, Sabido, & Rogers (2004).

Literacy. Literacy is vital for personal and national development. To reduce widespread illiteracy, the Mexican government launched a national self-study program. People who were skilled at reading were urged to organize small self-study groups in which they would teach others how to read with primers developed for this purpose. It was a good idea but enlisted few takers. Sabido therefore created a year-long serial with daily episodes to reach, enable, and motivate people to enlist in the program. A popular performer was cast in the role of the literate model. She recruits a diverse set of characters to represent the different segments of the population with problems of illiteracy. Assumed similarity enhances the power of social modeling.

A prior interview survey revealed several personal barriers that dissuaded people from enrolling in the literacy program. Many believed that they lacked the capabilities to master such a complex skill. Others believed that reading skills could be acquired only when one is young as the critical period was long gone. Still others felt that they were unworthy of having an educated person devote their time to them. These self-dissuading misbeliefs were modeled by the various characters and corrected by the mentor as she persuades them that they possess the capabilities to succeed.

The episodes included humor, conflicts, and engrossing discussions of the subjects being read. They portrayed the characters struggling in the initial phases of learning, and then gaining progressive mastery with self-pride in their accomplishments. To provide vicarious motivators to pursue the self-education program, the dramatic series depicted the substantial benefits of literacy both for personal development and for national efficacy and pride. One of the epilogues, by an admired movie star, informed the viewers of this national self-education program and encouraged them to take advantage of it. The next day 25,000 people showed up at the distribution center to enroll in the self-study program.

Millions of viewers watched this series faithfully. Compared to nonviewers, viewers of the dramatic series were much more informed about the national literacy program and expressed more positive attitudes about helping one another to learn. Enrollment in the literacy program was relatively low in the year before the televised series, but rose abruptly during the year of the broadcast (Sabido, 1981). As people develop a sense of efficacy and competencies that enable them to exercise better control over their lives, they serve as models, inspiration, and even tutors for others in the circles in which they travel. In the year following the televised series, another 400,000 people enrolled in the self-study literacy program.

Family Planning. Another serial drama in Mexico promoted family planning, as a means of confronting the social problem of unplanned childbearing and the cycle of poverty it can bring. The benefits of family planning were portrayed through a storyline that contrasted the lives of two married sisters. One experienced the benefits of life in a small family. The other was burdened with the responsibilities of a huge family living in impoverishment and hopelessness. Much of the drama focused on the married daughter from the huge family living in her parents' despairingly crowded and destitute environment. She had two children and was pregnant with the third; experienced marital conflict; was distressed over her desire for a voice in family life; and wanted to cease having babies who would be condemned to share an impoverished family life with inadequate personal care and supports. This woman and her husband served as a transition model; as the drama unfolded, the couple gained control over their family life with the help of a family planning center. This control, in turn, beneficially changed their family life. Televised epilogues informed viewers of family planning services, in order to facilitate the media-promoted changes.

The program proved to have its intended effect. Compared to nonviewers, heavy viewers were more likely to link lower childbearing to social, economic, and psychological benefits (Sabido, 1981). They also developed a more positive attitude toward helping others plan their family. Family planning centers reported a 32% increase in new contraceptive users over the number for the previous year. People reported that the televised program was the impetus for consulting the health clinics. National sales of contraceptives rose from low in the baseline years to a substantial increase in the year the program was aired.

The Status of Women. Efforts to reduce the rate of population growth must address not only the strategies and benefits of family planning but also the role and status of women, who are treated subserviently in so many societies. Gender inequity results sometimes from machismo dominance; sometimes from traditions in which women have no say in in the choice of husband or the number and spacing of children; and sometimes from dispossession by polygamous marriages.

A serial drama strategy designed to raise the status of women, as well as to promote a smaller family norm has been employed in India. The nation faces challenges. Its population not only is large but is growing at a pace that will make it the most populous of nations before the conclusion of the first third of this century. Its traditions commonly exclude women from decision making and positions of power. The serial drama in India addressed themes about family life in this sociohistorical context (Singhal & Rogers, 1999). Subthemes devoted particular attention to elevation of women's status in family, social, and economic life, and to educational opportunities and career options for women, son preference and gender bias in child rearing, the detriment of dowry requirements, choice in spouse selection, teenage marriage and parenthood, spousal abuse, family planning, youth delinquency, and community development. Some characters personified positive role models for gender equality, others supported women's traditional subservient roles, and yet others were transitional models. Epilogues reinforced the modeled messages.

The series, which was immensely popular, fostered more equitable attitudes toward women. The more aware viewers were of the messages being modeled, the greater was their support of women's freedom of choice in matters that affect them and limiting family size (Brown & Cody, 1991; Singhal & Rogers, 1999). Intensive interviews with village inhabitants revealed that the dramatizations sparked serious public discussions about the broadcast themes concerning child marriages, dowry requirements, education of girls, the benefits of small families, and other social issues (Papa, et al., 2000). The enrollment of girls in elementary and junior high schools rose from 10% to 38% in one year of the broadcasts.

A serial drama in Kenya illustrated the creative tailoring of storylines to cultural values. Land ownership is highly valued in Kenya. A dramatic storyline thus linked the impoverishing effect of large families to the inheritance of land. The production featured contrasting models: two brothers, one with a wife, son, and several daughters, and the other with multiple wives and larger numbers of sons and daughters. They squabble over how to pass on the inherited family farm to their next generation. In Kenya, only sons can inherit property. The monogamous brother argues that his lone male heir is entitled to half the land, the polygamous brother insists on dividing the farm into ten small plots which would provide, at best, a marginal subsistence for them all. In another concurrent plotline, a teacher pleads with parents, who want their young daughter to quit school, be circumcised and married off to an arranged partner, to allow her to continue her education, which she desperately desires.

The serial drama, broadcast via radio to reach rural areas, was very popular, attracting 40% of the Kenyan population each week. It also was very effective, as documented in quantitative analyses with multiple statistical controls for possible determinants (Westoff & Rodriguez, 1995). Contraceptive use increased by 58%, and desired family size declined 24%. A survey of women who came to health clinics reported that the radio series helped to persuade their husbands to allow them to seek family planning. Internal analyses of evaluation surveys further revealed that the media influence was a major factor in raising motivation to limit birthrate and adopt contraception practices.

In China, a serial drama addressed discriminatory gender norms and practices. This televised drama, which won numerous prestigious awards, employed intersecting plots to address a variety of societal issues: girl's education, arranged marriages, coerced pregnancy, son preference, and allowing women to have some voice in their lives. Dramatizations graphically portrayed the tragedy and injustice of social practices that force women into arranged marriages they do not want and that devalue baby girls. These issues are particularly pressing in our current age. Information technologies transform economic needs from brawn to intellect. Norms that impede women's independent entry into workforces are counter-productive for women and a nation's overall economy. The televised series tried to improve norms to match the challenges and opportunities of this era.

In this series, a father is desperate to receive a dowry payment so he can buy a bride for his son, his pride and joy. He demands that his daughter agree to an arranged marriage to an arrogant man of means. She resists because she is in love with a musician of modest means. But to spare her younger sister, who the father targets next, she eventually agrees to the arranged marriage. During the wedding procession, he shouts to her and plays a tune he played when they first met. Her husband, enraged by the boyfriend's intrusion, kicks out the guests after the wedding ceremony and rapes her. She finds herself trapped in a miserable marriage with an abusive husband. As the story unfolds, she gives birth to a female infant. He demands she get pregnant again to bear him a son. She leaves him, remarries, and pursues a successful career.

Viewers were inspired and strengthened by the determination and courage of female characters who challenged the subordinate status of women and strove to change detrimental cultural practices. The serial's central figure became an admired national model for valuing women and expanding their social and economic opportunities in Chinese society.

AIDS and Sexual Health. In Tanzania, a serial drama program targeted both family planning and sexual practices that increase vulnerability to infection with the AIDS virus, a raging epidemic at the time of the broadcast (Rogers, et al., 1999). At the time, the populace generally was well informed about contraception and AIDS prevention and was not unfavorably disposed toward such practices. People had access to contraceptive methods and family planning clinics. But positive attitudes did not translate into action. When other influences conflict with personal attitudes, people can find reasons to justify exemptions to them (as discussed in Chapter 5). The problem thus was not informational or attitudinal, but motivational. The dramatic series provided the impetus for change.

Of relevance to the study design is that the nation contains regions with separate radio transmitters. This enables an experimental comparison of the effectiveness of the serial drama. The series was broadcast on radio to one major region of the country, with another region serving as a control group. This experimental comparison verified the program's effectiveness. In comparison to the control region, the dramatizations raised viewers' perceived efficacy to determine their family size, increased the ideal age of marriage for women and approval of family planning methods, decreased desired number of children, stimulated spousal communication about family size, and enhanced use of family planning services and contraceptive methods (Rogers, et al., 1999). Study effects were replicated when the serial was later broadcast in the control region. The fertility rate declined more in the 2-year period of the serial dramas than in the previous 30 years without any change in socioeconomic conditions and little change in death rate (Vaughan, 2003). The more often people listened to the broadcasts, the more the married women talked to their spouses about family planning and the higher the rate of adoption of contraceptive methods. The diverse positive effects of the broadcast remained after statistically controlling for multiple other factors, such as prebroadcast education, access to family planning clinics, and rural-urban geographic differences.

A serial drama in Ethiopia also addressed the AIDS problem (Ryerson, 2006). Compared to their baseline status and to non-viewers, its viewers were more informed on how to determine their HIV status and were more likely to get a blood test for their HIV status. A radio serial in Sudan featured intersecting plotlines. These included the benefits of family planning to limit the number of children and their spacing, providing educational opportunities for daughters, the injustice of forced marriage and risks of early childbearing, domestic violence, embroilment in drug activities leading to a life of crime and narcotics, and prevention of HIV infection. A special theme centered on the devastating consequences of the widespread practice of genital mutilation. In the dramatization, Muslim clerics disapproved such practices as without religious justification. As the storyline unfolded, the dangers and deadly consequences of this practice were portrayed. The broadcasts reversed attitudes toward the brutal practice of genetical mutilation, with the majority, post-broadcast, favoring the abolishment of this procedure (Ryerson, 2006).

Modification of Consummatory Lifestyles

Environmental devastation is affected not only by population size, but also consumer patterns of consumption. The ecosystem is damaged not only by producing products but also by the technologies used to supply them to consumers (Ehrlich, Ehrlich, & Daily, 1995). There are limits to the earth's carrying capacity; our ecosystem cannot sustain burgeoning populations and high consumption of finite natural resources.

The agentic perspective of Social Cognitive Theory lends itself to strategies that promote lifestyle changes that help to preserve the environment. One such strategy was an Indian serial drama that included themes of environment preservation (Papa, et al., 2000). The series was designed to motivate villagers to take collective action to improve sanitation, reduce health hazards, adopt fuel conservation practices, and launch a tree-planting campaign. Qualitative and quantitative data attested to the impact of the broadcast on community life. Citizens did not listen passively to the broadcast content. They formed listener groups that collectively discussed program themes and their implications for their village's future.

Most people are probably unaware of how their purchases affect the environment. If they are to make decisions supportive of sustained development, they need to be informed of the ecological costs of their consummatory practices and enabled and motivated to turn enlightened concern into constructive courses of action. This change is best achieved through multiple modes of communication (Singhal & Rogers, 1999). Many of the lifelong consummatory habits are formed during childhood years. It is easier to prevent wasteful practices than to try to change them after they have become deeply entrenched as part of a lifestyle.

To address the environmental problems created by over-consumption, PCI produced a video, *The Cost of Cool*, for distribution to schools that focuses on the buying habits of teenagers (Tobias & Griffin, 2001). It tracks the ecological costs of the manufacture of everyday items such as T-shirts and sneakers. Providing teenagers with sound information helps them make informed choices in their buying habits. As one viewer put it, *"I'll never look at a T-shirt in the same way."* Popular entertainment formats, such as music concerts, recordings and videos, provide another vehicle for reaching mass youth populations. The themes address critical social issues, substance abuse, violence, teen sexuality, and gender equality. The impact of these complimentary approaches requires systematic evaluation. The increasing magnitude of the environmental problem calls for multifaceted efforts to alter behavioral practices that devastate the ecological supports of life.

Global problems can appear so large that they instill a sense of paralysis. But global effects are the cumulative products of local actions. The strategy of "Think globally, act locally" can restore a sense of efficacy that one can make a difference. The macrosocial approach implemented through mass media is a proven strategy for boosting the efficacy beliefs of individuals and communities and fostering local changes that accumulate into global benefits.[4]

Concluding Remarks

This relatively brief book has been a long journey. It has taken you, the reader, from general principles of human nature and causality; through concrete programs of research on observational learning, self-efficacy perception, self-regulatory processes, and moral behavior; to applications that have promoted individual well-being and fostered beneficial social change in societies in multiple regions of the world. Social Cognitive Theory strives to bring the best in others at both individual and social system levels.

The journey has been even longer for your Author. I began life in a rural hamlet in Northern Alberta. Its educational resources were meager. The primary local pastimes were drinking beer and playing pool. Common psychosocial predictors would not have predicted my life path. Viewed from a nonagentic perspective, I should not have gone to college, I should not have attained a doctoral degree, I should not have spent a career amidst the balmy palms of Stanford University, and I should not have written this book. But I am delighted that the course of events brought me here.

---

4 In 2017, the organization *Cinema for Change* extensively interviewed Professor Bandura on the topic of serial dramas for promoting social change. As of the time of this writing, this interview can be found online at https://www.cinemaofchange.com/albert-bandura-the-power-of-soap-operas-video/.

References

Adamovic, M., Gahan, P., Olsen, J. et al., (2021). Exploring the adoption of virtual work: The role of virtual work self-efficacy and virtual work climate, *The International Journal of Human Resource Management, 33*(17), 3492–3525.

Adler, L. L., & Adler, H. E. (1968). Age as a factor in observational learning in puppies. *American Dachshund*, 13–14.

Akamatsu, T. J., & Thelen, M. H. (1974). A review of the literature on observer characteristics and imitation. *Developmental Psychology, 10,* 38–47.

Alagna, S. W., & Reddy, D. M. (1984). Predictors of proficient technique and successful lesion detection in breast self- examination. *Health Psychology, 3,* 113–127.

Allan, L. G., Siegel, S., & Hannah, S. (2007). The sad truth about depressive realism. *The Quarterly Journal of Experimental Psychology, 60,* 482–495.

Allen, M. K., & Liebert, R. M. (1969). Effects of live and symbolic deviant-modeling cues on adoption of a previously learned standard. *Journal of Personality and Social Psychology, 11,* 253–260.

Alloy, L. B., & Abramson, L. Y. (1979). Judgment of contingency in depressed and nondepressed students: Sadder but wiser? *Journal of Experimental Psychology: General, 108,* 41–485.

Allport, F. H. (1924). *Social psychology*. Cambridge, MA:. Riverside Press.

Anderson, C. A., Bushman, B. J., Bartholow, B. D., Cantor, J., Christakis, D., Coyne, S. M., . . . Green, C. S. (2017). Screen violence and youth behavior. *Pediatrics, 140* (Supplement 2), S142–S147.

Andrus, B. C. (1969). *The infamous of Nuremberg*. London: Fravin.

Arbuthnot, J. (1975). Modification of moral judgment through role playing. *Developmental Psychology, 11,* 319–324.

Arch, E. C. (1992). Affective control efficacy as a factor in willingness to participate in a public performance situation. *Psychological Reports, 71,* 1247–1250.

Archer, J. (1996). Sex differences in social behavior: Are the social role and evolutionary explanations compatible? *American Psychologist, 51*(9), 909–917.

Aron, I. E. (1977). Moral philosophy and moral education. A critique of Kohlberg's theory. *School Review, 85*, 197–217.

Artistico, D., Berry, J. M., Black, J., Cervone, D., Lee, C., & Orom, H. (2011). Psychological functioning in adulthood: A self-efficacy analysis. In C. H. Hoare (Ed.), *The Oxford handbook of adult development and learning* (2nd ed., pp. 215–247). New York: Oxford University Press.

Arvey, P., & Dewhirst, H. (1976). Goal setting attributes, personality variables, and job satisfaction. *Journal of Vocational Behavior, 9*, 179–189.

Audia, P. G., Locke, E. A., & Smith, K. G. (2000). The paradox of success: An archival and a laboratory study of strategic persistence following radical environmental change. *Academy of Management Journal, 43*(5), 837–853.

Austen, V. D., Ruble, D. N., & Trabasso, T. (1977). Recall and order effects as factors in children's moral judgments. *Child Development, 48*, 470–474.

Austin, V. D., Ruble, D. N., & Trabasso, T. (1977). Recall and order effects as factors in children's moral judgments. *Child Development, 48*, 470–474.

Averill, J. R. (1973). Personal control over aversive stimuli and its relationship to stress. *Psychological Bulletin, 80*, 286–303.

Baer, O. M., & Sherman, J. A. 1964. Reinforcement control of generalized imitation in young children. *Journal of Experimental Child Psychology, l*, 37–49.

Baltes, P. B., & Labouvie, G. V. (1973). Adult development of intellectual performance: Description, explanation, and modification. In C. Eisdorfer & M. P. Lawton (Eds.), *The psychology of adult development and aging* (pp. 157–219). American Psychological Association.

Bandura, A. (1965a). Vicarious processes: A case of no-trial learning. In L. Berkowitz (Ed.), *Advances in experimental social psychology* (Vol. II, pp. 1–55). New York: Academic Press.

Bandura, A. (1965b). Behavioral modifications through modeling procedures. In L. Krasner & L. P. Ullmann (Eds.), *Research in behavior modification* (pp. 310–340). New York: Holt, Rinehart & Winston.

Bandura, A. (1965c). Influence of models' reinforcement contingencies on the acquisition of imitative responses. *Journal of Personality and Social Psychology, 1*, 589–595.

Bandura, A. (1969a). *Principles of behavior modification*. New York: Holt Rinehart & Winston.

Bandura, A. (1969b). Social-learning theory of identificatory processes. In A. Goslin (Ed.), *Handbook of socialization theory and research* (pp. 213–262). Chicago: Rand McNally.

Bandura, A. (1971a). Vicarious and self-reinforcement processes. In R. Glaser (Ed.), *The nature of reinforcement*. Columbus, OH: Merrill.

Bandura, A. (1971b). Psychotherapy based upon modeling principles. In A. E. Bergin & S. L. Garfield (Eds.), *Handbook of psychotherapy and behavior change* (pp. 653–708). New York: Wiley.

Bandura, A. (1973). *Aggression: A social learning analysis.* Englewood Cliffs, NJ: Prentice-Hall.

Bandura, A. (1974). Behavior and the models of man. *American Psychologist, 29*, 859–869.

Bandura, A. (1976). Effecting change through participant modeling. In J. Krumboltz & C. Thoresen (Eds.), *Counseling methods.* New York: Holt, Rinehart & Winston.

Bandura, A. (1977). Self-efficacy: Toward a unifying theory of behavioral change. *Psychological Review, 84*(2), 191.

Bandura, A. (1982). The psychology of chance encounters and life paths. *American Psychologist, 37,* 747–755.

Bandura, A. (1983). Temporal dynamics and decomposition of reciprocal determinism. *Psychological Review, 90,* 166–170.

Bandura, A. (1986). *Social foundations of thought and action: A social cognitive theory.* Englewood Cliffs, NJ: Prentice-Hall.

Bandura, A. (1988a). Self-regulation of motivation and action through goal systems. In V. Hamilton, G. H. Bower, & N. H. Frijda (Eds.), *Cognitive perspectives on emotion and motivation* (pp. 37–61). Dordrecht: Kluwer.

Bandura, A. (1988b). Perceived self-efficacy: Exercise of control through self-belief. In J. P. Dauwalder, M. Perrez, & V. Hobi (Eds,), *Annual series of European research in behavior therapy* (Vol. 2, pp. 27–59). Lisse: Swets & Zeitlinger.

Bandura, A. (1988c). Self-efficacy conception of anxiety. *Anxiety Research, 1,* 77–98.

Bandura, A. (1990). Reflections on nonability determinants of competence. In R. J. Sternberg & J. Kolligian Jr. (Eds.), *Competence considered* (pp. 315–362). New Haven, CT: Yale University Press.

Bandura, A. (1991). Self-efficacy mechanism in physiological activation and health-promoting behavior In J. I. V. Madden (Ed.), *Neurobiology of learning, emotion, and affect* (pp. 229–269). New York: Raven Press.

Bandura, A. (1991a). Self-regulation of motivation through anticipatory and self-reactive mechanisms. In R. A. Dienstbier (Ed.), *Perspectives on motivation: Nebraska Symposium on Motivation* (Vol. 38, pp. 69–164). Lincoln: University of Nebraska Press.

Bandura, A. (1991b). Social cognitive theory of moral thought and action. In W. M. Kurtines & J. L. Gewirtz (Eds.), *Handbook of moral behavior and development: Theory, research and applications* (Vol. 1, pp. 71–129). Hillsdale, NJ: Erlbaum.

Bandura, A. (1996). Failures in self-regulation. *Psychological Inquiry, 7,* 20–24.

Bandura, A. (1997). *Self-efficacy: The exercise of control.* New York: Freeman.

Bandura, A. (1999a). Social cognitive theory of personality. In D. Cervone & Y. Shoda (Eds.), *The coherence of personality: Social-cognitive bases of consistency, variability, and organization* (pp. 185–241) and in L. Pervin & O. John (Eds.), *Handbook of personality* (2nd ed., pp. 154–196). New York: Guilford.

Bandura, A. (1999b). Moral disengagement in the perpetration of inhumanities. *Personality and Social Psychology Review, 3,* 193–209.

Bandura, A. (2000). Exercise of human agency through collective efficacy. *Current Directions in Psychological Science, 9,* 75–78.

Bandura, A. (2000a). Health promotion from the perspective of social cognitive theory. In P. Norman, C. Abraham, & M. Conner (Eds.), *Understanding and changing health behaviour: From health beliefs to self-regulation* (pp. 239–339). Amsterdam: Harwood Academic.

Bandura, A. (2000b). Psychological aspects of prognostic judgments. In R. W. Evans, D. Baskin, & F. M. Yatsu (Eds.), Prognosis of neurological disorders (2nd ed., pp. 11–27). New York: Oxford University Press.

Bandura, A. (2001a). Social cognitive theory: An agentic perspective. *Annual Review of Psychology, 52,* 1–26.

Bandura, A. (2001b). Social cognitive theory of mass communications. In J. Bryant & D. Zillman (Eds.), *Media effects: Advances in theory and research* (2nd ed., pp. 121–153). Mahwah, NJ: Erlbaum.

Bandura, A. (2002). Environmental sustainability by sociocognitive deceleration of population growth. In P. Schmuck & W. Schultz (Eds.), *The psychology of sustainable development* (pp. 209–238). Dordrecht: Kluwer.

Bandura, A. (2002a). Social cognitive theory in cultural context. *Journal of Applied Psychology: An International Review, 51,* 269–290.

Bandura, A. (2002b). Growing primacy of human agency in adaptation and change in the electronic era. *European Psychologist, 7,* 2–16.

Bandura, A. (2004a). Health promotion by social cognitive means. *Health Education & Behavior, 31,* 143–164.

Bandura, A. (2004b). Selective exercise of moral agency. In T. A. Thorkildsen & H. J. Walberg (Eds.), *Nurturing morality* (pp. 35–57). Boston: Kluwer Academic.

Bandura A. (2005). The evolution of social cognitive theory. In K. G. Smith & M. A. Hitt (Eds.), *Great minds in management* (pp. 9–35). Oxford: Oxford University Press.

Bandura, A. (2006a). Going global with social cognitive theory: From prospect to paydirt. In S. I. Donaldson, D. E. Berger, & K. Pezdek (Eds.), *Applied psychology: New frontiers and rewarding careers* (pp. 53–79). Mahwah, NJ: Erlbaum.

Bandura, A. (2006b). On integrating social cognitive and social diffusion theories. In A. Singhal & J. Dearing (Eds.), *Communication of innovations: A journey with Ev Rogers* (pp. 111–135). Beverly Hills: Sage.

Bandura, A. (2006c). Toward a psychology of human agency. *Perspectives on Psychological Science, 1,* 164–180.

Bandura, A. (2008). The reconstrual of free will from the agentic perspective of social cognitive theory. In J. Baer, J. C. Kaufman, & R. F. Baumeister (Eds.), *Are we free? Psychology and free will* (pp. 86–127). Oxford: Oxford University Press.

Bandura, A. (2011a). Social cognitive theory. In P. A. M. van Lange, A. W. Kruglanski, & E. T. Higgins (Eds.), *Handbook of social psychological theories* (pp. 349–373). London: Sage.

Bandura, A. (2011b). The social and policy impact of social cognitive theory. In M. M. Mark, S. I. Donaldson, & B. Campbell (Eds.), *Social psychology and evaluation* (pp. 31–71). New York: Guilford.

Bandura, A. (2015). On deconstructing commentaries regarding alternative theories of self-regulation. *Journal of Management, 41,* 1025–1044.

Bandura, A. (2016). *Moral disengagement: How people do harm and live with themselves.* New York: Worth.

Bandura, A. (1991). Self-efficacy mechanism in physiological activation and health-promoting behavior. In J. Madden, IV (Ed.), Adaptation, learning and affect (pp. 229–269). New York: Raven.

Bandura, A. (1989). A social cognitive theory of action. In J. P. Forgas & M. J. Innes (Eds.), *Recent Advances in Social Psychology: An International Perspective* (pp. 127–138). North Holland: Elsevier.

Bandura, A., & Adams, N. E. (1977). Analysis of self-efficacy theory of behavioral change. *Cognitive Therapy and Research, 1,* 287–308.

Bandura, A., Adams, N. E., & Beyer, J. (1977). Cognitive processes mediating behavior change. *Journal of Personality and Social Psychology, 35,* 125–139.

Bandura, A., & Barab, P. G. (1971). Conditions governing nonreinforced imitation. *Developmental Psychology, 5,* 244–255.

Bandura, A., Barbaranelli, C., Caprara, G. V., & Pastorelli, C. (1996a). Mechanisms of moral disengagement in the exercise of moral agency. *Journal of Personality and Social Psychology, 71,* 364–374.

Bandura, A., Barbaranelli, C., Caprara, G. V., & Pastorelli, C. (1996b). Multifaceted impact of self-efficacy beliefs on academic functioning. *Child Development, 67,* 1206–1222.

Bandura, A., Barbaranelli, C., Caprara, G. V., & Pastorelli, C. (2001). Self-efficacy beliefs as shapers of children's aspirations and career trajectories. *Child Development, 72,* 187–206.

Bandura, A., Blanchard, E. B., & Ritter, B. (1969). The relative efficacy of desensitization and modeling approaches for inducing behavioral, affective, and attitudinal changes. *Journal of Personality and Social Psychology, 13,* 173–199.

Bandura, A., & Cervone, D. (1983). Self-evaluative and self-efficacy mechanisms governing the motivational effects of goal systems. *Journal of Personality and Social Psychology, 45,* 1017–1028.

Bandura, A., & Cervone, D. (1986). Differential engagement of self-reactive influences in cognitive motivation. *Organizational Behavior and Human Decision Processes, 38,* 92–113.

Bandura, A., Cioffi, D., Taylor, C. B., & Brouillard, M. E. (1988). Perceived self-efficacy in coping with cognitive stressors and opioid activation. *Journal of Personality and Social Psychology, 55,* 479–488.

Bandura, A., Grusec, J. E., & Menlove, F. L. (1966). Observational learning as a function of symbolization and incentive set. *Child Development, 37,* 499–506.

Bandura, A., & Harris, M. B. (1966). Modification of syntactic style. *Journal of Experimental Child Psychology, 4*(4), 341–352.

Bandura, A., & Jeffery, R. 1971. The role of symbolic coding, cognitive organization, and rehearsal in observational learning [Unpublished manuscript]. Stanford University.

Bandura, A., Jeffery, R. W., & Gajdos, E. (1975a). Generalizing change through participant modeling with self-directed mastery. *Behaviour Research and Therapy, 13,* 141–152.

Bandura, A., & Jourden, F. J. (1991). Self-regulatory mechanisms governing the impact of social comparison on complex decision making. *Journal of Personality and Social Psychology, 60,* 941– 951.

Bandura, A., & McDonald, F. J. (1963) The influence of social reinforcement and the behavior of models in shaping children's moral judgments. *Journal of Abnormal and Social Psychology, 67,* 274–281.

Bandura, A., & Menlove, F. L. (1968). Factors determining vicarious extinction of avoidance behavior through symbolic modeling. *Journal of Personality and Social Psychology, 8,* 99–108.

Bandura, A., & Mischel, W. (1965). Modification of self-imposed delay of reward through exposure to live and symbolic models. *Journal of Personality and Social Psychology, 2,* 698–705.

Bandura, A., Reese, L., & Adams, N. E. (1982). Microanalysis of action and fear arousal as a function of differential levels of perceived self-efficacy. *Journal of Personality and Social Psychology, 43,* 5–21.

Bandura, A., & Rosenthal, T. L. (1966). Vicarious classical conditioning as a function of arousal level. *Journal of Personality and Social Psychology, 3,* 54–62.

Bandura, A., Ross, D., & Ross, S. A. (1961). Transmission of aggression through imitation of aggressive models. *Journal of Abnormal and Social Psychology, 63,* 575–582.

Bandura, A., Ross, D., & Ross, S. A. (1963a). Imitation of film-mediated aggressive models. *Journal of Abnormal and Social Psychology, 66,* 3–11.

Bandura, A., Ross, D., & Ross, S. A. (1963b). A comparative test of the status envy, social power, and secondary reinforcement theories of identificatory learning. *Journal of Abnormal and Social Psychology, 67,* 527–534.

Bandura, A., & Schunk, D. H. (1981). Cultivating competence, self-efficacy, and intrinsic interest through proximal self-motivation. *Journal of Personality and Social Psychology, 41,* 586–598.

Bandura, A., & Simon, K. M. (1977). The role of proximal intentions in self-regulation of refractory behavior. *Cognitive Therapy and Research, 1,* 177–193.

Bandura, A., Taylor, C. B., Williams, S. L., Mefford, I. N., & Barchas, J. D. (1985). Catecholamine secretion as a function of perceived coping self-efficacy. *Journal of Consulting and Clinical Psychology, 53,* 406–414.

Bandura, A., Underwood, B., & Fromson, M. E. (1975b). Disinhibition of aggression through diffusion of responsibility and dehumanization of victims. *Journal of Research in Personality, 9,* 253–269.

Bandura, A., & Walters, R. H. (1959). *Adolescent aggression: A study of the influence of child-training practices and family interrelationships.* New York: Ronald.

Bandura, A., & Walters, R. H. (1963). *Social learning and personality development.* New York: Holt, Rinehart & Winston.

Bandura, A., & Wood, R. E. (1989). Effect of perceived controllability and performance standards on self-regulation of complex decision making. *Journal of Personality and Social Psychology, 56,* 805–814.

Baron, R. A., & Markman, G. D. (2003). Beyond social capital: The role of entrepreneurs' social competence in their financial success. *Journal of Business Venturing, 18,* 41–60.

Barrett, L. F. (2017). The theory of constructed emotion: An active inference account of interoception and categorization. *Social Cognitive and Affective Neuroscience, 12,* 1–23.

Baum, J. R. (1994). *The relation of traits, competencies, vision, motivation, and strategy to venture growth* [Unpublished doctoral dissertation]. University of Maryland.

Baylis, F., & Robert, J. (2004). The inevitability of genetic enhancement technologies. *Bioethics, 18,* 1–26.

Beach, F. A. (1969). It's all in your mind. *Psychology Today, 60,* 33–35.

Beck, A., Loeb, A., Diggory, J., & Tuthill, R. (1967). Expectancy, level of aspiration, performance, and self-evaluation in depression. In *Proceedings of the 75th Annual Convention of the American Psychological Association (2)* (pp. 193–194). Washington, DC: American Psychological Association.

Beck, K. H., & Lund, A. K. (1981). The effects of health threat seriousness and personal efficacy upon intentions and behavior. *Journal of Applied Social Psychology, 11,* 401–415.

Benton, A. A. (1967). Effect of the timing of negative response consequences on the observational learning of resistance to temptation in children. *Dissertation Abstracts, 27,* 2153–2154.

Bergin, A. E. (1962). The effect of dissonant persuasive communications upon changes in a self-referring attitude. *Journal of Personality, 30*, 423–438.

Berry, J. M. (1987, September). *A self-efficacy model of memory performance.* Paper presented at the meeting of the American Psychological Association, New York.

Berry, J. M. (1999). Memory self-efficacy in its social cognitive context. In T. M. Hess & F. Blanchard-Fields (Eds.), *Social cognition and aging* (pp. 69–96). San Diego, CA: Academic Press.

Berry, J. M., West, R. L., & Dennehey, D. M. (1989). Reliability and validity of the Memory Self-Efficacy Questionnaire. *Developmental Psychology, 25*, 701–713.

Betz, N. E., & Hackett, G. (1981). The relationship of career-related self-efficacy expectation to perceived career options in college women and men. *Journal of Counseling Psychology, 28*, 399–410.

Betz, N. E., & Hackett, G. (1986). Applications of self-efficacy theory to understanding career choice behavior. *Journal of Social and Clinical Psychology, 4*, 279–289.

Betz, N. E., & Hackett, G. (1997). Applications of self-efficacy theory to the career assessment of women. *Journal of Career Assessment, 5*, 383–402.

Biran, M., & Wilson, G. T. (1981). Cognitive versus behavioral methods in the treatment of phobic disorders: A self-efficacy analysis. *Journal of Consulting and Clinical Psychology, 49*, 886–899.

Blanchard, E. B. (1970). The relative contributions of modeling, informational influences, and physical contact in the extinction of phobic behavior. *Journal of Abnormal Psychology, 76*, 55–61.

Blasi, A. (1980). Bridging moral cognition and moral action: A critical review of the literature. *Psychological Bulletin, 88*, 1–45.

Bloom, A. H. (1986). Psychological ingredients of high-level moral thinking: A critique of the Kohlberg-Gilligan paradigm. *Journal of the Theory of Social Behaviour, 16*(1), 89–103.

Boag, S. (2011). Explanation in personality psychology: "Verbal magic" and the five-factor model. *Philosophical Psychology, 24*, 223–243.

Boag S. (2018). Personality dynamics, motivation, and the logic of explanation. *Review of General Psychology, 22*, 427–436.

Bolinger, D. (1982). *Language: The loaded weapon.* London: Longman.

Bong, M. (2001). Between- and within-domain relations of academic motivation among middle and high school students: Self-efficacy, task-value, and achievement goals. *Journal of Educational Psychology, 93*, 23–34.

Borsboom, D., Mellenbergh, G. J., & van Heerden, J. (2004). The concept of validity. *Psychological Review, 111*, 1061–1071.

Bouffard-Bouchard, T. (1990). Influence of self-efficacy on performance in a cognitive task. *The Journal of Social Psychology, 130*(3), 353–363.

Bower, G. H. (1983). Affect and cognition. *Philosophical Transactions of the Royal Society of London. B, Biological Sciences, 302*(1110), 387–402.

Boyer, D. A., Zollo, J. S., Thompson, C. M., Vancouver, J. B., Shewring, K., & Sims, E. (2000). A quantitative review of the effects of manipulated self-efficacy on performance. Poster session presented at the annual meeting of the American Psychological Society, Miami, FL.

Brock, T. C., & Buss, A. H. (1962). Dissonance, aggression, and evaluation of pain. *Journal of Abnormal and Social Psychology, 65*, 197–202.

Brock, T. C., & Buss, A. H. (1964). Effects of justification for aggression and communication with the victim on postaggression dissonance. *Journal of Abnormal and Social Psychology, 68*, 403–412.

Brod, M. I., & Hall, S. M. (1984). Joiners and non-joiners in smoking treatment: A comparison of psychosocial variables. *Addictive behaviors, 9*(2), 217–221.

Brody, G. H., & Henderson, R. W. (1977). Effects of multiple model variations and rationale provision on the moral judgments and explanations of young children. *Child Development, 48*, 1117–1120.

Brouwers, A., & Tomic, W. (2000). A longitudinal study of teacher burnout and perceived self-efficacy in classroom management. *Teaching and Teacher Education, 16*(2), 239–253.

Brown, R., & Bellugi, U. (1964). Three processes in the child's acquisition of syntax. *Harvard Educational Review, 34*, 133–151.

Brown, S. D., Lent, R. W., & Larkin, K. C. (1989). Self-efficacy as a moderator of scholastic aptitude-academic performance relationships. *Journal of Vocational Behavior, 35*(1), 64–75.

Brown, S. J., Lieberman, D. A., Gemeny, B. A., Fan, Y. C., Wilson, D. M., & Pasta, D. J. (1997). Educational video game for juvenile diabetes care: Results of a controlled trial. *Medical Informatics, 22*, 77–89.

Brown, W. J., & Cody, M. J. (1991). Effects of a prosocial television soap opera in promoting women's status. *Human Communication Research, 18*, 114–144.

Brown W. J., & Inouye, D. K. (1978). Learned helplessness through modeling: The role of perceived similarity in competence. *Journal of Personality and Social Psychology, 36*, 900–908.

Bryan, J. F., & Locke, E. A. (1967). Goal-setting as a means of increasing motivation. *Journal of Applied Psychology, 51*, 274–277.

Bruner, J. (1990). *Acts of meaning.* Cambridge, MA: Harvard University Press.

Bunge, M. (1977). Emergence and the mind. *Neuroscience, 2*, 501–509.

Burkhardt, M. E., & Brass, D. J. (1990). Changing patterns or patterns of change: The effects of a change in technology on social network structure and power. *Administrative Science Quarterly, 35*, 104–127.

Buss, D. M. (1995). Psychological sex differences: Origins through sexual selection. *American Psychologist, 50*, 164–168.

Bussey, K., & Bandura, A. (1992). Self-regulatory mechanisms governing gender development. *Child Development, 63,* 1236–1250.

Bussey, K., & Bandura, A. (1999). Social cognitive theory of gender development and differentiation. *Psychological Review, 106,* 676–713.

Campion, M. A., & Lord, R. G. (1982). A control systems conceptualization of the goal-setting and changing process. *Organizational Behavior and Human Performance, 30,* 265–287.

Cantor, J., & Wilson, B. J. (1988). Helping children cope with frightening media presentations. *Current Psychological Research and Reviews, 7,* 58–75.

Cao, Y., Wei, Q., Gui, S., & Li, F. (2020). The temporal course of vicarious embarrassment: An electrophysiological study. *Social Neuroscience, 15*(4), 435–446.

Caporael, L. (1997). The evolution of truly social cognition: The core configurations model. *Personality and Social Psychology Review, 1,* 276–298.

Caprara, G. V., & Cervone, D. (2000). *Personality: Determinants, dynamics, and potentials.* New York: Cambridge University Press.

Carroll, W. R., & Bandura, A. (1985). Role of timing of visual monitoring and motor rehearsal in observational learning of action patterns. *Journal of Motor Behavior, 17,* 269–281.

Carroll, W. R., & Bandura, A. (1987). Translating cognition into action: The role of visual guidance in observational learning. *Journal of Motor Behavior, 19,* 385–398.

Carroll, W. R., Rosenthal, T. L., & Brysh, C. G. (1969). *The social transmission of grammatical parameters* [Unpublished manuscript]. University of Arizona.

Carter, R. E. (1980). What is Lawrence Kohlberg doing? *Journal of Moral Education, 9,* 88–102.

Cervone, D. (1985). Randomization tests to determine significance levels for microanalytic congruences between self-efficacy and behavior. *Cognitive Therapy and Research, 9,* 357–365.

Cervone, D. (1997). Social-cognitive mechanisms and personality coherence: Self-knowledge, situational beliefs, and cross-situational coherence in perceived self-efficacy. *Psychological Science, 8,* 43–50.

Cervone, D. (1999). Bottom-up explanation in personality psychology: The case of cross-situational coherence. In D. Cervone & Y. Shoda (Eds.), *The coherence of personality: Social-cognitive bases of personality consistency, variability, and organization* (pp. 303–341). New York: Guilford.

Cervone, D. (2004). The architecture of personality. *Psychological Review, 111,* 183–204.

Cervone, D. (2005). Personality architecture: Within-person structures and processes. *Annual Review of Psychology, 56,* 423–452.

Cervone, D. (2008). Explanatory models of personality: Social-cognitive theories and the knowledge-and-appraisal model of personality architecture. In G. Boyle,

G. Matthews, & D. Saklofske (Eds.), *Handbook of Personality and Testing* (pp. 80–100). London: Sage Publications.

Cervone, D. (2021). The KAPA Model of personality structure and dynamics. In J. Rauthmann (Ed.), *Handbook of personality dynamics and processes* (pp. 601–620). San Diego, CA: Elsevier.

Cervone, D., Jiwani, N., & Wood, R. (1991). Goal-setting and the differential influence of self-regulatory processes on complex decision-making performance. *Journal of Personality and Social Psychology, 61*, 257–266.

Cervone, D., Mercurio, L., & Lilley, C. (2020). The individual STEM student in context: Idiographic methods for understanding self-knowledge and intra-individual patterns of self-efficacy appraisal. *Journal of Educational Psychology, 112*, 1597–1613.

Cervone, D., & Palmer, B. W. (1990). Anchoring biases and the perseverance of self-efficacy beliefs. *Cognitive Therapy and Research, 14*, 401–416.

Cervone, D., & Peake, P. K. (1986). Anchoring, efficacy, and action: The influence of judgmental heuristics on self-efficacy judgments and behavior. *Journal of Personality and Social Psychology, 50*, 492–501.

Cervone, D., & Pervin, L. A. (2023). *Personality: Theory and research* (15th ed.). Hoboken, NJ: Wiley.

Cervone, D., & Shoda, Y. (Eds.) (1999). *The coherence of personality: Social-cognitive bases of consistency, variability, and organization.* New York: Guilford.

Cervone, D., & Wood, R. (1995). Goals, feedback, and the differential influence of self-regulatory processes on cognitively complex performance. *Cognitive Therapy and Research, 19*, 521–547.

Chandler, M. J., Greenspan, S., & Barenboim, C. (1973). Judgments of intentionality in response to videotaped and verbally presented moral dilemma: The medium is the message. *Child Development, 44*, 315–320.

Chen, C. C., Greene, P. G., & Crick, A. (1998). Does entrepreneurial self-efficacy distinguish entrepreneurs from managers? *Journal of Business Venturing, 13*, 295–316.

Cheung, S., & Sun, S. Y. K. (2000). Effects of self-efficacy and social support on the mental health conditions of mutual-aid organization members. *Social Behavior and Personality, 28*, 413–422.

Chomsky, N. (1965). *Aspects of the theory of syntax.* Cambridge, MA: MIT Press.

Church, R. M. (1959). Emotional reactions of rats to the pain of others. *Journal of Comparative and Physiological Psychology, 52*, 132–134.

Ciminero, A. R., & Steingarten, K. A. (1978). The effects of performance standards on self-evaluation and self-reinforcement in depressed and nondepressed individuals. *Cognitive Therapy and Research, 2*, 179–182.

Cioffi, D. (1991). Beyond attentional strategies: A cognitive-perceptual model of somatic interpretation. *Psychological Bulletin, 109*, 25–41.

Clark, M., Ghandour, G., Miller, N. H., Taylor, C. B., Bandura, A., & DeBusk, R. (1997). *Development and evaluation of a computer based system for dietary management of hyperlipidemia, 97,* 146–150.

Clark, N., Gong, M., Kaciroti, N., Yu, J., Wu, G., Zeng, Z., et al. (2005). A trial of asthma self-management in Beijing schools. *Chronic Illness, 1,* 31–38.

Cleland, J., Bernstein, S., Ezeh, A., Faundes, A., Glasier, A., & Innis, J. (2006). Family planning: the unfinished agenda. *The Lancet, 368*(9549), 1810–1827.

Cline, V. B., Croft, R. G., & Courrier, S. (1973). Desensitization of children to television violence. *Journal of Personality and Social Psychology, 27,* 360–365.

Coates, B., & Hartup, W. W. 1969. Age and verbalization in observational learning. *Developmental Psychology, 1,* 556–562.

Codd, J. A. (1977). Some conceptual problems in the cognitive development approach to morality. *Journal of Moral Education, 6,* 147–157.

Coe, C. L., & Levine, S. (1989). Psychoimmunology: An old idea whose time has come. In P. R. Barchas (Ed.), *Social physiology of social relations.* Oxford: Oxford University Press,

Colby, A., Kohlberg, L., Gibbs, J. C., & Lieberman, M. (1983). A longitudinal study of moral judgment. *Monographs of the Society for Research in Child Development, 48*(1–2), 1–124.

Collins, J. L. (1982, March). *Self-efficacy and ability in achievement behavior.* Paper presented at the annual meeting of the American Educational Research Association, New York.

Corbin, C. (1972). Mental practice. In W. Morgan (Ed.), *Ergogenic aids and muscular performance* (pp. 93–118). New York: Academic Press.

Cowan, P. A., Longer, J., Heavenrich, J., & Nathanson, M. (1969). Social learning and Piaget's cognitive theory of moral development. *Journal of Personality and Social Psychology, 11*(3), 261–274.

Crooks, J. L. (1967). *Observational learning of fear in monkeys* [Unpublished manuscript] University of Pennsylvania.

Csikszentmihalyi, M. (1981) Leisure and socialization. *Social Forces* (1981): 332–340.

Cutrona, C. E., & Troutman, B. R. (1986). Social support, infant temperament, and parenting self-efficacy: A mediational model of postpartum depression. *Child Development, 57,* 1507–1518.

Darley, J. M., Klosson, E. C., & Zanna, M. P. (1978). Intentions and their contexts in the moral judgments of children and adults. *Child Development, 49,* 66–74.

Davis, F. W., & Yates, B. T. (1982). Self-efficacy expectancies versus outcome expectancies as determinants of performance deficits and depressive affect. *Cognitive Therapy and Research, 6*(1), 23–35.

Davis III, T. E., Ollendick, T. H., & Öst, L. G. (2019). One-session treatment of specific phobias in children: Recent developments and a systematic review. *Annual Review of Clinical Psychology, 15,* 233–256.

DeBusk, R. F., Clark, M., Kraemer, H. C., Bandura, A., Miller, N. H., Fisher, L., Greenwald, M. D., & Jaffe, M. (1999) Computer-assisted dietary intervention for hyperlipidemia: Results of a randomized trial and implications for clinical management. Submitted for publication.

DeBusk, R. F., Miller, N. H., Superko, H. R., Dennis, C. A., Thomas, R. J., Lew, H. T., et al. (1994). A case-management system for coronary risk factor modification. *Annals of Internal Medicine, 120,* 721–729.

DeHaene, S. (2009). *Reading in the brain.* New York: Penguin.

Devins, G. M., Binik, Y. M., Gorman, P., Dattel, M., McCloskey, B., Oscar, G., & Briggs, J. (1982). Perceived self-efficacy, outcome expectancies, and negative mood states in end-stage renal disease. *Journal of Abnormal Psychology, 91*(4), 241–244.

Diener, E. (1977). Deindividuation: Causes and consequences. *Social Behavior and Personality, 5,* 143–156.

Diener, E., Dineen, J., Endresen, K., Beaman, A. L., & Fraser, S. C. (1975). Effects of altered responsibility, cognitive set, and modeling on physical aggression and deindividuation. *Journal of Personality and Social Psychology, 31,* 328–337.

Dobzhansky, T. (1972). Genetics and the diversity of behavior. *American Psychologist, 27,* 523–530.

Dongbo, F., McGowan, P., Yi-e, S., Lizhen, Z., Huiqin, Y., Jianguo, M., et al. (2003). Implementation and quantitative evaluation of chronic disease self-management programme in Shanghai, China: Randomized controlled trial, *Bulletin of the World Health Organization, 81,* 174–182.

Dossett, D. L., Latham, G. P., & Mitchell, T. R. (1979). Effects of assigned versus participatively set goals, knowledge of results, and individual differences on employee behavior when goal difficulty is held constant. *Journal of Applied Psychology, 64*(3), 291–298.

Dowrick, P. W. (1999). A review of self modeling and related interventions. *Applied and preventive psychology, 8*(1), 23–39.

Dubbert, P. M., & Wilson, G. T. (1984). Goal-setting and spouse involvement in the treatment of obesity. *Behaviour Research and Therapy, 22*(3), 227–242.

Duncker, K. (1938). Experimental modification of children's food preferences through social suggestion. *Journal of Abnormal Social Psychology, 33,* 489–507.

Dysinger, W. S., & Ruckmick, C.A. (1933). *The emotional responses of children to the motion picture situation. Bound with Peters, C.C. Motion pictures and standards of morality.* New York: Macmillan.

Earley, P. C. (1993). East meets West meets Mideast: Further explanation of collectivistic and individualistic work groups. *Academy of Management Journal, 36,* 319–348.

Earley, P. C. (1994). Self or group? Cultural effects of training on self-efficacy and performance. *Administrative Science Quarterly, 39,* 89–117.

Earley, P. C., Connolly, T., & Ekegren, G. (1989a). Goals, strategy development, and task performance: Some limits on the efficacy of goal setting. *Journal of Applied Psychology, 74*(1), 24–33.

Earley, P. C., Connolly, T., & Lee, C. (1989b). Task strategy interventions in goal setting: The importance of search in strategy development. *Journal of Management, 15*(4), 589–602.

Eccles, J. (1974). Cerebral activity and consciousness. In F. S. Ayala & T. Dobzhansky (Eds.), *Studies in the philosophy of biology: Reductions and related problems* (pp. 87–107). Berkeley: University of California Press.

Ehrlich, P. R., Ehrlich, A. H., & Daily, G. C. (1995). *The stork and the plow: The equity answer to the human dilemma.* New Haven: Yale University Press.

Elder, G. (1994). Time, human agency, and social change: Perspectives on the life course. *Social Psychology Quarterly, 57,* 4–15.

Elkin, F., & Westley, W. A. (1955). The myth of adolescent culture. *American Sociological Review, 20,* 680–684.

Emmerich, W. (1959). Parental identification in young children. *Genetic Psychology Monographs, 60,* 257–308.

Emmons, R. A., & Diener, E. (1986). A goal–affect analysis of everyday situational choices. *Journal of Research in Personality, 20,* 309–326.

Englis, B. G., Vaughan, K. B., & Lanzetta, J. T. (1982). Conditioning of counter empathic emotional response. *Journal of Experimental Social Psychology, 18,* 375–391.

Epel, E. S. (2009). Psychological and metabolic stress: A recipe for accelerated cellular aging? *Hormones, 8,* 7–22.

Erez, M., & Zidon, I. (1984). Effect of goal acceptance on the relationship of goal difficulty to performance. *Journal of Applied Psychology, 69,* 69–78.

Ericsson, K. A., & Simon, H. A. (1980). Verbal reports as data. *Psychological Review, 87,* 215–251.

Ervin, S. M. (1964). Imitation and structural change in children's language. In E. H. Lenneberg (Ed.), *New directions in the study of language* (pp. 163–189). Cambridge, MA: MIT Press.

Feltz, D. L., & Landers, D. M. (1983). Effects of mental practice on motor skill learning and performance: A meta-analysis. *Journal of Sport Psychology, 5,* 25–57.

Fischer, K. W. (1983). Illuminating the processes of moral development. *Monographs of the Society for Research in Child Development, 38,* (1–2, Serial No. 200).

Flanders, J. P. (1968). A review of research on imitative behavior. *Psychological Bulletin, 69,* 316–337.

Flavell, J. H. (1996). Piaget's legacy. *Psychological Science, 7*(4), 200–203.

Foss, B. M. (1964). Mimicry in mynas (Gracula religiosa): A test of Mowrer's theory. *British Journal of Psychology, 55,* 85–88.

Frankfurt, H. G. (1971). Freedom of the will and the concept of a person. *The Journal of Philosophy, 68,* 5–20.

Freeman, M. A., & Bordia, P. (2001). Assessing alternative models of individualism and collectivism: A confirmatory factor analysis. *European Journal of Personality, 15,* 105–121.

Frese, M., Teng, E., & Cees, J. (1999). Helping to improve suggestion systems: Psychological predictors of giving suggestions in a Dutch company. *Journal of Organizational Behavior, 20,* 1139–1155.

Freud, A. (1917). *General Introduction to Psychoanalysis.* Garden City, NY: Garden City Publishing Co.

Freud, S. (1933). *New Introductory Lectures on Psychoanalysis* (W. J. H. Sprott, Trans). New York.

Freud, S. (1957). *Instincts and their vicissitudes.* Standard Edition (Vol. 14, pp. 117–140). London: Hogarth Press. (Original work published 1915).

Frey, K. S., & Ruble, D. N. (1990). Strategies for comparative evaluation: Maintaining a sense of competence across the lifespan. In R. J. Sternberg & J. Kolligian, Jr. (Eds.), *Competence considered* (pp. 167– 189). New Haven: Yale University Press.

Fries, J. F., & Crapo, L. M. (1981). *Vitality and aging: Implications of the rectangular curve.* San Francisco: Freeman.

Fuchs, V. (1974). *Who shall live? Health economics and social choice.* New York: Basic Books.

Gambino, R. (1973, November-December). Watergate lingo: A language of non-responsibility. *Freedom at Issue, 22,* 7–9, 15–17.

Garber, J., Hollon, S. D., & Silverman, V. (1979, December). *Evaluation and reward of self vs. others in depression.* Paper presented at the meeting of the Association for the Advancement of Behavior Therapy, San Francisco.

Garland, H. (1983) The influence of ability, assigned goals, and normative information on personal goals and performance: A challenge to the goal attainability assumption. *Journal of Applied Psychology, 68,* 20–30.

Geer, J. H., Davison, G. C, & Gatchel, R. K. (1970). Reduction of stress in humans through nonveridical perceived control of aversive stimulation. *Journal of Personality and Social Psychology, 16,* 731–738.

Gerst, M. S. (1971). Symbolic coding processes in observational learning. *Journal of Personality and Social Psychology, 19,* 7–17.

Gewirtz, J. L., & Stingle, K. G. (1968). Learning of generalized imitation as the basis for identification. *Psychological Review, 75,* 374–397.

Gibson, C. B. (1995). *Determinants and consequences of group-efficacy beliefs in work organizations in U.S., Hong Kong, and Indonesia* [Unpublished doctoral dissertation, University of California, Irvine].

Gibson, J. T., & Haritos-Fatouros, M. (1986). The education of a torturer. *Psychology Today, 20,* 50–58.

Gilligan, C. (1982). *In a different voice: Psychological theory and women's development.* Cambridge, MA: Harvard University Press.

Gillooly, S. N., Hardt, H., & Smith, A. E. (2021). Having female role models correlates with PhD students' attitudes toward their own academic success. *PLoS ONE 16*(8): e0255095.

Gjerde, P. F., & Onishi, M. (2000). Selves, cultures, and nations: The psychological imagination of the Japanese in the era of globalization. *Human Development, 43,* 216–226.

Glass, D. C., Singer, J. E., Leonard, H. S., Krantz, D., & Cummings, H. (1973). Perceived control of aversive stimulation and the reduction of stress responses. *Journal of Personality, 41,* 577–595.

Golin, S., & Terrill, F. (1977). Motivational and associative aspects of mild depression in skill and chance tasks. *Journal of Abnormal Psychology, 86,* 389–401.

Grueneich, R. (1982). The development of children's integration rules for making moral judgments. *Child Development, 53,* 887–894.

Gruman, J. (2006). Quantifying people particles. *Good behavior.* Washington, DC: Center for the Advancement of Health.

Grusec, J. E. (1971). Power and the internalization of self-denial. *Child Development, 42,* 93–105.

Gully, S. M., Incalcaterra, K. A., Joshi, A., & Beaubien, J. M. (2002). A meta-analysis of team-efficacy, potency, and performance: Interdependence and level of analysis as moderators of observed relationships. *Journal of Applied Psychology, 87,* 819–832.

Guthrie, E. R. 1952. *The psychology of learning.* New York: Harper.

Gutkin, D. C. (1972). The effect of systematic story changes on intentionality in children's moral judgments. *Child Development, 43,* 187–195.

Haan, N. (1985). Processes of moral development: Cognitive or social disequilibrium? *Developmental Psychology, 21*(6), 996–1006.

Hacker, P. M. S. (1996). *Wittgenstein mind and will: Volume 4 of an analytical commentary on the Philosophical Investigations.* Part I, Essays. Oxford: Blackwell.

Hacker, P. M. S. (2013). *The intellectual powers: A study of human nature.* Chichester: John Wiley & Sons.

Haggbloom, S. J., Warnick, R., Warnick, J. E., Jones, V. K., Yarbrough, G. L., Russell, T. M., . . . Monte, E. (2002). The 100 most eminent psychologists of the 20th century. *Review of General Psychology, 6,* 139–152.

Harré, R. (1998). *The singular self: An introduction to the psychology of personhood.* London: Sage.

Harré, R. (2021). Personality and public performance. *Journal for the Theory of Social Behaviour, 51*(2), 293–304.

Harré, R., & Gillet, G. (1994). Emotion words and emotional acts. *The Discursive Mind,* 144–166.

Haskell, W. L., Alderman, E. L., Fair, J. M., Maron, D. J., Mackey, S. F., Superko, H. R., et al. (1994). Effects of intensive multiple risk factor reduction on coronary atherosclerosis and clinical cardiac events in men and women with coronary artery disease. *Circulation, 89,* 975–990.

Hastorf, A. H. 1965. The "reinforcement" of individual actions in a group situation. In L. Krasner & L. P. Ullmann (Eds.), *Research in behavior modification* (pp. 268–284). New York: Holt, Rinehart & Winston.

Hatano, G. (1970). Subjective and objective cues in moral judgment. *Japanese Psychological Research, 12,* 96–106.

Heckhausen, J. (1987). Balancing for weaknesses and challenging developmental potential: A longitudinal study of mother-infant dyads in apprenticeship interactions. *Developmental Psychology, 23,* 762–770.

Helm, C., & Morelli, M. (1979). Stanley Milgram and the obedience experiment: Authority, legitimacy, and human action. *Political Theory, 7*(3), 321–345.

Henrich, J. (2020). *The weirdest people in the world : How the West became psychologically peculiar and particularly prosperous.* New York: Farrar, Strauss, Giroux.

Heyes, C. (2018). *Cognitive gadgets: The cultural evolution of thinking.* Cambridge, MA: Harvard University Press.

Heyes, C. (2021). Is morality a gadget? Nature, nurture and culture in moral development. *Synthese, 198,* 4391–4414.

Higgins, A., Power, C., & Kohlberg, L. (1984). Student judgments of responsibility and the moral atmosphere of high schools: A comparative study. In W. Kurtines & J. L. Gewirtz (Eds.), *Morality, moral behavior and moral development: Basic issues in theory and research* (pp. 74–106). New York: Wiley Interscience.

Hildebrandt, D. E., Feldman, S. E., & Ditrichs, R. A. (1973). Rules, models, and self-reinforcement in children. *Journal of Personality and Social Psychology, 25,* 1–5.

Hilgartner, S., Bell, R. C., & O'Connor, R. (1982). *Nukespeak: Nuclear language, visions, and mindset.* San Francisco: Sierra Club Books.

Hill, T., Smith, N. D., & Mann, M. F. (1987). Role of efficacy expectations in predicting the decision to use advanced technologies: The case of computers. *Journal of Applied Psychology, 72*(2), 307–313.

Hoffman, M. L. (1977). Sex differences in empathy and related behaviors. *Psychological Bulletin, 84,* 712–720.

Holahan, C. K., & Holahan, C. J. (1987a). Self-efficacy, social support, and depression in aging: A longitudinal analysis. *Journal of Gerontology, 42,* 65–68.

Holahan, C. K., & Holahan, C. J. (1987b). Life stress, hassles, and self efficacy in aging: A replication and extension. *Journal of Applied Social Psychology, 17,* 574–592.

Holden, G. (1991). The relationship of self-efficacy appraisals to subsequent health related outcomes: A meta-analysis. *Social Work in Health Care, 16,* 53–93.

Holden, G., Moncher, M. S., Schinke, S. P., & Barker, K. M. (1990). Self-efficacy of children and adolescents: A meta-analysis. *Psychological Reports, 66,* 1044–1046.

Holman, H., & Lorig, K. (1992). Perceived self-efficacy in self-management of chronic disease. In R. Schwarzer (Ed.), *Self-efficacy: Thought control of action* (pp. 305–323). Washington, DC: Hemisphere.

Holton, R. (2000). Globalization's cultural consequences. *Annals, AAPSS, 570,* 140–152.

Hyman D. J., Maibach E. W., Flora J. A., & Fortmann, S. P. (1992). Cholesterol treatment practices of primary care physicians. *Public Health Reports, 107,* 441–448.

Humphrey, G. 1921. Imitation and the conditioned reflex. *Pedadogical Seminary,* 28, 1–21.

Ismael, J. (2007). *The situated self.* New York: Oxford University Press

Ismael, J. (2016). How do causes depend on us? *The many faces of perspectivalism. Synthese, 193*(1), 245–267.

Ismael, J. T. (2006). *How physics makes us free.* New York: Oxford University Press.

Jacobs, B., Prentice-Dunn, S., & Rogers, R. W. (1984). Understanding persistence: An interface of control theory and self-efficacy theory. *Basic and Applied Social Psychology, 5,* 333–347.

Janis, I. (1972). *Victims of groupthink: A psychology study of foreign policy decisions and fiascoes.* Boston: Houghton Mifflin.

Jex, S. M., & Bliese, P. D. (1999). Efficacy beliefs as a moderator of the impact of work-related stressors: A multilevel study. *Journal of Applied Psychology, 84*(3), 349.

Jia, F., & Krettenauer, T. (2017). Recognizing moral identity as a cultural construct. *Frontiers in Psychology, 8.*

Jobe, L. D. (1984). *Effects of proximity and specificity of goals on performance* (Doctoral dissertation]. Murdoch University.

John, E. R., Chesler, P., Bartlett, F., & Victor, I. (1968). Observation learning in cats. *Science, 159*(3822), 1489–1491.

Joo, Y. J., Bong, M., & Choi, H. J. (2000). Self-efficacy for self-regulated learning, academic self-efficacy, and internet self-efficacy in web-based instruction. *Educational Technology Research and Development, 48*(2), 5–17.

Jorde-Bloom, P., & Ford, M. (1988). Factors influencing early childhood administrators' decisions regarding the adoption of computer technology. *Journal of Educational Computing Research, 4* (1), 31–47.

Jourden, F. (1991). *The influence of feedback framing on the self-regulatory mechanisms governing complex decision making* [Unpublished doctoral dissertation]. Stanford University.

Kagan, J. (1981). *The second year: The emergence of self-awareness.* Cambridge, MA: Harvard University Press.

Kagan, J. (1996). Three pleasing ideas. *American Psychologist, 51*, 901–908.

Kagan, J. (1998). *Three seductive ideas.* Cambridge, MA: Harvard University Press.

Kahneman, D., Slovic, S. P., Slovic, P., & Tversky, A. (Eds.). (1982). *Judgment under uncertainty: Heuristics and biases.* Cambridge: Cambridge University Press.

Kane, T. D., Marks, M. A., Zaccaro, S. J., & Blair, V. (1996). Self-efficacy, personal goals, and wrestlers' self-regulation. *Journal of Sport and Exercise Psychology, 18*, 36–48.

Kanfer, F. H., & Hagerman, S. (1981). The role of self-regulation. In L. P. Rehm (Ed.), *Behavior therapy for depression: Present status and future directions* (pp. 143–179). New York: Academic Press.

Kanfer, R., & Zeiss, A. M. (1983). Depression, interpersonal standard setting, and judgments of self-efficacy. *Journal of Abnormal Psychology, 92*, 319–329.

Kaplan, M. F. (1989). Information integration in moral reasoning: Conceptual and methodological implications. In J. Reykowski, N. Eisenberg, & E. Staub (Eds.), *Social and moral values: Individual and societal perspectives* (pp. 117–135). Hillsdale, NJ: Erlbaum.

Kaplan, R. M., Atkins, C. J., & Reinsch, S. (1984). Specific efficacy expectations mediate exercise compliance in patients with COPD. *Health Psychology, 3*(3), 223–242.

Kaplan, S. (1989a). The effects of management buyouts on operating performance and value. *Journal of Financial Economics, 24*(2), 217–254.

Kaplan, S. (1989b). Management buyouts: Evidence on taxes as a source of value. *The Journal of Finance, 44*(3), 611–632.

Karniol, R. (1989). The role of manual manipulative stages in the infant's acquisition of perceived control over objects. *Developmental Review, 9*, 205–233.

Kaufman, A., Baron, A., & Kopp, R. E. (1966). Some effects of instructions on human operant behavior. *Psychonomic Monograph Supplements, 1*, 243–250.

Kavanagh, D. J., & Bower, G, H. (1985). Mood and self-efficacy: Impact of joy and sadness on perceived capabilities. *Cognitive Therapy and Research, 9*, 507–525.

Kavanagh, D. J., & Wilson, P. H. (1988). *Prediction of outcome with a group version of cognitive therapy for depression* [Unpublished manuscript] University of Sydney.

Kazdin, A. E. (1978). Covert modeling—therapeutic application of imagined rehearsal. In J. L. Singer & K. S. Pope (Eds.), *The power of human imagination: New methods in psychotherapy. Emotions, personality, and psychotherapy* (pp. 255–278). New York: Plenum Press.

Kazdin, A. E. (1979). Imagery elaboration and self-efficacy in the covert modeling treatment of unassertive behavior. *Journal of Consulting and Clinical Psychology, 47*, 725–733.

Keasey, C. B. (1973). Experimentally induced changes in moral opinions and reasoning. *Journal of Personality and Social Psychology, 26,* 30–38.

Keeney, J., Cannizzo, S. R., & Flavell, J. H. (1967). Spontaneous and induced verbal rehearsal in a recall task. *Child Development, 38,* 953–966.

Kelman, H. C. (1973). Violence without moral restraint: Reflections on the dehumanization of victims and victimizers. *Journal of Social Issues, 29,* 25–61.

Keniston, K. (1970a). Student activism, moral development, and morality. *American Journal of Orthopsychiatry, 40*(4), 577–592.

Keniston, K. (1970b). Youth: A "new" stage of life. *The American Scholar, 39*(4), 631–654.

Kent, G. (1987). Self-efficacious control over reported physiological, cognitive and behavioural symptoms of dental anxiety. *Behaviour Research and Therapy, 25,* 341–347.

Kent, G., & Gibbons, R. (1987). Self-efficacy and the control of anxious cognitions. *Journal of Behavior Therapy & Experimental Psychiatry, 18,* 3340.

Kim, U., Triandis, H. D., Kâitçibasi, C., Choi, S., & Yoon, G. (1994). *Individualism and collectivism: Theory, method, and applications.* Thousand Oaks, CA: Sage Publications.

King (2009). Overcoming structure and agency: Talcott Parsons, Ludwig Wittgenstein and the theory of social action. *Journal of Classical Sociology, 9,* 260–288.

Kirschenbaum, D. S., Humphrey, L. L., & Malett, S. D. (1981). Specificity of planning in adult self-control: an applied investigation. *Journal of Personality and Social Psychology, 40*(5), 941.

Kirschenbaum, D. S., Tomarken, A. J., & Ordman, A. M. (1982). Specificity of planning and choice applied to adult self-control. *Journal of Personality and Social Psychology, 42*(3), 576–585.

Kleingeld, A., van Mierlo, H., & Arends, L. (2011). The effect of goal setting on group performance: A meta-analysis. *Journal of Applied Psychology, 96*(6), 1289–1304. Epub 2011 Jul 11. PMID: 21744940

Kluckhohn, C. E., & Murray, H. A. (1948). *Personality in nature, society, and culture.* New York: Knopf.

Kohlberg, L. (1963a). The development of children's orientations toward a moral order I. Sequence in the development of moral thought. *Vita Humana, 6,* 11–33.

Kohlberg, L. (1963b). Moral development and identification. In H. W. Stevenson (Ed.) & J. Kagan, C. Spiker (Collaborators) & N. B. Henry & H. G. Richey (Eds.), *Child psychology: The sixty-second yearbook of the National Society for the Study of Education, Part 1* (pp. 277–332). Chicago: National Society for the Study of Education; University of Chicago Press.

Kohlberg, L. (1971). From is to ought: How to commit the naturalistic fallacy and get away with it in the study of moral development. In T. Mischel (Ed.),

Cognitive development and epistemology (pp. 151–232). New York: Academic Press.

Kohlberg, L. (1976). Moral stages and moralization. In T. Lickona (Ed.), *Moral development and behavior* (pp. 31–53). New York: Holt, Rinehart, & Winston.

Kohlberg, L., & Candee, D. (1984). The relationship of moral judgment to moral action. *Morality, Moral Behavior, and Moral Development, 52,* 73.

Korsgaard, C. M. (1989a). Personal identity and the unity of agency: A Kantian response to Parfit. *Philosophy & Public Affairs, 18*(2) 101–132.

Korsgaard, C. M. (1989b). Morality as freedom. In *Kant's practical philosophy reconsidered* (pp. 23–48). Dordrecht: Springer.

Krueger Jr., N. F., & Dickson, P. R. (1993). Perceived self-efficacy and perceptions of opportunity and threat. *Psychological Reports, 72*(3 suppl), 1235–1240.

Krueger Jr., N. F, & Dickson, P. R. (1994). How believing in ourselves increases risk taking: Perceived self-efficacy and opportunity recognition. *Decision Sciences, 25*(3), 385–400.

Kurtines, W., & Greif, E. B. (1974). The development of moral thought: Review and evaluation of Kohlberg's approach. *Psychological Bulletin, 81*(8), 453–470.

Kuzyk, O., Grossman, S., & Poulin-Dubois, D. (2020). Knowing who knows: Metacognitive and causal learning abilities guide infants' selective social learning. *Developmental Science, 23,* e12904.

Laajaj, R., & Macours, D.A., et al., (2019). Challenges to capture the big five personality traits in nonweird populations. *Science Advances, 5*(7): eaaw5226.

Lachman, M. E. (1986). Locus of control in aging research: A case for multidimensional and domain-specific assessment. *Psychology and Aging, 1*(1), 34–40.

Lachman, M. E., & Leff, R. (1989). Perceived control and intellectual functioning in the elderly: A 5-year longitudinal study. *Developmental Psychology, 25*(5), 722.

Lane, J., & Anderson, N. H. (1976). Integration of intention and outcome in moral judgment. *Memory & Cognition, 4*(1), 1–5.

Langer, J. (1969). Disequilibrium as a source of development. In P. Mussen, J. Langer, & M. Covington (Eds.), *Trends and issues in developmental psychology* (pp. 22–37). New York: Holt, Rinehart, & Winston.

Laschruger, H. K. S., & Shamian, J. (1994). Staff nurses' and nurse managers' perceptions of job-related empowerment and managerial self-efficacy. *Journal of Nursing Administration, 24,* 38–47.

Latham, G. P., & Locke, E. A. (2018). Goal setting theory: Controversies and resolutions. In D. S. Ones, N. Anderson, C. Viswesvaran, & H. K. Sinangil (Eds.), *The SAGE handbook of industrial, work and organizational psychology: Organizational psychology* (pp. 145–166). Sage Reference.

Latham, G. P., & Marshall, H. A. (1982). The effects of self-set, participatively set and assigned goals on the performance of government employees. *Personnel Psychology, 35*(2), 399–404.

Latham, G. P., & Yukl, G. A. (1976). Effects of assigned and participative goal setting on performance and job satisfaction. *Journal of Applied Psychology, 61*(2), 166–171.

LaVoie, J. C. (1974). Cognitive determinants of resistance to deviation in seven-, nine-, and eleven-year-old children in low and high maturity of moral judgment. *Developmental Psychology, 10*(3), 393–403.

Lazarus, R. S., & Folkman, S. (1984). *Stress, appraisal, and coping.* New York: Springer.

Lazowick, L. M. (1955). On the nature of identification. *The Journal of Abnormal and Social Psychology, 51*(2), 175–183.

Le Furgy, W. G., & Woloshin, G. W. (1969). Immediate and long-term effects of experimentally induced social influence in the modification of adolescents' moral judgments. *Journal of Personality and Social Psychology, 12*(2), 104.

Leiter, M. P. (1992a). Burn-out as a crisis in self-efficacy: Conceptual and practical implications. *Work & Stress, 6*(2), 107–115.

Leming, J. S. (1978a). Cheating behavior, situational influence, and moral development. *The Journal of Educational Research, 71*(4), 214–217.

Leming, J. S. (1978b). Intrapersonal variations in stage of moral reasoning among adolescents as a function of situational context. *Journal of Youth and Adolescence, 7*(4), 405–416.

Lenneberg, E. H. (1967). The biological foundations of language. *Hospital Practice, 2*(12), 59–67.

Lent, L. (1982). The perception of causality in infants. *Perception, 11,* 173–186.

Lent, R., Brown, S., & Larkin, K. C. (1987). Comparison of three theoretically derived variables in predicting career and academic behavior: Self-efficacy, interest congruence, and consequence thinking. *Journal of Counseling Psychology, 34,* 293–298.

Lent, R., Brown, S., Nota, L., & Soresi, S. (2003). Testing social cognitive interest and choice hypothesis across Holland types in Italian high school students. *Journal of Vocational Behavior, 62,* 101–118.

Lent, R. W., Brown, S. D., & Hackett, G. (1994). Toward a unifying social cognitive theory of career and academic interest, choice, and performance. *Journal of Vocational Behavior, 45,* 79–122.

Lent, R. W., Brown, S. D., & Larkin, K. C. (1984). Relation of self-efficacy expectations to academic achievement and persistence. *Journal of Counseling Psychology, 31,* 356–362.

Lent, R. W., Brown, S. D., & Larkin, K. C. (1986). Self-efficacy in the prediction of academic performance and perceived career options. *Journal of Counseling Psychology, 33,* 265–269.

Lent, R. W., & Hackett, G. (1987). Career self-efficacy: Empirical status and future directions. *Journal of Vocational Behavior, 30,* 347–382.

Lent, R. W., Larkin, K. C., & Brown, S. D. (1989). Relation of self-efficacy to inventoried vocational interests. *Journal of Vocational Behavior, 34*(3), 279–288.

Lent, R. W., Lopez, F. G., & Bieschke, K. J. (1993). Predicting mathematics-related choice and success behaviors: Test of an expanded social cognitive model. *Journal of Vocational Behavior, 42,* 223–236.

Leon, M. (1980). Integration of intent and consequences information in children's moral judgments. In F. Wilkening, J. Becker, & T. Trabasso (Eds.), *Information integration by children* (pp. 71–97). Hillsdale, NJ: Erlbaum.

Leon, M. (1982). Rules in children's moral judgments: Integration of intent, damage, and rationale information. *Developmental Psychology, 18*(6), 835–842.

Leon, M. (1984). Rules mothers and sons use to integrate intent and damage information in their moral judgments. *Child Development, 55*(6) 2106–2113.

Levine, S., & Ursin, H. (Eds.). (1980). *Coping and health.* New York: Plenum Press.

Lewis, M., & Brooks-Gunn, J. (1979). Toward a theory of social cognition: The development of self. *New Directions for Child and Adolescent Development, 1979*(4), 1–20.

Li, R., Liang, N., Bu, F., & Hesketh, T. (2020). The effectiveness of self-management of hypertension in adults using mobile health: Systematic review and meta-analysis *JMIR Mhealth Uhealth, 8*(3): e17776.

Litt, M. D. (1988). Self-efficacy and perceived control: cognitive mediators of pain tolerance. *Journal of personality and social psychology, 54*(1), 149.

Lieberman, D. A., & Brown, S. J. (1995). Designing interactive video games for children's health education. R. M. Satava, K. Morgan, H. B. Sieburg, R. Mattheus, & H. I. Christensen (Eds.), *Interactive technology and the new paradigm for healthcare* (pp. 201–210). IOS Press.

Lieberman, H. (Ed.). (2001). *Your wish is my command: Programming by example.* San Francisco: Morgan Kaufmann.

Liebert, R. M., Odom, R. D., Hill, J. H., & Huff, R. L. (1969). Effects of age and rule familiarity on the production of modeled language constructions. *Developmental Psychology, 1,* 108–112.

Liebert, R. M., & Ora Jr, J. P. (1968). Children's adoption of self-reward patterns: Incentive level and method of transmission. *Child Development, 39*(2) 537–544.

Liebert, R. M., & Sprafkin, J. (1988). *The early window: Effects of television on children and youth* (3rd ed.). Oxford: Pergamon Press.

Leiter, M. P. (1992b). Burnout as a crisis in professional role structures: Measurement and conceptual issues. *Anxiety, Stress, and Coping, 5*(1), 79–93.

Lin, J., & Epel, E. (2022). Stress and telomere shortening: Insights from cellular mechanisms. *Ageing Research Reviews, 73*, 101507.

Lindsley, D. H., Mathieu, J. E., Heffner, T. S., & Brass, D. J. (1994). Team efficacy, potency, and performance: A longitudinal examination of reciprocal processes. In *Annual Meeting of the Society for Industrial and Organizational Psychology*, Nashville.

Litt, M. D., Nye, C., & Shafer, D. (1993). Coping with oral surgery by self-efficacy enhancement and perceptions of control. *Journal of Dental Research, 72*, 1237–1243.

Little, B. L., & Madigan, R. M. (1994). Motivation in work teams: A test of the construct of collective efficacy. In *Annual Meeting of the Academy of Management*, Houston, TX (Vol. 70).

Livinti, R., Gunnesch-Luca, G., & Iliescu, D. (2021). Research self-efficacy: A meta-analysis. *Educational Psychologist, 56*, 215–242.

Locke, D. (1979). Cognitive stages or developmental phases? A critique of Kohlberg's stage-structural theory of moral reasoning. *Journal of Moral Education, 8*(3), 168–181.

Locke, D. (1980). The illusion of stage six. *Journal of Moral Education, 9*, 103–109.

Locke, E. A. (1968). Toward a theory of task motivation and incentives. *Organizational Behavior and Human Performance, 3*, 157–189.

Locke, E. A., Bryan, J. F., & Kendall, L. M. (1968). Goals and intentions as mediators of the effects of monetary incentives on behavior. *Journal of Applied Psychology, 52*(2), 104–121.

Locke, E. A., Cartledge, N., & Knerr, C. S. (1970). Studies of relationships between satisfaction, goal setting, and performance. *Organizational Behavior and Human Performance, 5*, 135–158.

Locke, E, A., Frederick, E., Lee, C., & Bobko, P. (1984). Effect of self-efficacy, goals, and task strategies on task performance. *Journal of Applied Psychology, 69*, 241–251.

Locke, E. A., & Latham, G. P. (1990). *A theory of goal setting and task performance.* Englewood Cliffs, NJ: Prentice-Hall.

Loeb, A., Beck, A. T., Diggory, J. C., & Tuthill, R. (1967, January). Expectancy level of aspiration performance and self-evaluation in depression. *In American Psychologist, 22*(7), 479.

Lorig, K., Chastain, R. L., Ung, E., Shoor, S., & Holman, H. (1989a). Development and evaluation of a scale to measure perceived self-efficacy in people with arthritis. *Arthritis and Rheumatism, 32*, 37–44.

Lorig, K. R., González, V., & Ritter, P. L. (1999a). Community-based Spanish language arthritis education program: A randomized trial. *Medical Care, 37*, 957–963.

Lorig, K. R., & Holman, H. R. (2003). Self-management education: History, definition, outcomes, and mechanisms. *Annals of Behavioral Medicine, 26,* 1–7.

Lorig, K. R., Hurwicz, M., Sobel, D., & Hobbs, M. (2006). A national dissemination of an evidenced based self-management program: A translation study. *Patient Education and Counseling, 59,* 69–79.

Lorig, K., Seleznick, M., Lubeck, D., Ung, E., Chastain, R. L., & Holman, H. R. (1989b). The beneficial outcomes of the arthritis self-management course are not adequately explained by behavior change. *Arthritis and Rheumatism, 32,* 91–95.

Lorig, K. R., Sobel, D. S., Stewart, A. L., Brown, B. W., Bandura, A., Ritter, P., et al. (1999b). Evidence suggesting that a chronic disease self-management program can improve health status while reducing hospitalization: A randomized trial. *Medical Care, 37,* 5–14.

Lovass, O. I. (1967). A behavior therapy approach to the treatment of childhood schizophrenia. In J. P. Hill (Ed.), *Minnesota symposia on child psychology* (Vol. 1, pp. 108–159). Minneapolis: University of Minnesota Press.

Luchins, A. S., & Luchins, E. H. (1966). Learning a complex ritualized social role. *Psychological Record, 16,* 177–187.

Maier, S. E., Laudenslager, M. L., & Ryan, S. M. (1985). Stressor controllability, immune function, and endogenous opiates. In E. R. Brush & J. B. Overmier (Eds.), *Affect, conditioning, and cognition: Essays on the determinants of behavior* (pp. 183–201). Hillsdale, NJ: Erlbaum.

Manderlink, G., & Harackiewicz, J. M. (1984). Proximal versus distal goal setting and intrinsic motivation. *Journal of Personality and Social Psychology, 47*(4), 918.

Mandler, J. M. (1992a). How to build a baby: II. Conceptual primitives. *Psychological Review, 99*(4), 587–604.

Mandler, J. M. (1992b). The foundations of conceptual thought in infancy. *Cognitive Development, 7*(3), 273–285.

Markman, G. D., & Baron, R. A. (1999, May). *Cognitive mechanisms: Potential differences between entrepreneurs and non-entrepreneurs.* Paper presented at the Babson College/Kauffman Foundation Entrepreneurship conference.

Marquis, D. P. (1941). Learning in the neonate: the modification of behavior under three feeding schedules. *Journal of Experimental Psychology, 29*(4), 263–282.

Matefy, R. E., & Acksen, B. A. (1976) The effect of role-playing discrepant positions on change in moral judgments and attitudes, *The Journal of Genetic Psychology, 128*(2), 189–200, 10.1080/00221325.1976.10533989

Matsui, T., Okada, A., & Kakuyama, T. (1982). Influence of achievement need on goal setting, performance, and feedback effectiveness. *Journal of Applied Psychology, 67*(5), 645–648.

Matsui, T., & Onglatco, M. L. (1992). Career self-efficacy as a moderator of the relation between occupational stress and strain. *Journal of Vocational Behavior, 41*(1), 79–88.

Matsumoto, D., Kudoh, T., & Takeuchi, S. (1996). Changing patterns of individualism and collectivism in the United States and Japan. *Culture & Psychology, 2,* 77–107.

McAuley, E. (1985). Modeling and self-efficacy: A test of Bandura's model. *Journal of Sport Psychology, 7,* 283–295.

McCann, H. J. (1998). *The works of agency: On human action, will, and freedom.* Ithaca, NY: Cornell University Press

McCaul, K. D., & Malott, J. M. (1984). Distraction and coping with pain. *Psychological Bulletin, 95*(3), 516–533.

McCrae, R. R., & Costa, P. T. (1996). Toward a new generation of personality theories: Theoretical contexts for the five-factor model. In J. S. Wiggins (Ed.), *The five-factor model of personality. Theoretical perspectives* (pp. 51–87). New York: Guilford.

McDonald, T., & Siegall, M. (1992). The effects of technological self-efficacy and job focus on job performance, attitudes, and withdrawal behaviors. *The Journal of Psychology: Interdisciplinary and Applied, 126*(5), 465–475.

McDougall, W. (1908). *An introduction to social psychology.* London: Methuen.

McGuire, W. J. (1985) Attitudes and attitude change. In G. Lindzey & E. Aronson, E. (Eds.), *Handbook of Social Psychology* (3rd ed., Vol. 2, pp. 233–346). New York: Random House.

McKenna, M. D., & Coates, J. (2021). Compatibilism. In E. N. Zalta (Ed.), *The Stanford Encyclopedia of Philosophy* (Fall 2021 ed.). Retrieved from https://plato.stanford.edu/archives/fall2021/entries/compatibilism/

McMains, M. J., & Liebert, R. M. (1968). Influence of discrepancies between successively modeled self-reward criteria on the adoption of a self-imposed standard. *Journal of Personality and Social Psychology, 8*(2, Pt.1), 166–171.

McMullin, D. J., & Steffen, J. J. (1982). Intrinsic motivation and performance standards. *Social Behavior and Personality: An International Journal, 10*(1), 47–56.

Meece, J. L., Wigfield, A., & Eccles, J. S. (1990). Predictors of math anxiety and its influence on young adolescents' course enrollment intentions and performance in mathematics. *Journal of Educational Psychology, 82,* 60–70.

Meichenbaum, D. H. (1977). *Cognitive-behavior modification: An integrative approach.* New York: Plenum Press.

Mento, A. J., Steel, R. P., & Karren, R. J. (1987). A meta-analytic study of the effects of goal setting on task performance: 1966–1984. *Organizational Behavior and Human Decision Processes, 39,* 52–83.

Menyuk, P. (1964). Comparison of grammar of children with functionally deviant and normal speech. *Journal of Speech and Hearing Research, 7*(2), 109–121.

Miao, C., Humphrey, R. H., & Qian, S. (2017a). A meta-analysis of emotional intelligence effects on job satisfaction mediated by job resources, and a test of moderators. *Personality and Individual Differences, 116*, 281–288.

Miao, C., Qian, S., & Ma, D. (2017b). The relationship between entrepreneurial self-efficacy and firm performance: A meta-analysis of main and moderator effects. *Journal of Small Business Management, 51*, 87–107.

Michael, D. N., & Maccoby, N. (1961). Factors influencing the effects of student participation on verbal learning from films: Motivating versus practice effects, "feedback," and overt versus covert responding. In A. A. Lumsdaine (Ed.), *Student response in programmed Instruction* (pp. 271–293). Washington: National Academy of Sciences, National Research Council.

Milgram, S. (1974). *Obedience to authority: An experimental view*. New York: Harper & Row.

Millar, W. S. (1972). A study of operant conditioning under delayed reinforcement in early infancy. *Monographs of the Society for Research in Child Development, 37*(2), Serial No. 147), 1–44.

Millar, W. S., & Schaffer, H. R. (1972). The influence of spatially displaced feedback on infant operant conditioning. *Journal of Experimental Child Psychology, 14*(3), 442–452.

Miller, N. E., & Dollard, J. 1941. *Social learning and imitation*. New Haven: Yale University Press.

Miller, R. E., Caul, W. F., & Mirsky, I. A. (1967). Communication of affects between feral and socially isolated monkeys. *Journal of Personality and Social Psychology, 7*(3, Pt.1), 231–239.

Miller, S. M. (1980). Why having control reduces stress: If I can stop the roller-coaster I don't want to get off. In J. Garber & M. E. P. Seligman (Eds.), *Human helplessness: Theory and applications* (pp. 71–95). New York: Academic Press.

Mineka, S. (1987). A primate model of phobic fears. In H. J. Eysenck & I Martin (Eds.) *Theoretical foundations of behavior therapy* (pp. 81–111). Boston: Springer.

Mischel, W. (1981). Objective and subjective rules for delay of gratification. In G. d'Ydewalle & W. Lens (Eds.), *Cognition in human motivation and learning* (pp. 33–58). Leuven, Belgium, & Hillsdale, NJ: Leuven University Press & Lawrence Erlbaum.

Mischel, W. (2008). The toothbrush problem. *APS Observer, 21*.

Mischel, W., & Liebert, R. M. (1967). The role of power in the adoption of self-reward patterns. *Child Development, 38*(3), 673–683.

Mischel, W., & Mischel, H. N. (1976). A social-cognitive learning approach to morality and self-regulation. In T. Lickona (Ed.), *Moral development and behavior* (pp. 84–107). New York: Holt, Rinehart, & Winston.

Mischel, W., & Shoda, Y. (1995). A cognitive-affective system theory of personality: Reconceptualizing situations, dispositions, dynamics, and invariance in personality structure. *Psychological Review, 102,* 246–286.

Mischel, W., & Shoda, Y. (1999). Integrating dispositions and processing dynamics within a unified theory of personality: The cognitive-affective personality system. In L. A. Pervin & O. P. John (Eds.), *Handbook of personality: Theory and research* (pp. 197–218). New York: Guilford.

Morelli, S. A., Sacchet, M. D., & Zaki, J. (2015). Common and distinct neural correlates of personal and vicarious reward: A quantitative meta-analysis. *NeuroImage, 112,* 244–253.

Morgan, C. L. (1896). *Habit and instinct.* London: Arnold.

Morgan, M. (1985). Self-monitoring of attained subgoals in private study. *Journal of Educational Psychology, 77*(6), 623–630.

Moritz, S. E., Feltz, D. L., Fahrbach, K. R., & Mack, D. E. (2000). The relation of self-efficacy measures to sport performance: A meta-analytic review. *Research Quarterly for Exercise and Sport, 71*(3), 280–294.

Mossholder, K. W. (1980). Effects of externally mediated goal setting on intrinsic motivation: A laboratory experiment. *Journal of Applied psychology, 65*(2), 202–210.

Mowrer, O. H. (1950). Identification: A link between learning theory and psychotherapy. In *Learning theory and personality dynamics* (pp. 573–615). New York: Ronald.

Multon, K. D., Brown, S. D., & Lent, R. W. (1991). Relation of self-efficacy beliefs to academic outcomes: A meta-analytic investigation. *Journal of Counseling Psychology, 38,* 30–38.

Muñoz, R. F., Lenert, L. L., Delucchi, K., Stoddard, J., Perez, J. E., Penilla, C., & Pérez-Stable, E. J. (2006). Toward evidence-based Internet interventions: A Spanish/English web site for international smoking cessation trials. *Nicotine & Tobacco Research, 8*(1), 77–87.

Mynatt, C., & Herman, S. J. (1975). Responsibility attribution in groups and individuals: A direct test of the diffusion of responsibility hypothesis. *Journal of Personality and Social Psychology, 32,* 1111–1118.

Nahmias, E. (2002). When consciousness matters: A critical review of Daniel Wegner's "The illusion of conscious will." *Philosophical Psychology, 15*(4), 527–541.

Nolen-Hoeksema, S. (1987). Sex differences in unipolar depression: Evidence and theory. *Psychological Bulletin, 101,* 259–282.

Nordin, I. (1999). The limits of medical practice. *Theoretical Medicine and Bioethics, 20,* 105–123.

Nozick, R. (1981). *Philosophical explanations.* Cambridge, MA: Belknap.

Odom, R. D., Liebert, R. M., & Hill, J. H. (1968). The effects of modeling cues, reward, and attentional set on the production of grammatical and ungrammatical syntactic constructions. *Journal of Experimental Child Psychology, 6,* 131–140.

Oh, C., Carducci, B., Vaivada, T., & Bhutta, Z. A. (2022). Digital interventions for universal health promotion in children and adolescents: a systematic review. *Pediatrics, 149*(Supplement 6).

Oh, S. (2020). How future work self affects self-efficacy mechanisms in novel task performance: Applying anchoring heuristic under uncertainty. *Personality and Individual Differences, 167,* 110–166.

O'Leary, A., Shoor, S., Lorig, K., & Holman, H. R. (1988). A cognitive-behavioral treatment for rheumatoid arthritis. *Health Psychology, 7,* 527–544.

Olejnik, A. B. (1980). Adults' moral reasoning with children. *Child Development, 51*(4) 1285–1288.

Osgood, C. E., Suci, G. J., & Tannenbaum, P. H. (1957). *The measurement of meaning.* Urbana: University of Illinois Press.

Ostrow, A. C. (1976). Goal-setting behavior and need achievement in relation to competitive motor activity. *Research Quarterly, 47*(2), 174–183.

Ozer, E., & Bandura, A. (1990). Mechanisms governing empowerment effects: A self-efficacy analysis. *Journal of Personality and Social Psychology, 58*(3), 472–486.

Pajares, F., & Miller, M. D. (1994). Role of self-efficacy and self-concept beliefs in mathematical problem solving: A path analysis. *Journal of Educational Psychology, 86,* 193–203.

Pajares, F., & Schunk, D. H. (2001). Self-beliefs and school success: Self-efficacy, self-concept, and school achievement. In R. J. Riding & S. G. Rayner (Eds.), *Self perception* (pp. 239–265). Norwood, NJ: Ablex Publishing.

Papa, M. J., Singhal, A., Law, S., Pant, S., Sood, S., Rogers, E. M., et al. (2000), Entertainment-education and social change: An analysis of parasocial interaction, social learning, collective efficacy, and paradoxical communication. *Journal of Communication, 50,* 31–55.

Park, Y. S., Kim, U., Chung, K. S., Lee, S. M., Kwon, H. H., & Yang, K. M. (2000). Causes and consequences of life-satisfaction among primary, junior high, senior high school students. *Korean Journal of Health Psychology, 5,* 94–118.

Parke, R. D. (1974). Rules, roles, and resistance to deviation: Recent advances in punishment, discipline, and self-control. In A. D. Pick (Ed.), *Minnesota symposia on child psychology* (Vol. 8, pp. 111–143). Minneapolis: University of Minnesota Press.

Parsons, T. 1951. *The social system.* New York: The Free Press of Glencoe.

Parsons, T. (1955). Family structure and the socialization of the child. In T. Parsons & R. F. Bales, *Family, socialization and interaction process* (pp. 35–131). Glencoe, IL: Free Press.

Pastorelli, C., Caprara, G. V., Barbaranelli, C., Rola, J., Rozsa, S., & Bandura, A. (2001). Structure of children's perceived self-efficacy: A cross-national study. *European Journal of Psychological Assessment, 17*, 87–97.

Patterson, G. R. (1976). The aggressive child: Victim and architect of a coercive system. In E. J. Mash, L. A. Hamerlynck, & L. C. Handy (Eds.), *Behavior modification and families* (pp. 267–316). New York: Brunner/Mazel.

Peake, P. K., & Cervone, D. (1989). Sequence anchoring and self-efficacy: Primacy effects in the consideration of possibilities. *Social Cognition, 7*(1), 31–50.

Perloff, B. F. (1970). *Influence of muscular relaxation, positive imagery, and neutral imagery on extinction of avoidance behavior through systematic desensitization.* Stanford: Stanford University.

Perry, D. C, & Bussey, K. (1984) *Social development.* Englewood Cliffs, NJ: Prentice-Hall.

Perry, D. G., & Bussey, K. (1979). The social learning theory of sex differences: Imitation is alive and well. *Journal of Personality and Social Psychology, 37*(10), 1699–1712.

Peters, G. R. (1971). Self-conceptions of the aged, age identification, and aging. *The Gerontologist, 11*(4, Pt. 2), 69–73.

Peters, R. S. (1966). *Ethics and education.* London: Allen & Unwin.

Piaget, J. (1960). *The child's conception of the world.* Lanham, MD: Littlefield.

Poindexter, D. O. (2004). A history of entertainment-education, 1958–2000: The origins of entertainment-education. In A. Singhal, M. J. Cody, E. M., Rogers, & M. Sabido (Eds.), *Entertainment-education and social change: History, research, and practice* (pp. 21–31). Mahwah, NJ: Erlbaum..

Poulin-Dubois, D., & Brosseau-Liard, P. (2016). The developmental origins of selective social learning. *Current Directions in Psychological Science, 25*, 60–64.

Powers, W. (1973). *Perceptual control theory.* Hawthorne, NY: Aldine DeGruyter

Powers, W. T. (1978). Quantitative analysis of purposive systems: Some spadework at the foundations of scientific psychology. *Psychological Review, 85*, 417–435.

Powers, W. T. (1991). Comment on Bandura's "human agency." *American Psychologist, 46*, 151–153.

Pritchard, R. D., & Curtis, M. I. (1973). The influence of goal setting and financial incentives on task performance. *Organizational Behavior and Human Performance, 10*, 175–183.

Prussia, G. E., & Kinicki, A. J. (1996). A motivational investigation of group effectiveness using social cognitive theory. *Journal of Applied Psychology, 81*, 187–199.

Rapoport, D. C., & Alexander, Y. (Eds.). (1982). *The morality of terrorism: Religious and secular justification.* Elmsford, NY: Pergamon Press.

Reed, P. G. (1987). Spirituality and well-being in terminally ill hospitalized adults. *Research in Nursing & Health, 10*(5), 335–344.

Reichard, G. A. (1938). Social life. In F. Boas (Ed.), *General anthropology* (pp. 409–486). Boston: Health.

Reid, C. M., Murphy, B., Murphy, M., Maher, T., Ruth, D., & Jennings, G. (1994). Prescribing medication versus promoting behavioural change: A trial of the use of lifestyle management to replace drug treatment of hypertension in general practice. *Behaviour Change, 11,* 77–185.

Rest, J. R. (1973). The hierarchical nature of moral judgment: A study of patterns of comprehension and preference of moral stages. *Journal of Personality, 41*(1), 86–109.

Rest, J. R. (1975). Longitudinal study of the Defining Issues Test of moral judgment: A strategy for analyzing developmental change. *Developmental Psychology, 11*(6), 738–748.

Rest, J., Turiel, E., & Kohlberg, L. (1969). Level of moral development as a determinant of preference and comprehension of moral judgments made by others. *Journal of Personality, 37*(2), 225–252.

Richter, N. F., Martin, J., Hander, S. V., Taras, V., & Alon, I. (2021). Motivational configurations of cultural intelligence, social integration, and performance in global virtual teams. *Journal of Business Research, 129,* 351–367.

Riley, A. H., Sangalang, A., Critchlow, E., Brown, N., Mitra, R., & Campos Nesme, B. (2021). Entertainment-education campaigns and COVID-19: How three global organizations adapted the health communication strategy for pandemic response and takeaways for the future. *Health Communication, 36*(1), 42–49.

Rogers, E. M., Vaughan, P. W., Swalehe, R. M. A., Rao, N., Svenkerud, P., & Sood, S. (1999). Effects of an entertainment-education radio soap opera on family planning behavior in Tanzania. *Studies in Family Planning, 30,* 1193–1211.

Rosen J. B., Asok, A., & Chakraborty, T. (2015). The smell of fear: innate threat of 2,5-dihydro-2,4,5-trimethylthiazoline, a single molecule component of a predator odor. *Frontiers in Neuroscience, 9,* 292.

Rosenbaum, M., & Hadari, D. (1985). Personal efficacy, external locus of control, and perceived contingency of parental reinforcement among depressed, paranoid, and normal subjects. *Journal of Personality and Social Psychology, 49*(2), 539.

Rosenhan, D., Frederick, F., & Burrowes, A. (1968). Preaching and practicing: Effects of channel discrepancy on norm internalization. *Child Development, 39*(1) 291–301.

Rosenthal, T. L., & Whitebook, J. S. (1970). Incentives versus instructions in transmitting grammatical parameters with experimenter as model. *Behaviour Research and Therapy, 8*(2), 189–196.

Rosenthal, T. L., & Zimmerman, B. J. (1970). Observationally induced changes in children's interrogative classes. *Journal of Personality and Social Psychology, 16*(4), 681–688.

Rottinghaus, P. J., Larson, L. M., & Borgen, F. H. (2003). The relation of self-efficacy and interests: A meta-analysis of 60 samples. *Journal of Vocational Behavior, 62*, 221–236.

Rottschaefer, W. (1986). Willard A. Young, fallacies of creationism. *Philosophy in Review 6*, 411–412.

Rozin, P., Dow S., Moscovitch, M., & Rajaram S. (1998). What causes humans to begin and end a meal? A role for memory for what has been eaten, as evidenced by a study of multiple meal eating in amnesic patients. *Psychological Science*, 9, 392–396.

Rudd, P. (1997). Compliance with antihypertensive therapy: Raising the bar of expectations. *American Journal of Managed Care, 4*, 957–966.

Rushton, J. P. (1975). Generosity in children: Immediate and long-term effects of modeling, preaching, and moral judgment. *Journal of Personality and Social Psychology, 31*(3), 459–466.

Rutte, C., Taborsky, M., & Brinkhof, M. W. G. (2006). What sets the odds of winning and losing? *Trends in Ecology and Evolution, 21*, 16–21.

Ryerson, W. N. (1999). *Population media center.* Shelburne, VT. Retrieved from https://www.populationmedia.org/people/william-ryerson-mphil

Ryerson, W. N. (2006). *Reduction of support for genital mutilation in Sudan.* Raw data.

Sabido, M. (1981). *Towards the social use of soap operas.* Mexico City: Institute for Communication Research.

Sadri, G., & Robertson, I. T. (1993). Self-efficacy and work-related behavior: A review and meta-analysis. *Applied Psychology: An International Review, 42*, 139–152.

Safari, R., Jackson, J., & Sheffield, D. (2020). Digital self-management interventions for people with osteoarthritis: systematic review with meta-analysis. *Journal of Medical Internet Research, 22*(7), e15365.

Safire, W. (1979, May 13). The fine art of euphemism. *San Francisco Chronicle*, p. 13.

Salkovskis, P. M., & Harrison, J. (1984). Abnormal and normal obsessions-A replication. *Behaviour Research and Therapy, 22*, 549–552.

Sanderson, W. C., Rapee, R. M., & Barlow, D. H. (1989). The influence of an illusion of control on panic attacks induced via inhalation of 5.5% carbon dioxide-enriched air. *Archives of General psychiatry, 46*(2), 157–162.

Sanford, N., & Comstock, C. (1971). *Sanctions for Evil: Sources of Social Destructiveness.* Boston: Beacon Press.

San Francisco Chronicle. (1979), April 22). Would you believe it? p. B5.

Sarason, I. G. (1975). Anxiety and self-preoccupation. In I. G. Sarason & D. C. Spielberger (Eds.), *Stress and anxiety* (Vol. 2, pp. 27–44). Washington, DC: Hemisphere.

Schaie, K. W. (1974). Translations in gerontology: From lab to life: Intellectual functioning. *American Psychologist, 29*(11), 802–807.

Schaubroeck, J., & Merritt, D. E. (1997). Divergent effects of job control on coping with work stressors: The key role of self-efficacy. *Academy of Management Journal, 40*(3), 738–754.

Schechtman, M. (1997). The brain/body problem. *Philosophical Psychology, 10,* 149–164.

Schleifer, M., & Douglas, V. I. (1973). Moral judgments, behaviour and cognitive style in young children. *Canadian Journal of Behavioural Science/Revue canadienne des sciences du comportement, 5*(2), 133–144.

Schunk, D. H. (1982a). Effects of effort attributional feedback on children's perceived self-efficacy and achievement. *Journal of Educational Psychology, 74,* 548–556.

Schunk, D. H. (1982b). Progress self-monitoring: Effects on children's self-efficacy and achievement. *The Journal of Experimental Education, 51*(2), 89–93.

Schunk, D. H. (1984). Self-efficacy perspective on achievement behavior. *Educational Psychologist, 19*(1), 48–58.

Schunk, D. H., & Rice, J. M. (1993). Strategy fading and progress feedback: Effects on self-efficacy and comprehension among students receiving remedial reading services. *The Journal of Special Education, 27,* 257–276.

Schunk, D. H., & Zimmerman, B. J. (Eds.). (1994). *Self-regulation of learning and performance.* Hillsdale, NJ: Erlbaum.

Schwartz, R. A., (1974). An economic model of trade credit, *Journal of Financial and Quantitative Analysis, 9*(4), 643–657.

Schwarzer, R., & Jerusalem, M. (1995). Generalized self-efficacy scale. In J. Weinman, S. Wright, & M. Johnston, *Measures in health psychology: A user's portfolio. Causal and control beliefs* (pp. 35–37). Windsor: NFER-Nelson.

Sears, R. R., Maccoby, E. E., & Levin, H. (1957). *Patterns of child rearing.* Evanston, IL: Row, Peterson.

Shapiro, M. J. (2003). Perpetual war. *Body & Society, 9*(4), 109–122.

Shavit, Y., & Martin, F. C. (1987). Opiates, stress, and immunity: Animal studies. *Annals of Behavioral Medicine, 9*(2), 11–15.

Shih, S., & Alexander, J. M. (2000). Interacting effects of goal setting and self- or other-referenced feedback on children's development of self-efficacy and cognitive skill within the Taiwanese classroom. *Journal of Educational Psychology, 92,* 536–543.

Shoda, Y., Cervone, D., & Downey, G. (Eds.) (2007). *Persons in context: Building a science of the individual.* New York: Guilford.

Shoji, K., Cieslak, R., Smoktunowicz, E., Rogala, A., Benight, C. C., & Luszczynska, A. (2016). Associations between job burnout and self-efficacy: A meta-analysis. *Anxiety, Stress, & Coping, 29*(4), 367–386.

Short Jr., J. F. (1968). *Gang delinquency and delinquent subcultures.* New York: Harper & Row.

Shweder, R. A. (1982). Beyond self-constructed knowledge: The study of culture and morality. *Merrill-Palmer Quarterly, 28*(1), 41–69.

Shweder, R. A. (1999). Humans really are different. *Science, 283,* 798–799

Simon, K. M. (1979a). *Effects of self-comparison, social comparison, and depression on goal setting and self-evaluative reactions* [Unpublished manuscript]. Stanford University.

Simon, K. M. (1979b). Self-evaluative reactions: The role of personal valuation of the activity. *Cognitive Therapy and Research, 3,* 111–116.

Simpson, E. L. (1974). Moral development research. *Human Development, 17*(2), 81–106.

Singhal, A., Cody, M. J., Rogers, E. M., & Sabido, M. (Eds.). (2003). *Entertainment-education and social change: History, research, and practice.* London: Routledge.

Singhal, A., & Rogers. E. M. (1999). *Entertainment-education: A communication strategy for social change.* Mahwah, NJ: Erlbaum.

Skinner, B. F. (1953). *Science and human behavior.* New York: Macmillan.

Skinner, B. F. (1971). *Beyond freedom and dignity.* New York: Knopf.

Slobin, D. I. (1968). Imitation and grammatical development in children. In N. S. Endler, L. R. Boulter, & H. Osser (Eds.), *Contemporary issues in developmental psychology* (pp. 437–443). New York: Holt, Rinehart & Winston.

Smaldino, P. E., Lukaszewski, A., von Rueden, C., & Gurven, M. (2019). Niche diversity can explain cross-cultural differences in personality structure. *Nature Human Behaviour, 3,* 1276–1283.

Snyder, M. (1980). Seek, and ye shall find: Testing hypotheses about other people. In E. T. Higgins, C. P. Herman, & M. P. Zanna (Eds.), *Social cognition: The Ontario symposium on personality and social psychology* (Vol. 1, pp. 105–130). Hillsdale, NJ: Erlbaum.

Snyder, M., & Campbell, B. H. (1982). Self-monitoring: The self in action. In J. Suls (Ed.), *Psychological perspectives on the self* (pp. 185–207). Hillsdale, NJ: Erlbaum.

Sobesky, W. E. (1983). The effects of situational factors on moral judgments. *Child Development, 54*(3), 575–584.

Speier, C., & Frese, M. (1997). Generalized self-efficacy as a mediator and moderator between control and complexity at work and personal initiative: A longitudinal field study in East Germany. *Human Performance, 10*(2), 171–192.

Sperry, R. W. (1991). In defense of mentalism and emergent interaction. *The Journal of Mind and Behavior,* 221–245.

Sperry, R. (1993). The impact and promise of the cognitive revolution. *American Psychologist, 48,* 878–885.

Stajkovic, A. D., & Lee, D. S. (2001, August). *A meta-analysis of the relationship between collective efficacy and group performance.* Paper presented at the national Academy of Management meeting, Washington, DC.

Stajkovic, A. D., & Luthans, F. (1998). Self-efficacy and work-related performance: A meta-analysis. *Psychological Bulletin, 124,* 240–261.

Stanley, M. A., & Maddux, J. E. (1986). Cognitive processes in health enhancement: Investigation of a combined protection motivation and self-efficacy model. *Basic and Applied Social Psychology, 7*(2), 101–113.

Staples, D. S., Hulland, J. S., & Higgins, C. A. (1998). A self-efficacy theory explanation for the management of remote workers in virtual organizations. *Journal of Computer-Mediated Communication, 3*(4).

Sternberg, R. J., & Kolligian, J. (Eds.). (1990). *Competence considered*. New Haven: Yale University Press

Stewart, G. L., & Manz, C. C. (1995). Leadership for self-managing work teams: A typology and integrative model. *Human Relations, 48*(7), 747–770.

Stoke, S. M. (1950). An inquiry into the concept of identification. *Journal of Genetic Psychology, 76,* 163–189.

Stumphauzer, J. S. (1969). Application of reinforcement contingencies with a 23-year-old anorexic patient. *Psychological Reports, 24*(1), 109–110.

Sua, Y. S., Jiang, Y., Thompson, D. R., & Wang, W. (2020). Effectiveness of mobile phone-based self-management interventions for medication adherence and change in blood pressure in patients with coronary heart disease: A systematic review and meta-analysis. *European Journal of Cardiovascular Nursing, 19*(3), 192–200.

Sullivan, E. V. 1967. The acquisition of conservation of substance through film-mediated models. In D. W. Brison & E. V. Sullivan (Eds.), *Recent research on the acquisition of conservation of substance. Education Monograph*. Toronto: Ontario Institute for Studies in Education.

Surber, C. F. (1977). Development processes in social inference: Averaging of intentions and consequences in moral judgment. *Developmental Psychology, 13*(6), 654–665.

Surber, C. F. (1985). Measuring the importance of information in judgment: Individual differences in weighting ability and effort. *Organizational Behavior and Human Decision Processes, 35*(2), 156–178.

Talhelm, T., Zhang, X., Oishi, S., Shimin, C., Duan, D., Lan, X., & Kitayama, S. (2014). Large-scale psychological differences within China explained by rice versus wheat agriculture. *Science, 344,* 603–608.

Tarde, G. (1903). *The laws of imitation*. New York: Holt, Rinehart, & Winston.

Taylor C. (1985). *Human agency and language: Philosophical papers I*. Cambridge: Cambridge University Press.

Taylor, C., Bryson, S., Luce, K., Cunning, D., Celio, A., Abascal, L., et al. (2006). Prevention of eating disorders in at-risk college-age women. *Archives of General Psychiatry, 63,* 831–888.

Taylor, C., Winzelberg, A., & Celio, A. (2001). Use of interactive media to prevent eating disorders. In R. Striegel-Moor & L. Smolak (Eds.), *Eating disorders: New direction for research and practices* (pp. 255–270). Washington, DC: American Psychological Association.

Taylor, M. S., Locke, E. A., Lee, C., & Gist, M. E. (1984). Type A behavior and faculty research productivity: What are the mechanisms? *Organizational Behavior and Human Performance, 34,* 402–418.

Taylor, S. E., & Brown, J. D. (1988). Illusion and well-being: A social psychological perspective on mental health. *Psychological Bulletin, 103,* 193–210.

Thase, M. E., & Moss, M. K. (1976). The relative efficacy of covert modeling procedures and guided participant modeling on the reduction of avoidance behavior. *Journal of Behavior Therapy and Experimental Psychiatry, 7*(1), 7–12.

Thorndike, E. L. 1898. Animal intelligence: An experimental study of the associative processes in animals. *Psychological Review Monograph Supplements, 2* (4) (Whole No. 8).

Tilker, H. A. (1970). Socially responsible behavior as a function of observer responsibility and victim feedback. *Journal of Personality and Social Psychology, 14,* 95–100.

Times Higher Education (2009, March 26). *Most cited authors of books in the humanities, 2007.* Retrieved from http://www.timeshighereducation.co.uk/405956.article

Tobias, M., & Griffin, M (Directors). (2001). *The cost of cool.* [Film] PCI Media.

Turiel, E. (1966). An experimental test of the sequentiality of developmental stages in the child's moral judgments. *Journal of Personality and Social Psychology, 3*(6), 611–618.

Tversky, A., & Kahneman, D. (1974). Judgment under uncertainty: Heuristics and biases: Biases in judgments reveal some heuristics of thinking under uncertainty. *Science, 185*(4157), 1124–1131.

Umstot, D. D., Bell, C. H., & Mitchell, T. R. (1976). Effects of job enrichment and task goals on satisfaction and productivity: Implications for job design. *Journal of Applied Psychology, 61*(4), 379–394.

United Nations (2022). Global issues: Population. https://www.un.org/en/global-issues/population#:~:text=The%20world%20population%20is%20projected,surrounding%20these%20latest%20population%20projections

Vandello, J. A., & Cohen, D. (1999). Patterns of individualism and collectivism across the United States. *Journal of Personality and Social Psychology, 77,* 279–292.

Van Gulick, R. (2001). Reduction, emergence and other recent options on the mind/body problem. A philosophic overview. *Journal of Consciousness Studies, 8*(9–10), 1–34.

Van Hekken, S. M. J. (1969). The influence of verbalization on observational learning in a group of mediating and a group of non-mediating children. *Human Development, 12,* 204–213.

Vaughan, P. W. (2003). *The onset of fertility transition in Tanzania during the 1990's: The role of two entertainment-education radio dramas* [Unpublished manuscript]. Minneapolis.

Vaughan, P. W., Roger, E. M., Singhal, A., & Swalehe, R. M. (2000). Entertainment-education and HIV/AIDS prevention: A field experiment in Tanzania. *Journal of Health Communications, 5,* 81–100.

Wachs, T. D. (1977). The optimal stimulation hypothesis and early development. In I. Č. Užgiris & F. Weizmann (Eds.), *The structuring of experience* (pp. 153–177). Boston, MA: Springer.

Walker, L. J. (1983). Sources of cognitive conflict for stage transition in moral development. *Developmental Psychology, 19,*103–110.

Walker, L. J., & Richards, B. S. (1976). The effects of a narrative model on children's moral judgments. *Canadian Journal of Behavioural Science/Revue canadienne des sciences du comportement, 8*(2), 169–177.

Walker, W. B., & Franzini, L. R. (1983). *Self-efficacy and low-risk aversive group treatments for smoking cessation.* Paper presented at the annual convention of the Western Psychological Association, San Francisco.

Walters, G. C., & Grusec, J. E. (1977). *Punishment.* New York; W. H. Freeman.

Walters, R. H., & Parke, R. D. (1964). Influence of response consequences to a social model on resistance to deviation. *Journal of Experimental Child Psychology, 1,* 269–280.

Walters, R. H., Parke, R. D., & Cane, V. A. (1965). Timing of punishment and the observation of consequences to others as determinants of response inhibition. *Journal of Experimental Child Psychology, 2,* 10–30.

Watson, J. (1979). Perception of contingency as a determinant of social responsiveness. In E. B. Thoman (Ed.), *Origins of the infant's social responsiveness* (Vol. 1, pp. 33–64). New York: Halsted.

Watson, J. B. (1908). Imitation in monkeys. *Psychological Bulletin, 5,* 169–178.

Wei, D., Talwar, V., & Lin, D. (2021). Neural circuits of social behaviors: Innate yet flexible. *Neuron, 109,* 1600–1620.

Weinberg, R. S., Bruya, L., & Jackson, A. (1985). The effects of goal proximity and goal specificity on endurance performance. *Journal of Sport Psychology, 7*(3), 296–305.

Weinberg, R. S., Gould, D., & Jackson, A. (1979). Expectations and performance: An empirical test of Bandura's self-efficacy theory. *Journal of Sport Psychology, 1,* 320–331.

Weinberg, R. S., Gould, D., Yukelson, D., & Jackson, A. (1981). The effect of preexisting and manipulated self-efficacy on a competitive muscular endurance task. *Journal of Sport Psychology, 4,* 345–354.

Weinberg, R. S., Yukelson, D., & Jackson, A. (1980). Effect of public and private efficacy expectations on competitive performance. *Journal of Sport Psychology, 2*(4), 340–349.

West, J. A., Bandura, A., Clark, E., Miller, N. H., Ahn, D., Greenwald, G., et al. (1999). *Self-efficacy predicts adherence to dietary sodium limitation in patients with heart failure* [Manuscript]. Stanford University.

Westoff, C. F., & Rodriguez, G. (1995). The mass media and family planning in Kenya. *International Family Planning Perspectives, 21,* 26–31.

Wheeler, L. (1966a). Toward a theory of behavioral contagion. *Psychological Review, 73*(2), 179–192.

Wheeler, L. (1966b). Motivation as a determinant of upward comparison. *Journal of Experimental Social Psychology, 1,* 27–31.

Whelton, P. K., Appel, L. J., Espeland, M. A., Applegate, W. B., Ettinger, W. H., Kostis, J. B., et al. (1998). Sodium reduction and weight loss in the treatment of hypertension in older persons. *Journal of American Medical Association, 279,* 839–846.

White, J. (1982). *Rejection.* Reading, MA: Addison-Wesley.

White, M. J. (1985). *Agency and integrality.* Dordrecht: Reidel.

Whyte, G., & Saks, A. (1999). Expert decision making in escalation situations: The role of self-efficacy. Manuscript submitted for publication.

Whyte, G., Saks, A., & Hook, S. (1997). When success breeds failure: The role of perceived self-efficacy in escalating commitment to a losing course of action. *Journal of Organizational Behavior, 18,* 415–432

Williams, S. L. (1992). Perceived self-efficacy and phobic disability. In R. Schwarzer (Ed.), *Self-efficacy: Thought control of action* (149–176). London: Routledge.

Williams, S. L., Dooseman, G., & Kleifield, E. (1984). Comparative effectiveness of guided mastery and exposure treatments for intractable phobias. *Journal of Consulting and Clinical Psychology, 52*(4), 505–518.

Williams, S. L., Kinney, P. J., & Falbo, J. (1989). Generalization of therapeutic changes in agoraphobia: The role of perceived self-efficacy. *Journal of Consulting and Clinical Psychology, 57*(3), 436–442.

Williams, S. L., Turner, S. M., & Peer, D. F. (1985). Guided mastery and performance desensitization treatments for severe acrophobia. *Journal of Consulting and Clinical Psychology, 53*(2), 237–247.

Wilson, B. J., & Cantor, J. (1985). Developmental differences in empathy with a television protagonist's fear. *Journal of Experimental Child Psychology, 39*(2), 284–299.

Wittgenstein, L. (1953). *Philosophical investigations* (G. E. M. Anscombe Trans.). Oxford: Blackwell.

Wonderly, D. M., & Kupfersmid, D. M. (1980). Moral maturity and behavior: Failure to find a link. *Journal of Youth and Adolescence, 9*(3), 249–261.

Wood, R. E., & Bandura, A. (1989a). Social cognitive theory of organizational management. *Academy of Management Review, 14,* 361–384.

Wood, R. E., & Bandura, A. *(*1989b*)*. Impact of conceptions of ability on self-regulatory mechanisms and complex decision making. Journal of Personality and Social Psychology, *5*(3), 407–415.

Wood, R. E., Mento, A. J., & Locke, E. A. (1987). Task complexity as a moderator of goal effects: A meta-analysis. *Journal of Applied Psychology, 72*(3), 416–425.

Yamada, M., & Sakurai, Y. (2018). An observational learning task using Barnes maze in rats. *Cognitive Neurodynamics, 12*, 519–523.

Yamagishi, T. (1988). The provision of a sanctioning system in the United States and Japan. *Social Psychology Quarterly, 51*, 265–271.

Yukl, G. A., & Latham, G. P. (1978). Interrelationships among employee participation, individual differences, goal difficulty, goal acceptance, goal instrumentality, and performance. *Personnel Psychology, 31*(2), 305–323.

Zentall, T. R. (2012). Perspectives on observational learning in animals. *Journal of Comparative Psychology, 126*, 114–128.

Zimbardo, P. (1969). The human choice: Individuation, reason, and order versus deindividuation, impulse, and chaos. In W. J. Arnold & D. Levine (Eds.), *Nebraska Symposium on Motivation* (pp. 237–309). Lincoln: University of Nebraska Press.

Zimmerman, B. J. (1989). A social cognitive view of self-regulated academic learning. *Journal of Educational Psychology, 81*(3), 329–339.

Zimmerman, B. J., Bandura, A., & Martinez-Pons, M. (1992). Self-motivation for academic attainment: The role of self-efficacy beliefs and personal goal-setting. *American Educational Research Journal, 29*, 663–676.

Zimmerman, B. J., & Blom, D. E. (1983). Toward an empirical test of the role of cognitive conflict in learning. *Developmental Review, 3*(1), 18–38.

Author Index

Social Cognitive Theory: An Agentic Perspective on Human Nature, First Edition. Albert Bandura.
© 2023 John Wiley & Sons, Inc. Published 2023 by John Wiley & Sons, Inc.

Subject Index

Please note that page references to Figures are followed by the letter 'f'.
References to Notes will contain the letter 'n' following the Note number.

Social Cognitive Theory: An Agentic Perspective on Human Nature, First Edition. Albert Bandura.
© 2023 John Wiley & Sons, Inc. Published 2023 by John Wiley & Sons, Inc.

Printed in Australia
06 Jun 2025
LP01560z

Printed in Australia
06 Jun 2023
LP015902